YO-BST-361

INTERPERSONAL

COMMUNICATION COMPETENCE

Brian H. Spitzberg
William R. Cupach

Sage Series in Interpersonal Communication
Volume 4

SAGE PUBLICATIONS
Beverly Hills   London   New Delhi

For information address:

SAGE Publications, Inc.
275 South Beverly Drive
Beverly Hills, California 90212

SAGE Publications India Pvt. Ltd.
C-236 Defence Colony
New Delhi 110 024, India

SAGE Publications Ltd
28 Banner Street
London EC1Y 8QE, England

Printed in the United States of America

Library of Congress Cataloging in Publication Data

Spitzberg, Brian H.
    Interpersonal communication competence.

    (Sage series in interpersonal communication ; v. 4)
    Bibliography: p.
    Includes index.
    1. Interpersonal communication. 2. Communicative
competence. I. Cupach, William R. II. Title.
BF637.C45S67   1984   153.6   84-6847
ISBN 0-8039-2306-6
ISBN 0-8039-2307-4 (pbk.)

FIRST PRINTING

CONTENTS

Series Editor's Introduction

One of the most common and basic reactions we human beings exhibit is our tendency to evaluate things. Is it good or bad? positive or negative? successful or unsuccessful? Communication behavior is no exception. We are constantly making judgments about our own communication behavior and the behavior of others. But do we know what competent communication behavior really is? This book provides a valuable resource for answering this question.

For this volume, Spitzberg and Cupach gathered and synthesized an enormous body of literature from a variety of academic disciplines. The compilation of this scattered research and theory should, alone, be a prized feature for anyone whose teaching or research focuses on the issue of competence in communicating.

In addition to the thorough review of the literature, the authors of this volume also tackle the complex and difficult, yet central, issues surrounding the study of communicative competence. The following are illustrative of the questions arising out of two of these issues:

- *Trait vs. State Behavior.* To what extent is a communicator's competence grounded in qualities that are carried from one situation to another? To what extent is competence the result of situation-specific behavior?

- *Goals and Awareness.* Should the conceptualization of competence be limited to goal-directed behavior? What about situations in which communicators are not fully aware of their goals? Should communicative competence focus on both long- and short-range goals? Is it possible for a communicator to be too aware of his or her own communication behavior?

For me, the two most provocative concepts about competence in this book concern the notion of communicator interdependence and the identification of competence as an interpersonal impression.

- *Communicator Interdependence.* This issue strikes at the very heart of *where competence resides.* Virtually all prior accounts of communicative competence have conceived of competence as something exhibited or possessed by a single individual. To say that competent interaction is rooted in the configuration of behavior manifested by both interactants is a radical departure from previous ways of thinking about this issue — although it seems more in line with current communication theory. By taking into account the responses of one's interaction partner, our whole previous understanding of what is competent, normal, and problematic seems subject to revision.

- *Competence as an Interpersonal Impression.* Although at first glance this concept may seem to be axiomatic, it has important implications if we fully subscribe to it. For example, if competence is not based on an absolute standard, communicator *behaviors* are likely to represent only a part of the competence judgment — and sometimes only a small part. This has important implications for training in social skill improvement, which is based on the assumption that behavioral changes will result in improved competence judgments. Also embedded in this issue is the question of *who should rate competence.* If it is an interpersonal impression, it may be an impression of the actors as well as the observers. Typically, research has not given much attention to the actors as a source of data. Further, the concept of impressions suggests the possibility of a much more complex judgment than competent-incompetent — that is, perceiving some behavior as more competent and some as less during a single action sequence. This response option has not characterized much of our past efforts in this area.

To say that people believe it is important to strive for competence in communicating is to state the obvious. Corporations spend millions of dollars training managers how to communicate more effectively; the Dale Carnegie courses and others like them enroll thousands of people who desire to improve their communication skills; and the federal government, as well as various education associations, have identified speaking and listening as "basic skills"— skills in which everyone should attain competence. Despite the recognized importance of communicating competently, we still have much to learn about the subject. Comunication textbooks are too often woefully simplistic in prescribing competent behavior — for example, admonishing communicators to "avoid manipulating others," to "always be clear," and to "avoid jumping to conclusions." But the need to understand communicative competency extends beyond the teaching function. Whether it is stated explicitly or not, communication research studies are often guided and justified by the assumption that the findings will somehow contribute to improved understanding and/or performance of communication behavior. *Interpersonal Communication Competence* does not pretend to have all the answers, but it does make an important contribution toward understanding this very complex issue.

—Mark L. Knapp

PREFACE

INTERACTANTS AND RESEARCHERS alike are fundamentally concerned with competence in communicating. That is also the focus of this book: communication quality. Our aim is to understand (and ultimately produce) communicators with *savoir faire* and conversations that are gratifying. We have attempted to lay a foundation for future scholarly inquiry into communication competence.

It should be apparent that the topic of communication competence is as expansive as the topic of communication itself. Consequently, we have limited our content primarily to interpersonal communication. We have emphasized communication situations that entail essentially dyadic, face-to-face interaction. We recognize the intrinsic relevance of interpersonal communication to many contexts, such as small groups and organizations, but we do not take up the issues *unique* to these contexts in this volume.

Our exploration begins in Chapter 1 with the rather uncontroversial premise that competent communication is important in everyday life. At the same time, the scholarly import of the competence construct is highlighted as we trace its conceptual and empirical roots. The diverse paths that have given rise to current interest in competence are numerous. The intent is Chapter 2 attempts to sort out the vast literatures on competence by characterizing the major theoretical/conceptual vantage points that undergird the modern study of competence. To facilitate our review, categories of competence constructs are delineated, and the relevant literature is examined for each category. In Chapter 3, a critical analysis of issues related to the conceptualization and measurement of competence is presented. The discussion of these definitional issues serves as a backdrop for the model of relational competence elaborated in Chapter 4. The model represents our synthesis of the assumptions and components we believe are most useful for understanding competence in communication. We hope the model stimulates academic argument, empirical research, and theory construction. The final chapter explores some theoretical, methodological, and pedagogical implications of relational competence and suggests some priorities for future work.

Many individuals have been unwitting accomplices in the development of this book. We wish to thank our friends, colleagues, students, and mentors for their encouragement, support, and ideas. In particular, we appreciate their operational (walking, talking) definitions of competence as exhibited in their everyday discourse. We also grudgingly recognize the contribution of those persons who—from time to time—felt free to identify instances of *in*competence in our own communicative behavior. It is the irony of talking and writing about competence that those who do so are expected to demonstrate it as well as know about it.

We sincerely thank Professor Mark Knapp for his incisive criticism and invaluable editorial guidance. His feedback was always timely and wise. He freely shared his excellent ideas with us while still allowing us tremendous discretion. Given this latitude, we hope that any deficiencies in content will be attributed solely to us. We also appreciate the assistance of Grace Foote in transforming the bibliography from its raw state to its present state.

Finally, this book is dedicated to the dedicated...Shelley and Betty.

1

Competent Communication in Everyday Life

COMPETENCE IS AN ISSUE both perennial and fundamental to the study of communication. We use communication in virtually every facet of our lives, and it is a particularly salient feature in interviewing, conflict management and negotiation, initiation and maintenance relationships, of public speaking, political persuasion, social conversation, and a multitude of other interpersonal events. The importance of communication in our daily lives has been a topic of concern for more than 2,500 years (Fisher, 1978). Despite this continuing interest, there is still a lack of consensus regarding the nature of competence in communicating, or the best way to identify the ability to communicate well.

The need to specify the nature of communication competence is significant. It is the yardstick for measuring the quality of our interpersonal relationships. Moreover, the acquisition of communication competence is necessary to fulfill the general need of all humans to control their environment—what White (1959) termed "effectance motivation." Effective environmental control requires successful interface with other people who are an integral part of that environment.

In addition to facilitating fulfillment of the general motive for environmental control, people must display competence in achieving many specific personal and interpersonal objectives. Gaining or resisting compliance, eliciting or disseminating information, mediating conflict, and attaining physical or psychological gratification are only some of the common functions served by communication. Breen, Donlon, and Whitaker (1977) conclude that "the pure enjoyment of life... is directly related to the level of interpersonal competence" while "deficiency in interpersonal skills may also be the most prevalient source of discord and unpleasantness in our personal lives" (p. 1). Anomia (Parks, 1977a), alienation (Giffin, 1970), mental illness (Jackson, King, & Heller, 1981; Trower, Bryant, & Argyle, 1978), and loneliness (Spitzberg & Canary, 1983) are some of the more unpleasant potential consequences of communication incompetence.

That communication competence is important seems axiomatic. Certain cultural trends add to the demands that communicators face. Modern technology is rapidly making possible an environment in which information on virtualy any subject is available "at the push of a button." In open societies, world events become news almost instantaneously. Television, radio, cinema, teleconferencing, electronic funds transfer, computer information processing, and satellite linkages function not only to transfer information but also to alter the ways in which we use and produce communication. With each new medium (such as video conferring and video phones) comes a new mode of communication to master (Naisbett, 1982). Moreover, the information explosion made possible by the media may even have expanded the *topoi* with which typical communicators need to be familiar in order to be competent.

Parallel to the rapid innovations on technological fronts is the increasing mobility of society in general. Individuals and families travel and relocate more now than in the past. Assuming that needs for human contact remain relatively constant (an interesting but largely unexplored assumption), increasing social mobility brings with it a need to establish and maintain interpersonal relationships more frequently and perhaps more quickly.

Finally, our mobility, combined with our massive exposure to information on world events and peoples, may accelerate the diffusion of social change and provide more opportunities for intercultural contact than ever before. People may therefore find that they must adapt their communication more often and in response to a greater number of communicative situations, media and people than in the past. This is not to say that interaction is necessarily more difficult. There may be compensating developments. Expanded information and media repertoires may be mastered and used efficiently. Nonetheless, today's communication environment presents many unique challenges that make competence an important and highly relevant concern. The study of communication competence is also problematic when people bestow upon themselves an unwarranted expertise. The sheer ubiquity of interaction renders the ability to communicate as something easily taken for granted (see Fisher, 1978, p. 6). Many individuals seem to believe that they need no training or education in an activity they perform (quite well, thank you) every day.

A variety of indicators reveal that our educational institutions are not meeting the communicative needs of enough students. The solution being sought by policy makers and educators is organized loosely under the aegis of "competency-based education" (Spady, 1977; Spady & Mitchell, 1977). As Johnson and Powell (1981b) have noted, in the decade of the 1970s, "among the most fashionable educational movements was 'competency based' curriculum, particularly in the areas of language arts and mathematics" (p. 1). Consequently, as of June 1981, 31 states have established, or intend to establish, some form of communication competency standards for high school graduation.

One study of the communication competence of college students concluded that

> 11 percent of the students tested had problems asking a question; 33 percent could not organize ideas well; 32 percent could not give accurate directions; 35 percent could not adequately express and defend a point of view; 10 percent didn't understand the difference between a fact and an opinion; and 49 percent could not describe the point of view of a person who disagreed with them. (Rubin, 1981b, p. 30)

This finding is corroborated by a nationwide study of 7,500 adults by the Adult Performance Level Research Project at the University of Texas-Austin. It was concluded that, "taking the

U.S. population as a whole, approximately one-fifth of adults are estimated to be functionally incompetent" (as reported in Bassett, Whittington, & Staton-Spicer, 1978, p. 294). Elsewhere, Argyle (1981) provides a more conservative estimate of the extent of incompetence: "It seems likely that at least 7 percent of the normal adult population have fairly serious difficulties with social behavior" (p. 264). These findings suggest that skill in communicating is *not* something that can be taken for granted. The field of communication studies is recognizing this and responding both with active academic dialogue and significant pragmatic research (Allen & Brown, 1976; Backlund, Brown, Gurry & Jandt, 1982; Barbatsis, 1980; Berryman-Fink & Pederson, 1981; Breen et al, 1977; Brown, Ecroyd, Hopper, McCambridge, & Nance, 1977; Johnson & Powell, 1981a; Larson, Backlund, Redmond, & Barbour, 1978; Mead, 1980a, 1980b; Moore & Levison, 1977; Rubin, 1981a, 1982; Tortoriello & Phelps, 1975; Zimmerman, 1980).

Fortunately, there are numerous concomitant trends in our culture, technology, educational systems, and organizations that highlight the increasing importance of communication skills and the correspondent value placed on these skills. Evidence of such trends includes increased research activity and textbook space (see, for example, DeVito, 1980; Glaser, 1980; Knapp, 1978; Ross & Ross, 1982; Verdeber & Verdeber, 1980; Wilmot, 1979) devoted to the topic of communication competency, as well as a recent federal law (PL 95-561) that identifies spoken communication as an essential curriculum component in our schools. In an attempt to access all competence-related articles referenced in *Psychological Abstracts* from 1927 to 1977, Garmezy, Masten, Nordstrom, and Ferrarese (1979) found 929 relevant entries using terms such as "social" and "interpersonal competence." When plotted against the general psychological literature, the number and relative percentage of "competence-related articles appears to be increasing" (p. 38). The back-to-basics movement in American education seems to have recognized the need for a fourth "R": relating.

The ability to engage in appropriate and effective interpersonal interaction (that is, competent communication) is the concern of this book. We will attempt to bring clarity, integration, and direction to the mass of material that informs the conceptualization of interpersonal communication competence. Before reviewing and evaluating recent approaches to this topic, we will summarize the diverse historical foundations which preceded them.

HISTORICAL ROOTS

The Rhetorical Tradition

"The importance of effective interpersonal behavior has been stressed by nearly all philosophical and scientific theorists concerned with the nature of human social relationships" (Eisler, 1978, p. 369). The study of effective interpersonal behavior has its roots in the discipline of rhetoric. In Western society, the specific origins of this interest apparently began with the sophistic rhetorics of ancient Sicily (around 467 B.C.). These arts of rhetoric were developed to aid citizens of Syracuse in regaining properties that they had lost to the recently deposed tyrants. Because this was a courtroom context for rhetoric, the original arts were oriented almost exclusively toward persuasion (that is, the accomplishment of a desired effect—a courtroom victory—with the audience or judge). This persuasion bias dominated the subject of rhetoric for centuries thereafter. This bias eventually led the sophists into ill repute. Sophists developed reputations among many for winning at all costs, for trickery and deceit, and for twisting facts around in order to make the untrue appear true.

Probably the single most influential ancient rhetorical figure is Aristotle (384-322 B.C.). A student of Plato, Aristotle sought to develop a rhetoric that would not suffer the abuses that had brought the sophistic rhetorics into disrepute. Aristotle systematized the art of rhetoric, revealing that it could be codified into a set of principles that could be taught and learned. He defined rhetoric as "the faculty of discovering in every case the available means of persuasion" (1926, p. 5). It is here that the relevance of "context" is first implied. Aristotle specifically stressed the analysis of and adaptation to one's audience—that is, the target of persuasion. Although his definition of rhetoric was circumscribed to situations of persuasion, the idea of matching strategy to context emerges at this point. The principal focus of this rhetorical theory was on the *substance and grammar* of rhetoric (Ehninger, 1968), and it was not until much later that *conceptualizations* of context were expanded and refined.

Another implication of Aristotle's conception of rhetoric is that persuasion is contingent, in part, upon the impression that a speaker creates or maintains. According to Aristotle,

> since the object of rhetoric is judgment...it is not only necessary to consider how to make a speech itself demonstrative and convincing, but also that the speaker should show himself to be of a certain character and should know how to put the judge into a certain frame of mind. (1926, p. 169)

The "character" to which Aristotle refers is composed of good sense, virtue, and goodwill. Thus, an interest in persuasion necessarily implies an interest in impression management as well.

Later, around 55 B.C., borrowing heavily from Aristotle's rhetoric, Cicero expanded the scope of rhetoric, or the art of oratory. According to Cicero, "the complete and finished orator is he who on any matter whatever can speak with fullness and variety" (1959, p. 59.) A perfect orator needed to be conversant with all possible topics. In addition, this conversational ability was to be demonstrated with "tact." After suggesting that no other word in the Latin language was more significant, Cicero points out that tactlessness

> is most amply illustrated in our ordinary conversation, inasmuch as whosoever fails to realize the demands of the occasion, or talks too much, or advertises himself, or ignores the prestige or convenience of those with whom he has to deal, or, in short, is in any way awkward or tedious, is described as "tactless." (1959, pp. 209, 211)

This passage points to an interest in contexts other than strictly courtroom rhetoric, even though rhetorical teaching in ancient Rome was still oriented heavily toward political concerns. More than a century after Cicero, Quintilian went to Rome and, about A.D. 88, wrote the *Institutes of Oratory*, concerning the education of an orator. Again, indicating a more expansive view of rhetoric than that of persuasion, Quintilian posited that *"ora-tory is the art of speaking well"* (1903, p. 147). While persuasion continued to be the major focus of the classical rhetoricians, the seeds of a conversational art seem to have been planted in this era as well.

In the Renaissance, rhetorics based largely upon Cicero and Quintilian appeared to shift their emphasis to an aesthetic art, adapted to the "gracious" and political life of the royal court. In reviewing *The Civile Conversation,,* authored by the Renaissance writer Stephano Guazzo, Mohrmann (1972) discovered that the ultimate criterion of proper conversational delivery was "decorum." Decorum requires delivery to be adapted with appropriate discretion to the context encountered, in both vocal quality and content. This is a fairly modern concept, suggesting the importance of pleasing the "other" person. It is not surprising, then, that Ehninger (1975) refers to "the stylistic rhetoric of the Renaissance as an aesthetically oriented art of ingratiation" (p. 448). Once again, rhetorical theorists of the Renaissance revealed an interest in the art of everyday conversation generally and the art of being "other-oriented" specifically.

The rhetorics of the eighteenth and early nineteenth centuries (such as those of George Campbell, Joseph Priestly, Thomas Sheridan, Hugh Blair, and Richard Whately) reveal a variety of theoretical derivations. While the elocutionary movement stressed delivery over content through the "just and graceful management of the voice, countenance, and gesture in speaking" (Sheridan, 1762, p. II, 1), the rhetorics of Campbell and Whately were grounded in the prevailing faculty psychology of the day. Rhetorical speeches were classified by their presumed ability to affect an audience's faculties—"to enlighten the understanding, to please the imagination, to move the passions, or to influence the will" (Campbell, 1963, p. 1). To some extent, the diversity of the rhetorics in this era prompt diverse characterizations of them. Whereas Ehninger (1975) refers to "British rhetoric of the later eighteenth century as a psychologically oriented art of adapting means to purposes" (p. 448), Scott (1975) depicts the same rhetoric as "managerial" in its emphasis on methods by which speakers "manage" the audience according to its salient faculties. Common to both of these characterizations is the idea of *adapting* speech to the needs of the audience.

To a large extent, therefore, rhetorical theorists have been interested in the ability to communicate effectively (and persuasively) for centuries. Aristotle established rhetoric as an art that can be systematized, learned, and taught. Despite emphasis on the persuasive uses of rhetoric, Aristotle included in his writings the critical concepts of audience adaptation, contextual analysis, topoi (an early version of a strategy repertoire), and credibility (an early version of impression management). Armed with the legitimacy and tools introduced by Aristotle, other rhetoricians stressed particular features of rhetoric. Cicero and Quintilian continued the focus on persuasion but also assured the role of general communicative skills for all occasions. Cicero's use of tact and Quintilian's "art of speaking well" indicated that a skilled speaker is not skilled simply in public speaking. Renaissance rhetorics shifted the emphasis somewhat away from persuasion and more toward ingratiation (an early version of other-oriented interaction), while eighteenth-century rhetorics identified the importance of adapting one's communication to the psychological characteristics of the audience. As P. A. Duhamel (1949) stated,

> All rhetoricians have had one object: the teaching of effective expression. That object can be considered as the "least common denominator" of mental notes which undergo accretion and modification in accordance with an author's conception of what constitutes eloquence. (pp. 344-345)

But what has *constituted* effective expression, and the *contexts* in which such expression is encountered, vary greatly from one rhetorician to another and from one time period to another.

Perhaps the foremost rhetorician of the twentieth century is Kenneth Burke. Burke's rhetoric (1945, 1950, 1966), with its sociological emphasis, attempts to explain the nature of human symbolic interaction. Rhetoric is conceived as a necessary mechanism to overcome the conditions of divisiveness and estrangement endemic to society. For Burke, the purposes of rhetoric are to induce cooperation and facilitate the sharing of motives among humans. This broad conception of rhetoric is amenable to application to interpersonal interaction. Although Burke does not directly address the issue of competence, his core concept of identification implies a standard of competence. Identification is the process of relating to other communicators via symbols in order to achieve consubstantiality—commonality or sharedness. The consequences of increasing consubstantiality are greater shared meaning and enhanced understanding among communicators.

Another contemporary rhetorician concerned with shared meaning is I. A. Richards. Rhetoric, in Richards's view, involves the "study of misunderstanding and its remedies" (1965, p. 3). Consequently, the aim of rhetoric is to facilitate what can be considered an essential element of competent communication: accuracy in meaning. Although Richards's concerns (and definition of rhetoric) are more narrow and focused than Burke's, both authors exemplify the tendency of modern rhetorics to be broader in scope than the ancient rhetorics of persuasion. Nor are the modern rhetorics restricted to the speaker-audience situation. Interpersonal interaction more clearly falls within the purview of rhetoric in modern conceptualizations than it did in classical and eighteenth-century approaches.

Certain rhetorical theorists concern themselves specifically with the notion of competent interaction. For example, W. R. Fisher (1978) examines the realm of discourse in which value-based reasons and arguments are used. In establishing a "logic" whereby interlocutors can examine the values and reasons underlying their discourse, Fisher (1978) provides a scheme whereby interactants may manifest rhetorical competence. For Fisher (1980), rhetorical competence "is a term that not only encompasses knowledge and ability in the rational arts—the logic of good reasons—it would also refer to proficiency in the arts of invention, composition, presentation, and audience analysis" (p. 122). Fisher seems to be addressing an "ideal" speech situation.

Rooted less in philosophy and more in the social psychology of communicative development, Clark and Delia (1979) define rhetorical competence broadly as "purposive, strategic message formulation." Specifically, a rhetorically competent "speaker must not only define communicative goals, but must control the full resources of communication in fitting a message to concrete circumstances in accomplishing those defined ends" (p. 193). In viewing competence as an ability to construct communicative strategies that achieve purposive goals in given contexts, Clark and Delia implicitly expand the scope of rhetoric to *all* communicative functions—not just the persuasive function.

In a related sense, Hart and his colleagues (Eadie & Paulson, 1983; Hart & Burks, 1972; Hart, Carlson, & Eadie, 1980) developed the construct of rhetorical sensitivity. The rhetorically sensitive person manifests "a particular attitude toward encoding spoken messages" (Hart et al., 1980, p. 2). This attitude incorporates five principles: (a) acceptance of personal complexity (that is, conversants are multifaceted in their roles); (b) avoidance of stylized behavior and communicative rigidity; (c) interaction consciousness, an avoidance of both extreme altercentrism and egocentrism, focusing instead on the communicative transaction itself; (d) appreciation of the communicability of information and ideas, in which the conversant "seeks to distinguish between all information and information acceptable for communication" (Hart & Burks, 1972, p. 76); and (e) tolerance for, and acceptance of, inventional searching (that is, a recognition that ideas can be expressed in many ways and that it is at times difficult to search for the most appropriate expression). This last approach appears as one example of Ehninger's (1975) characterization of modern rhetoric "as a socially oriented art aimed at promoting healthy and productive human relationships" (p. 448). It is also this aspect of modern rhetoric that best represents the focus of this chapter. Whereas the classical rhetorics tended to stress persuasion and strategic communication, modern rhetorics tend to look for ways to alleviate the problems involved in communication and the human condition. Burke sees communication as a vital tool to compensate for the isolation and division intrinsic in being human. Richards views rhetoric as a way of managing misunderstandings and differences of meaning. Fisher attempts to provide the tools for discovering the underlying differences in communicator values and for managing the issues that divide people. These theorists, therefore, view rhetoric as a means of overcoming the divisions among humans. Thus, while ancient rhetorics concentrated on the persuasive functions of communication, modern rhetorics appear to be more concerned with the social and epistemological functions of communication.

Clark and Delia resurrect classical rhetoric to some extent by stressing persuasion and strategic uses of communication to accomplish specific objectives. They are among the first rhetorical theorists to cast this traditional concern into a competence framework. Hart and colleagues attempt to develop a more interpersonal rhetoric in which "sensitivity" plays a central role. Modern rhetoricians, therefore, have elaborated the broader social functions of communication. We turn now to a consideration of the social-psychological roots of competence-related constructs. In reviewing these contributions, note will be made of the importance of competent communication to mental health and quality of life.

Psychiatric Approaches to Competence

In an attempt to untangle some of the diffuse origins of competence in the psychiatric literature, Wine (1981) identifies three dominant historical "models" of human functioning: the demonological and medical *defect* models and the recent *competence* model. The primary assumptions of the defect models are that

> (1) the aspects of human functioning that are most important to observe are those that are deviant and abnormal; (2) these deviant characteristics are assumed to be manifestations of a pathological state located within the individual; (3) the cause of the intraindividual state, whether supernatural, physical, or psychic, occurred at some time in the past. (Wine, 1981, pp. 7-8)

The demonological instantiation of the defect model reflects the scientific world view of the medieval era. Deviant human behavior was thought to be a result of demonological possession or partnership. This model not only conformed to prevailing social ideology but also helped to enforce societal and religious morals (e.g., the Spanish Inquisition and the European witch craze).

Not until the late fifteenth and early sixteenth centuries did the demonological model begin to give way to the medical model. According to Wine (1981), the medical model presents both a physical and a psychic metaphor. The physical approach attributes deviant or disturbed behavior to underlying physiological disturbances (toxic substances, lesions, genetic abnormalities, and the like). The psychic or psychoanalytic approach views behavioral disturbances as reflections of underlying problems in mental apparatus or processes, usually caused by events in the childhood of the subject. It was the medical model that spawned the emphasis on mental illness and pathology. Wine (1981) suggests that this model was sustained until after World War II, at which point rising criticisms of the accuracy, labeling, and resulting rights violations of this model led to a new conceptualization—a mental *health* model, that is, the competence model. This model seeks to identify the characteristics of positive human functioning and adjustment.

In a lucid review of psychiatric trends from the nineteenth century to the present, Jurgen Ruesch (1951) indicates that for the most part, it was not until the 1940s and 1950s that psychiatry began to recognize the importance of communication in understanding mental illness and health. Earlier references to competence rarely emphasize the role of communication. For example, the earliest references to the notion of "social competence" appear to be in the 1930s (Doll, 1935, 1939; Bassett, Longwell, & Bulow, 1939; Bradway, 1937, 1938; Otness, 1941). Social competence was used as a criterion of mental health, or conversely, as Doll (1935) stated, "Mental deficiency is usually defined as a condition of social incompetence due to arrested mental development" (p. 103). As conceived by Doll (1953), social competence was "defined as the functional ability of the human organism for exercising personal independence and social responsibility" (p. 10). While communication was a component of Doll's measurement approach, it was a relatively unimportant and static conception. Sullivan (1950, 1953) was among the first to elaborate an entire psychiatric theory of human development in which the interpersonal system was the primary unit of analysis and in which competence was a central notion. Sullivan's psychiatry identified stages of psychosocial development (infancy, childhood, juvenile, preadolescence, late adolescence, and maturity) in which relations with others provided the basis for developing "mature competence for life in a fully human world" (p. 371). If an individual is prevented from fully developing in any stage, later stages will be impaired, resulting in mental disturbances (such as anxiety) and incompetence.

Ruesch (1951) was even more explicit in his reliance on communication as a central psychiatric construct. Ruesch (1972) traces the role of communication in psychiatric theories from Freud's analysis of transference to Sullivan's interpersonal theory of psychiatry. But Ruesch goes further than these theorists by viewing communication as both a cause and an effect of mental disturbance.

> The ability to mutually correct the meaning of messages and to mutually influence each other's behavior to each other's satisfaction is the result of successful communication. This is the only criterion we possess, and if we achieve such a state, it indicates mental health. . . . It is obvious that people are mentally healthy only when their means of communication permit them to manage their surroundings successfully. (1951, p. 87)

Some time after making this statement, Ruesch detailed the manifold ways in which communication can become "disturbed," thereby producing mental illness in the receiver or indicating it in the sender (1972). Still later, psychiatrists of the Palo Alto group, relying to some extent on Ruesch's conceptions, developed a communication-based theory of schizophrenia (Watzlawick, Beavin, & Jackson, 1967).

In a series of studies on social competence as measured by the Vineland Social Maturity scale, Doll (1953) found that social competence consistently discriminated degrees and types of mental illness. Beginning in 1960, Zigler and Phillips developed a research program investigating the relationship between social competence and mental illness (Phillips & Zigler, 1961; Zigler & Phillips, 1960, 1961, 1962; see also Tanaka & Bentler, 1983; Zigler & Levine, 1981). While their operationalization of social competence assessed communication very indirectly (that is, through the variables of age, intelligence, education, occupational skill level, employment history, and marital status), they nevertheless found significant evidence that competent persons were less likely to manifest certain psychopathological symptoms, were less likely to be institutionalized, were institutionalized for shorter periods of time, and were less likely to be reinstitutionalized than socially incompetent persons, although the evidence is not entirely consistent (see Rosen, Klein, Levenstein, & Shahinian, 1969).

In a related line of research, several studies and reviews have found a relationship between impaired social networks or social incompetence and the onset or perpetuation of psychological dysfunction (Brim, Witcoff, & Wetzel, 1982; Carkhuff & Truax, 1966; Finch & Wallace, 1977; Goldsmith & McFall, 1975; Griffiths, 1980; Gunzberg, 1973; Monti, Corriveau, & Curran, 1982; Paul, 1969; Rumsey & Justice, 1982; Wolf & Wenzl, 1982).

These findings stress the importance of identifying the elements of social competence (see Farina, Arenberg, & Guskin, 1957; Aumack, 1962; Jones, 1977; McConkey & Walsh, 1982; Reynolds, 1981; Ulmer & Timmons, 1966). Gladwin (1967), a clinical psychologist, concurs. According to Gladwin (1967), "Social competence can be gauged in terms of the ability of persons to participate effectively in the legitimate activities of their society" (p. 31). Thus, social competence develops along three factors: the possession of a versatile response repertoire, the ability to manage and move among a variety of social systems, and effective reality testing. Social competence, therefore, provides a positive indicator of mental health rather than a negative one.

More recently, psychiatrists and clinical psychologists have begun to elaborate the various behavioral facets of maladaptive behavior and to discover ways to teach adaptive behaviors (see Bellack & Hersen, 1978; Trower et al., 1978). Such approaches will be dealt with in greater detail in the social skills section of Chapter 2.

In summary, the concept of mental health is strongly grounded in the way we interact in social contexts. At this point, the context remains an abstract concept. Increasingly, however, clinical psychologists are beginning to differentiate their areas of specialization into various contextual concerns. One of these concerns that is particularly germane to competent interaction is the marital context. A clear and consistent element of context to be reckoned with by communicators is the co-communicator—that is, the relational partner.

Marital Adjustment and Satisfaction

The relevant literature on marriage and the family focuses on marital satisfaction as it is contingent on spousal communication. This body of literature attempts to uncover those aspects of communicative behavior which, when enacted within a salient relationship context, typify competent and satisfying marriages.

Marital research represents one of the first contextually specific approaches to competent interaction. The major question has been: "What communication behaviors, patterns, and perceptions are associated with greater marital adjustment and success?"

Spanier (1976) offers an integrative definition of marital (or dyadic) adjustment that encompasses the view of adjustment as both process and end state. That is, adjustment can be viewed as a state of positive qualitative evaluation at a given point in time and

> as a process, the outcome of which is determined by the degree of: (1) troublesome dyadic differences; (2) interpersonal tensions and personal anxiety; (3) dyadic satisfaction; (4) dyadic cohesion; and (5) consensus on matters of importance to dyadic functioning. (p. 17)

Although Spanier found support for the importance of these factors, communication itself is more noticeably a part of his process definition. Other research efforts on marital adjustment have also found communication to be a vital component of well-adjusted and satisfying marital relationships. Kieren and Tallman (1972) define marital competence as an ability to solve or cope with interpersonal marital problems. Specifically, adaptability is cast as the critical skill involved in marital competence. Adaptability, as the ability to alter roles and strategies in concurrence with situational demands, is defined by three components: flexibility, empathy, and motivation. However, these three components were found to be inseparable empirically. D. K. Synder (1979) attempted to examine 11 dimensions of marital satisfaction (conventionalization, global distress, affective communication, problem-solving communication, time together, disagreement about finances, sexual dissatisfaction, role orientation, family history of distress, dissatisfaction with children, and conflict over child rearing) and found that "measures of affective and problem-solving communication are consistently the best single predictors of global marital satisfaction " (p. 818). Similarly, Tucker and Horowitz (1981) investigated the relative importance of sexual satisfaction and adjustment, several demographic variables, and verbal and nonverbal communication in predicting marital adjustment. They found that frequency of verbal and nonverbal communication is far more predictive of adjustment than either demographic variables or sexual adjustment.

These studies, for the most part, examined relatively abstract spousal perceptions of communication. Increasingly, communication researchers and social psychologists are attempting to specify the form of effective communication in successful marital relationships (Larson, 1967; Watson & Petelle, 1981). Navran (1967) concluded that happily married couples, relative to unhappy married couples, talked more to each other, conveyed understanding more, had more topics available for discussion, personalized their language, and used more supplementary nonverbal forms of communication. Bienvenu (1970) found numerous communication items on self-report questionnaires to differentiate between couples receiving counseling and nondistressed couples. The items reflected behaviors such as saying things better left unsaid, use of irritating tone of voice, use of insults, failing to express disagreement, hesitating to discuss topics that might hurt the spouse's feelings, failing to express feelings, nagging, talking things over, pretending to listen, and accuracy of understanding. Royce and Weiss (1975) investigated the relationship among specific interaction behaviors enacted during a videotaped conversation, marital satisfaction, and third-party ratings of the couples' marital satisfaction. The tendency for couples to compromise, show attention, laugh, show positive physical behavior, and provide agreement significantly predicted the couples' reported satisfaction ($R = .71$). Talk time equivalence, laughing, compromising, showing attention, positive physical behavior, and the use of humor significantly predicted judges' ratings of couples' marital satisfaction ($R = .73$). Boyd and Roach (1977) found three clusters of communication behaviors that discriminated between high and low adjusted couples: sending clear and direct messages (for example, "I say what I really think"), active listening (for example, "I listen and attend when my spouse expresses a point of view"), and verbal expressions of respect or esteem for spouse (for example, "I make statements that tell my spouse that she[he] really counts with me") (p. 541). Jacob, Kornblith, Anderson, and Hartz (1978) discovered that distressed and normal couples could be discriminated by, among other things, the degree of reported "shared activities and positive affectional/emotional interchanges" (p. 289). Wegener, Revenstorf, Hahlweg, and Schindler (1979) coded the verbal dialogues of distressed and nondistressed couples in an experimental conflict situation and found that distressed couples asked fewer questions, used less self-criticism and agreements, and used more rejecting responses. Mettetal and Gottman (1980), similar to Vincent, Weiss, and Birchler (1975), found that distressed couples are characterized by greater *reciprocity* of negative behavior than are nondistressed couples. That is, nondistressed couples are less likely to respond with a negative statement when confronted with one than are distressed couples. Several other studies have also examined the communication used by marital couples during conflict. Billings (1979), for example, found that "maritally distressed couples make more negative and fewer positive cognitive and problem-solving communications in conflict situations than those reporting a satisfactory marriage" (p. 374). These findings are consistent with the data obtained by Margolin and Wampold (1981), who found that nondistressed couples exhibited higher rates of problem-solving, neutral, and verbal and nonverbal positive behaviors than did distressed couples. Koren, Carlton, and Shaw (1980) found that distressed couples were more likely to utilize criticism during a conflict, while nondistressed couples were more likely to be verbally responsive to each other's influence efforts. These behaviors were also shown to predict the outcomes of mutual satisfaction and the attainment of objective conflict resolution.

Collectively, these studies indicate that certain types of communication behaviors are functional in the marital context (and even within certain types of marital relationships), whereas other types are dysfunctional (Fitzpatrick & Indvik, 1982). There is a sound basis, therefore, for pursuing a context-specific approach to competent interaction—that is, for examining communication behaviors as they relate to positive outcomes in specific types of relationships.

Relationship Development

There has been a recent and dramatic increase in social-scientific efforts to understand the development of interpersonal relationships (Altman, Vinsel, & Brown, 1981; Burgess & Huston, 1979; Duck, 1980). This trend is also reflected in the numerous publications offering advice on how to improve communication in various relationships (see, for example, Bach & Deutsch, 1970; Buley, 1979; Guerney, 1977; Hocker-Wilmot, 1981; Rasmussen, Day, & Cllie, 1981).

Altman and Taylor (1973) provide one theoretical perspective on relationship development. Relying on social exchange theory, they make a series of basic assumptions regarding the "social penetration process." First, relationships that progress move from relatively nonintimate, uninvolving, and superficial forms of interpersonal exchange to intimate, involving and intense forms of exchange. This basic assumption has been echoed by different theorists and theories (for example, Berger & Calabrese, 1975; Berger, Gardner, Clatterbuck, & Schulman, 1976; Miller & Steinberg, 1975; Miller & Sunnafrank, 1982). Second, Altman and Taylor (1973) theorize that the progression of a relationship is a function of perceived (and expected) rewards relative to costs and foregone alternatives. To the extent that past and present exchange—communication—optimizes rewards relative to costs, a relationship is likely to advance toward greater intimacy. One of the fundamental modes of exchange is self-disclosure, and it is predicted that as relationships evolve, self-disclosure increases in depth (that is, in the intimacy of the information disclosed) and breadth (the range of topic areas disclosed). Altman and Taylor's theory has been elaborated by Knapp (1978) and Altman et al. (1981).

As a basic prediction, Knapp (1978) suggests that relationships progress through identifiable stages of "growing together" and "growing apart." Characteristic of the growth stages, communication is likely to become increasingly broad, unique, efficient, flexible, smooth, personal, spontaneous, and judgmentally expressive. Conversely, as relationships decay or dissolve, communication is likely to become more narrow, stylized, difficult, rigid, awkward, public, hesitant, and judgmentally inexpressive. Implicit in this and other conceptions of relationship evolution is the assumption that com-

municative messages to his or her partner with greater likelihood of achieving desired outcomes. Although this assumption
is mitigated by alternative psychological processes in many
relationships, it nevertheless provides a usefull framework for
understanding the role of communication in relationship evolution.

With enhanced prediction, a communicator can adapt communicative messages to his or her partner with greater likelihood of achieving desired outcomes. Although this assumption
is mitigated by alternative psychological processes in many relationships, it nevertheless provides a useful framework for understanding the role of communication in relationship evolution.

A somewhat divergent approach is provided by Altman et
al. (1981). Instead of "averaging" a relationship's patterns, or
cycles, of increasing self-disclosure, they presume two opposing needs of relational partners: intimacy and privacy. Given
these opposing needs, it is predicted that developing relationships fluctuate over time in their manifestation of open and
closed communication patterns. In the early stages of a relationship, it is proposed that interactants display frequent,
brief, and unstable cycles of openness and closedness
"perhaps as they scan one another in a variety of areas, and
then back off to assess their interaction" (p. 145). In later
stages, these cycles are more infrequent, involve greater total
change (amplitude), and are more stable in their rate of
change. This approach would seem to predict cycles of competent interaction as well. As relational participants withdraw
from the relationship (that is, become more closed), the appropriateness and effectiveness of interaction may become less
probable, although for many relationships, withdrawal may be
the most competent strategy for the relational partners in the
long run. Some research provides support for such a curvilinear (Eidelson, 1980) or cycling (Baxter & Wilmot, 1983)
approach to relationship development.

A theoretic orientation that makes several similar predictions is the uncertainty reduction approach, grounded in attribution theory. Attribution theory posits a basic human need
to understand social events. This need stimulates a proclivity
to attribute events to perceived underlying causes. Applied to
relationship development, this means that initial interactions

involve considerable ambiguity and uncertainty. In order to reduce this uncertainty and to make one's fellow interactant comprehensible and predictable, one will invoke a series of characteristic communication processes (Berger, 1975, 1979; Berger & Bradac, 1982; Clatterbuck, 1979). The basic sequence expected is that, as relationships develop, more and more information will be disclosed, making both partners more and more predictable and therefore more gratifying to interact with (Berger & Calabrese, 1975; Miller & Sunnafrank, 1982). From this perspective, the prediction can be made that as relationships evolve, the information exchanged evolves from being largely cultural and sociological (superficial or general, for example) to being more psychological (intimate or idiosyncratic). A second implication is that as partners become better understood and more predictable, so do their communication behaviors. Again, this suggests a smoother, less awkward (and more competent) form of interaction in the highly intimate relationship.

Although the prediction that interaction becomes more competent as a relationship evolves is overly simplistic (Delia, 1980), it does underscore the idea that relationships tend to display characteristic patterns, contingent on certain motivational forces. One of the largely unexplored facets of these patterns and forces is that of competence in relationship management. What is involved in the competent initiation of relationships? How are impressions managed in order to provide the desired image to another to whom one is attracted? What factors influence the way in which we create an impression of competence in another's eye? Once a relationship is established, what kind of communication is most satisfying? These questions are only now being investigated in the study of human communication. Needless to say, the answers are not yet clear and may not be for some time. Our effort here is an attempt to identify the various approaches that have been taken toward competent communication, to examine the issues raised by these approaches, and to identify a model of relational competence that integrates much of the extant research and theory.

SUMMARY

Rhetoric, psychiatry, marital relations, and interpersonal communication have added to the concept we now call competence. Rhetoric introduced the systematic "art" of effective communication and provided a forum for accumulating knowledge about using actions and symbols to accomplish specific objectives. Psychiatry, in its search to explain human behavior and its psychological origins, introduced the concept of social competence. Psychiatry viewed social competence as an abstract ability to participate successfully in society. As such, social competence, and its implicit association with mental health, serves as a theoretical package in which communication can be housed. The study of marital relations indicated the importance of relational interaction and the dyadic context. Finally, the study of interpersonal communication has established the theoretical interest in communication specifically as it affects relational evolution. A comprehensive treatment of competence in communicating necessarily borrows heavily from the efforts in these fields. Notions of strategic and effective communication, context, social competence, and adaptation all have their origins in prior works.

The study of competent communication has evolved from a diffuse and circuitous historical path. The concerns of the rhetorical theorist for effective expression eventually became the concerns of the behavioral scientist as well. Psychiatry was interested in the relation of social competence and adjustment to the etiology of mental illness and mental health. Marital therapists and psychologists were interested in identifying the competencies that facilitated marital adjustment and satisfaction. More recently, interpersonal communication theorists and social psychologists have revealed an interest in the interface between competent interaction and relationship evolution. All of these theoretical interests are still active and, in fact, thriving. Evidence suggests that the notion of competence is a major theme of our times. Current communication textbooks routinely discuss interpersonal communication competence (see, for example, Morse & Phelps, 1980; Scott & Powers, 1978; Wilmot, 1979). This is not surprising. Competent communication is defining a core for the emerging area of interpersonal communication for several reasons.

As indicated throughout this chapter, competence in communicating is integral to an individual's quality of life. In general, competent communication has been shown to facilitate psychological health (Barrios, 1980; Doll, 1953; Myers, 1982; Paul, 1981; Trower et al., 1978; Zigler & Phillips, 1961), educational success (Breen et al., 1977, Kohn, 1977; Trenholm & Rose, 1981), occupational success (Clinard, 1979; Krembs, 1980; Moment & Zeleznik, 1963), intercultural adjustment (Bannai, 1980; Buckingham & Rosenfeld, 1978; LaFromboise & Rowe, 1983; Ruben, 1976), and social effectiveness (Campbell & Yarrow, 1961; Fitts, 1970; Gottman, Gonso, & Rasmussen, 1975). Stated succinctly, "communicative competence is essential for social, personal, and educational growth" (Simon, 1979, p. vii).

These are the concerns which this book addresses, both directly and indirectly. Having just identified some of the diverse historical origins of our interest in competent communication and having indicated its importance to everyday conversation and quality of life, we will now identify the various theoretic orientations toward competent interaction and effective communication (Chapter 2). A critical analysis will then be applied to the prominent theoretic approaches (Chapter 3). Having thus indicated some critical criteria, the assumptions and components of a relational competence model will be elaborated (Chapter 4). Finally, in an attempt to look to the future, a series of theoretical, methodological, and pedagogical issues will be discussed, and certain recommendations and suggestions will be explored in each of these areas (Chapter 5).

2

Approaches to the Conceptualization of Competence

THE WRITING AND RESEARCH associated with competence can be found under any one of the following labels: competence, social adjustment, psychosocial competence, environmental competence, social competence, rhetorical competence, rhetorical sensitivity, grammatical competence, linguistic competence, referential competence, communicative competence, conversational competence, social skills, interpersonal problem solving, interactional competence, interpersonal competence, interpersonal communication competence, and relational competence. It is the purpose of the present chapter to provide some order and focus for the many competence constructs that have been proposed. It is not our intent to provide an in-depth review of all the writing and research in this area. We have however, tried to capture the breadth and diversity of the scholarly conceptualization of competence in communicating. In later chapters, we will examine in more detail some of the concepts we perceive as especially central to competence in communicating.

Our review is organized around seven generic competence constructs that can be derived from the literature: fundamental competence, social competence, social skills, interpersonal competence, linguistic competence, communicative competence, and relational competence. These seven categories represent conceptual clusters around which work may be organized. It is important to recognize that these are neither pure nor exclusive classes of constructs. Often writers use these terms in ways unlike other researchers. Some writers incorporate features from several of the construct types. In the process of classifying constructs into one category or another, we attended to certain features that consistently differentiated the various authors. Thus, a person purporting to study communicative competence may be classified in our scheme as studying interpersonal competence, and a construct labeled social competence by its authors may be placed within the relational competence category. This is not intended to muddy the waters further but instead to ground the labels themselves in an underlying conceptual framework. Therefore, we differentiate the constructs according to the degree to which they emphasize *outcomes* of interaction relative to the actual *messages* produced in interaction. For the most part, fundamental competence, social competence, and interpersonal competence constructs focus on the outcomes of interaction. The defining criterion of "possessing" competence is whether some end state is successfully attained, be it psychological adjustment, the achievement of a relatively satisfactory level of peer relationships, or the negotiation of a desired contract in a particular episode. In contrast, the notions of linguistic and communicative competence stress the message itself. Social skills and relational competence represent hybrid constructs that attempt to explore the functional association of message behavior with the attainment of relatively desirable outcomes. Aside from this rather broad distinction, each construct label also represents at least one fairly unique feature. For example, fundamental competence theorists are concerned primarily with the development of competence and its relationship to mental health. Social competence theorists typically look for a set of traits that qualify a person to function well within certain social role relationships. Interpersonal competence theorists are interested in effectiveness, that is, any traits or psychological processes that consistently enable a person to achieve specific interpersonal objectives. Linguistic competence theorists limit their inquiry to knowledge structures and processes as they pertain to the production and interpretation of language, while communicative competence theorists investigate the use of interactive behavior that is appropriate to a given context. Social skills studies examine the relationship of specific behaviors to perceptions of competence, anxiety, attractiveness, and the like, in prototypical types of contexts. While social skills are concerned with typical context types, relational competence examines the relationship of specific behaviors to perceptions of competence in a particular episode, context, and situation. The differences among these constructs are further elaborated in the review that follows.

OUTCOME-FOCUSED APPROACHES

Fundamental Competence

The most general and most basic conceptualization of competence is that of *fundamental competence*: an individual's ability to *adapt* effectively to the surrounding environment over time (see Connolly & Bruner, 1974; Coulter & Morrow, 1978; Smith & Greenberg, 1979) to achieve goals. In this sense, competence refers to the general fitness of a person to interact with the physical and social environment in order to survive, grow, and thrive (White, 1968). An individual possessing fundamental competence has the ability to achieve desired outcomes; adaptability is considered essential for cross-contextual effectiveness. Such an individual is referred to as psychologically well adjusted. Psychological adjustment is viewed as an end state of having developed competence in interactions generally.

No other aspect of competence and effective social functioning seems so universally accepted as the ability to adapt to changing environmental and social conditions (see Baldwin, 1958; Brunner & Phelps, 1979; Flavell, Botkin, Fry, Jarvis, & Wright, 1968; Foote & Cottrell, 1955; Hale & Delia, 1976; Hart & Burks, 1972; Ivey & Hurst, 1971; Moment & Zaleznik, 1963; Ritter, 1979; Sundberg, Snowden, & Reynolds, 1978). Rigidity

or behavioral inflexibility, on the other hand, is often associated with abnormal or even pathological orientations
(Braen, 1960; Breskin, 1968; Cervin, 1957; Colton & Lan-
golois, 1976; Muhar, 1974; Schaie, 1955; Scott, 1966; Wolpert,
1955; Zelen & Levitt, 1954). "Adaptability," "behavioral flexibility," "behavioral repertoires," "creativity," and "style flexing" are
all terms used to represent a stable individual ability to produce consistent and effective responses in others by adjusting
to varied situations.

Because the notion of adaptability is at the core of nearly
all competence constructs, fundamental competence serves as
a conceptual building block for more specific and elaborate approaches to competence. The literature under the rubric of
"fundamental competence" is unique in its *focus* on the
phenomenon of *general adaptability*. The term "fundamental"
is appropriate for characterizing this literature because of its
direct concern with the most basic and encompassing of competence-related concepts.

Theories of fundamental competence reflect two interrelated concerns: (a) the cognitive capacities leading to consistent personal effectiveness and (b) the developmental
processes that facilitate or inhibit the acquisition of general
adaptability. Consequently, fundamental competence theorists
tend to restrict their analyses to *psychological* (that is, mentalistic) elements. Elements of performance and skill are *assumed* rather than elaborated. Indeed, many writers use the
terms "skills" and "abilities" interchangeably. It is the ability to
adapt that is of most interest to these writers rather than the
exhibited behaviors that presumably lead to successful outcomes.

Most theorists consider an "awareness" of one's physical
and social environment to be a cognitive requisite for adaptability. Such awareness entails a discriminative ability to identify
the context in which one is embedded. But recognition and discrimination of contexts alone are not sufficient—adaptability
also implies the capacity to *accommodate* to changing elements of the environment. An element of *creativity* in meeting
environmental contingencies is implied (Athay & Darley, 1981;
Foote & Cottrell, 1955). Thus, at a minimum, fundamental
competence involves the cognitive abilities to (a) process relevant information from the environment, (b) select information
most relevant to a specific task, and (c) "construct innovative

patterns of performance by reconstructing familiar practiced paradigms to meet the instrumental demands of constantly varying interaction situations." (Athay & Darley, 1981, p. 299). Some writers have insisted that competence goes even further than simply meeting the requirements of an environmental context. It is argued that the competent person also has the ability to alter his or her environment in order to achieve personal goals (Connolly & Bruner, 1974; Steele, 1980). This expanded conception of adaptability implies an "operative intelligence" of "*knowing how* rather than simply knowing that" (Connolly & Bruner, 1974). The competent individual is thus able to achieve some degree of personal autonomy and independence without impairing the context(s) within which this achievement is made (Doll, 1953; Inkeles, 1966). Theorists from a sociological perspective tend to emphasize the social dimension of environment (rather than the physical). The criterion for successful interaction is the effective performance of social roles (Havighurst, 1957; Smith, 1968). Roles define social expectations for behavior that are internalized by individuals in society. In a sense, then, the sociological approach to fundamental competence equates *effective* interaction with *appropriate* interaction. That is, knowing and performing socially prescribed behavior is tantamount to effective adaptation to the environment.

An enormous amount of literature pertains to the *development* of competence and adaptive behavior (e.g., Appleton, Clifton, & Goldberg, 1975; Marsh, 1982; O'Malley, 1977; Stohl, 1982; Waters & Sroufe, 1983). Much of this literature has been devoted to studying the emergence of adaptive or communication competencies according to age or over time, from infancy to adolescence (see Burke & Clark, 1980; Kagan, 1979; Keenan, 1974, Krauss & Glucksberg, 1969; Mayo & La France, 1978; Piaget, 1955; Ritter, 1979; Rothenberg, 1970). This research generally has found that as infants grow older, they develop greater abilities to take on the role of others, understand the causes of behavior, and adapt their verbal and nonverbal behavior to listeners. In an attempt to integrate and understand the relevance of this literature to competence, we will examine three theories that have been advanced to explain the development or growth of competence from infancy through adulthood: effectance motivation, sense of efficacy, and self-efficacy theory.

R. H. White (1959, 1968, 1976) developed the theory of effectance motivation to describe "what the neuromuscular system wants to do when it is otherwise unoccupied or is gently stimulated by the environment" (1959, p. 321). Humans have an anatomical urge that motivates them to interact with the environment through causing change and being causal agents. An infant experiences pleasure upon shaking a rattle and recognizing the he or she is the cause of the sound produced. White observed many such examples of environmental mastery activities and proposed that they be considered forms of competence. These activities, according to White, have no apparent function other than that of effectance itself.

Assuming an effectance motivation (that is, a motivation to master one's environment), gratification and satisfaction represent outcomes of successful effectance. This satisfaction, however, depends on the recognition of a "contingency experience" (Bronson, 1974; Goldberg, 1977). In other words, a person must realize or perceive that he or she is responsible for the environmental effect observed. It is obvious, moreover, that some environmental effects are not gratifying. Telling a joke to someone who takes extreme offense at it may produce a clear, observable effect, but the embarrassment that results is likely to outweigh any effectance gratification that results.

As the social realm of family and peers begins to permeate the infant's world, the processes of play, fantasy, role identification, and language emerge. As children enter into social interaction, they begin to develop a sense of self and identity (Mead, 1974). The self develops only in relationship to others, because only in others is there a basis for self-comparison. So the effectance urge, largely biological in nature, is transformed into a sense of self-esteem in the social context. White (1968), Harter (1978), Broucek (1979), and Franks and Morolla (1976) all propose that largely anatomical effectance urges are redefined by social perception processes. The effectance motive becomes a desire for a sense of competence; that is, a sense of self-esteem and social effectiveness. Effective social interactions over time become subjective measures of self-worth by gratifying the actor's sense of self-capability and resulting in satisfaction. Self-esteem is thus a function of one's feelings of efficacy and is viewed as a criterion of fundamental competence. This sense of self-esteem is what White (1968) and Harter (1978) refer to as a "sense of efficacy."

The importance of developing a sense of efficacy has been echoed by many theorists. Smith (1968) and Williams (1979) suggest that a competent individual perceives self to be an agent of change and accepts responsibility when desired effects are not accrued. This has been described elsewhere as an *internal locus of control* or sense of agency—the perception that self (rather than external events) is responsible for outcomes in the world (Tyler, 1978, 1979; Tyler & Gatz, 1977). Harter (1978) considers an internal locus of control to be essential to the furtherance of effectance motivation. To some extent, this is a necessary outcome of perceiving a "contingency experience." Collectively, then, efficacy theorists view the competent person as possessing a positive self-concept, an internal locus of control, and a history of successful mastery attempts.

The concept of a history of successful mastery attempts deserves further consideration. Smith (1968) explains that the reinforcement history of an individual exerts a strong influence on the development of fundamental competence. A self-fulfilling prophecy occurs such that once an individual is on the right track, successes multiply and accumulate. These successes, in turn, enhance the individual's attitude, knowledge, and skills, making subsequent success more likely. On the other hand, a series of failures can inhibit an individual from further attempts. Consequently, the knowledge and skills that are required for success (when the individual *does* try) are not properly acquired or developed. Research generally supports the notion that fostering the sense of self-responsibility and success in contingency experiences of infants enhances their eventual development of fundamental competence (Ainsworth & Bell, 1974; Baumrind & Black, 1967). Part of this process must involve unsuccessful contingency experiences if the development is to be a true learning experience in which the more effective strategies can be differentiated from the less effective strategies.

One theory compatible with this line of analysis is that of self-efficacy (Bandura, 1977; Mischel, 1973; Saltzer, 1982; Sherer et al., 1982). Self-efficacy theory posits that efficacy expectations mediate the initiation and persistence of a given set of behaviors. Specifically, people acquire new behavior patterns by observing behaviors in others, using these "models" as guides, and self-correcting their own behavior once enacted on the basis of social feedback and outcome achievement. The degree to which an individual believes he or she *can* enact a behavioral routine successfully, in turn, determines his or her likelihood of initiating and persisting in these behaviors (assuming that the objective of these behaviors is positively balanced). This belief provides an efficacy expectation for the individual. "An efficacy expectation is the conviction that one can successfully execute the behavior required to produce the outcomes" (Bandura, 1977, p. 193). This efficacy expectation is to a large extent based on current and past successes and the perceived locus of origin. Thus, the greater the degree to which people perceive the actual attainment of desired outcomes and positive reinforcement as contingent on self-originated behavior, the more confident they are likely to become in their efficacy expectations and the more persistently will these behaviors be enacted. Consistent with the self-efficacy perspective (although not grounded on it), research has found a relationship between social effectiveness (defined as success in interpersonal influence attempts and/or popularity) and competence (Campbell & Yarrow, 1961; Gottman et al., 1975; Sherer et al., 1982; Wright, 1980). The more a person experiences success in social relations and influence efforts (the conditions underlying self-efficacy expectations), the more likely that person is to enhance general fundamental competence.

In summary, the sine qua non of fundamental competence is cross-situational adaptability. Literature on fundamental competence is at a general level; that is, theories are concerned with the acquisition and development of adaptability and its cognitive precursors. The explanations for competence are generally cognitive and person-centered. Messages, per se, are not focal points for this literature. Interaction is *assumed* but not elaborated in fundamental competence theories. Nor are the exact goals or outcome events specified. Instead, the emphasis is on generic adaptive capabilities that *lead to* cross-situational effectiveness.

Social Competence and Social Skills. The literature on fundamental competence is concerned with a person's general ability to perform successfully certain socially defined roles. Competence as an ability frequently is conceptualized in terms of skills. The term "skill" refers "to the organization of actions into a purposeful plan which is executed with economy;...the essence of the skill lies in the ability to achieve a goal" (Elliot & Connolly, 1974, p. 135). Thus, skills may be considered as abilities focused on goal accomplishment, wheter the goal is as specific as speaking without a trembling voice or is as general as learning to manage the greeting ritual in a variety of contexts. Whereas fundamental competence concerns *the* ability to be *generally* adaptive, social skills and social competence models turn their focus to the *specific* abilities underlying (or manifested in) the performance of competent behavior.

In the last two decades, an enormous amount of literature has emerged under the heading of social skills. Consequently, this review is very selective. (For other reviews and critiques, see Argyle, 1979; Arkowitz, 1977; Ballack & Hersen, 1978; Curran, 1979a, 1979b; Eisler, 1978; Eisler & Frederiksen, 1980; Gambrill, 1977; Hersen & Bellack, 1977; Morrison & Bellack, 1981; Rathjen, 1980; Wine, 1981; Yardley, 1979.) A useful distinction for reviewing the social skills literature is provided by McFall (1982). He identifies two general models of social skills: the trait and the molecular models. Trait models, which are more common, view social skills as relatively enduring personality dispositions. The less common molecular models treat social skills as particular, situation-specific behavioral responses, which are not necessarily related to underlying personality characteristics. The distinction between trait and molecular models is most clear in the research conducted within these approaches. Since the trait model presumes that socially competent behavior is largely a function of personal dispositions, this line of research relies heavily upon self-report measures of traits supposed to be relevant to competent behavior. As a prototype of this approach, consider the study by Steffen, Greenwald, and Langmeyer (1979). In an attempt to discover the important components of social competence, these researchers factor-analyzed several self-report trait measures that were intended as operationalizations of social competence (assertiveness, social self-esteem, anxiety, dating satisfaction, and so on). In contrast, the molecular model, in its pure form, is almost entirely concerned with investigating the relationship between the performance of specific discrete message behaviors and molar ratings of competence (or anxiety, or attractiveness). The molar ratings are made on the basis of an observed performance, not on a general cross-situational characteristic. Prototypical of this model is Greenwald's (1977) study, in which female college students' role-playing episodes were videotaped. These videotapes were then viewed by judges who first rated the social skill and social anxiety of the interactants' performances and then indicated that behaviors they thought were important in making those ratings. These behaviors were then coded and related to the judges' ratings of social skill and anxiety. Of course, these approaches can be combined. For example, subjects can be selected on the basis of their extreme scores (high and low) on trait measures, placed in role-playing situations, and then compared in terms of their discrete behaviors performed. For our purposes, if the study actually identifies, codes, and relates molecular behaviors to ratings of social skill (or a related construct), it will be considered a molecular approach. We make this distinction because it preserves the theoretical differences between the approaches. The trait models assume that the sources of competence are the traits of the person, whereas the molecular model presumes that the sources of competence are in the specific behaviors performed. In an effort to preserve the term "skills" as a behaviorally focused term, we choose to refer to the social skills trait approaches as social competence models and the social skill molecular approaches as social skills models. Social competence, therefore, represents a type of trait (or set of traits) that facilitate performance of certain social roles. Social skills, in our usage, are specific behaviors associated with perceptions of social skillfulness.

Social Competence Models

Many of these studies have attempted to identify what specific enduring characteristics facilitate competent interaction. Among the personality traits that have been hypothesized to enhance one's social competence are nonverbal sensitivity (Christensen, Farina, & Boudreau, 1980), nonverbal expressiveness (Friedman, DiMatteo, & Taranta, 1980), extraversion, self-monitoring, social anxiety, assertiveness, locus of control (Henderson & Furnham, 1982), empathy, self-congruence, unconditional regard (Pierce & Zarle, 1972; Rosen, 1967), assertiveness (Rose, 1975), androgyny (Brunner & Phelps, 1979, 1980), and attentiveness (Spitzberg, 1982a). Other research has specifically viewed social or heterosocial anxiety as a primary trait of incompetence in social interaction (see Curran, Corriveau, Monti, & Haberman, 1980; Montgomery & Hammerlie, 1982; Prisbell, 1982; Steffen et al., 1979; Wallander, Conger, Mariotto, Curran, & Farrell, 1980). Still other researchers have investigated the relationship between trait-oriented styles of interaction and competence (Jones & Brunner, 1981; Moment & Zaleznik, 1963; Walters & Snavely, 1981). Collectively, these studies have provided a varied and inconsistent picture of the traits underlying competent interaction. Most of the authors simply isolated one or two traits that the literature suggested should facilitate a person's competence in interacting. There is little attempt to develop a theoretical framework that would identify an interdependent set of general social competence traits within which the others could be interpreted.

In examining the literature on traits associated with competence in interaction, four constellations of skill traits emerge as broad enough to encompass many of the more specific traits listed above yet focused enough to be measured. These four constellations of skills that appear to bear a strong conceptual and empirical relation to competent interaction are cognitive complexity, empathy, role taking, and interaction management. These four constructs collectively tap a broad range of behavioral, affective, and cognitive processes associated with interaction.

Cognitive complexity pertains to the number and interrelatedness of cognitive schemata that a person utilizes in processing information about the social environment (Bruch, Heisler, & Conroy, 1981). "Cognitive complexity may be defined as the capacity to construe social behavior in a multidimensional way" (Bieri et al., 1966, p. 185). These dimensions or schemas are also referred to as interpersonal constructs, which "are the cognitive structures within which the behavior, appearance, and utterances of others are interpreted and given meaning" (Hale & Delia, 1976, p. 198). The more complex a person's construct system is, the more differentiated and flexible are the impressions of processed information. A person who is cognitively complex is more capable of assessing situations and other people from a number of different perspectives and is able to incorporate contradictory information in an organized fashion (Olson & Partington, 1977). In order to become interpersonally competent, an individual must develop the cognitive skills necessary for interpreting people and social situations. Such skills allow for the flexible and strategic adaptation of messages (Hale & Delia, 1976).

In studies of the relationship between cognitive complexity and competence (frequently operationalized by the level of message adaptation, number of messages generated, or degree of perspective taking implicit in a strategic message), the evidence is mixed. Hale and Delia (1976) found a strong positive relationship between cognitive complexity and the ability to represent another person's perspective ($r = .61$, $p < .01$). Borden (1981) found that cognitive differentiation and abstractness related inconsistently to message adaptation. Differentiation was not significantly related to overall level of message adaptation, and abstractness was moderately and positively related to degree of specific types of message adaptation ($r = .44$, $p < .001$). Bruch et al. (1981) found that conceptually complex subjects were more assertive in complex situations than low complex subjects ($t = 2.11$, $p < .05$), and they were more persistent in their assertiveness ($x^2 = 3.89$, $p < .05$). Rubin and Henzl (1982), however, utilized a multiple communication competence and skill assessment strategy and related it to cognitive complexity only to find a nonsignificant effect ($r = .15$, ns). Reardon (1982) discovered a significant positive relationship between cognitive complexity and social perspective taking ($r = .50$, $p < .05$) and communication adaptation ($r = .50$, $p < .05$). In an extensive study of children's social relationships in a summer camp, Campbell and Yarrow (1961) did not find a consistent relationship between cognitive complexity/abstractness and social popularity or effectiveness. The results of several studies, then, suggest a small to moderate positive relationship between cognitive complexity and competence in communicating. One of the reasons for the inconsistent or attenuated relationships found in the literature is that other relevant variables are not accounted for. A person may be very cognitively complex but not motivated to adapt to another person. Furthermore, message adaptation is only one aspect of competent interaction. As this review indicates, several other skills are involved. Just as likely is that different measures of cognitive complexity may be measuring different constructs (O'Keefe & Sypher, 1981).

Empathy is commonly defined synonymously with role-taking ability (see Cottrell & Dymond, 1949; Dymond, 1948, 1949; Dymond, Hughes, & Raabe, 1952; Foote & Cottrell, 1955; Weinstein, 1969). Kelly, Osborne, & Hendrick (1974) avoid this equivocality by positing that "empathy is not synonymous with role-taking." In general, empathy refers to some kind of motor mimicry. Empathy does not, however, involve one's taking account of, analysis of, and adaptation to the role of another as does role-taking" (p. 67). This implies a basic difference between vicarious affective experience and cognitive decentering (Campbell, Kagan, & Krathwohl, 1971; Hoffman, 1977; Keefe, 1976; Mehrabian & Epstein, 1972; Stotland, Mathews, Sherman, Hansonn, & Richardson, 1978). In other words, role taking involves a mental and imaginative construction of another's role for purposes of managing interaction, whereas empathy is an emotional reaction to, or an affective experience of, another's emotional state (Spitzberg, 1980). Although distinct processes, empathic responses may inform the cognitions involved in role taking, and role taking in turn may provide constructive frameworks for interpreting empathic experiences. Together, these two abilities account for much of the generic concept of adaptiveness (Flavell et al., 1968; Hale & Delia, 1976; Hart & Burks, 1972; Howell, 1982; Stryker, 1957). By role taking or empathizing with another person, one is better able to predict the responses of that other to messages and communicative cues (Gompertz, 1960; Keefe, 1976; Konsky & Murdock, 1980; Lane, 1981; Ritter, 1979). The understanding and prediction of others afforded by these abilities provide one with the requisite information to adapt to the other and the situation. In addition, by taking the role of others, a person acquires the various roles, cognitive constructs, and behavioral lines of action of others. This allows an individual to internalize a behavioral repertoire of acts and to adapt to the construct system of the listener (Hale, 1980). Additionally, highly empathic individuals are likely to possess prosocial motivations that facilitate interaction and other-oriented behavior (Hoffman, 1977; Lane, 1981; Pierce and Zarle, 1972; Staub, 1978).

The importance of role taking and empathy to competent interaction is demonstrated by the findings of three studies. Cottrell and Dymond (1949) contrasted two groups of individuals differing in empathy and role-taking ability. The highly empathic individuals were described by the authors as emotionally expressive, outgoing, optimistic, warm, and flexible. In contrast, rigidity and introversion characterized those individuals with low empathy scores. In a study of interpersonal skills, D'Augelli (1973) described a strikingly similar finding. Individuals rated as high in interpersonal skills "were seen as significantly more empathetically understanding, as more honest and open with their feelings, as warmer and more accepting and...less set in their ways" (p. 533). There appears to be considerable isomorphism between socially competent behavior and the skills of empathy and role taking (Marsh, Serafica, & Barenboim, 1981). As Bochner and Yerby (1977) showed, persons high in empathy are likely to acquire other, related interpersonal skills as well. Decentering leads to the vicarious experience of other people's interactional repertoires and, for highly empathic persons, the internalization of these repertoires. However, it is important to recognize that these studies used self-report measures of empathy rather than physiological measures. The dependent measures were observational, indicating that the empathy constructs did affect the subjects' behavior, but it becomes more difficult to interpret exactly what the empathy items are measuring.

The aforementioned studies also suggest that role taking and empathic abilities may enhance the skillful management of dialogue. Interaction management (Wiemann, 1977) concerns the ability to handle the procedural aspects of structuring and maintaining a conversation. These include negotiation of topics discussed, turn taking, entering and exiting episodes, and handling topical development smoothly. By enhancing the interpretation of identity and message information, role-taking and empathic abilities allow better adjustment of responses and directions of dialogue in response to other interactants (Bronfenbrenner, Harding, & Gallwey, 1958). As a result, management of communication should be more satisfying to the interactants. While interaction management commonly is referred to as if it were an individual skill or ability, there has been little research to discover whether it is a cross-situational or a stable personal trait.

Social Skills Models. The molecular approach to social skills generally reflects the assumption that any behavior a person manifests can be reproduced. Reproducible behaviors are, in turn, representative of an underlying motor process or skill. The reasoning seems to be that a person performing a behavior (such as mutual eye gaze) must possess the ability to *produce* that behavior and, therefore, *reproduce* that behavior. Thus, the intent of most research in the molecular approach is either to identify what specific microscopic behaviors differentiate competent groups from incompetent groups of subjects or to find out what behaviors are related to third-party impressions of competence. Many of the studies operationalize social competence in terms of perceived confidence or assertiveness. By discovering the particular behaviors that are related to impressions of assertiveness or anxiety, researchers can infer which skills (behaviors) need to be taught or extinguished in therapeutic contexts.

Most of these studies have as their research question: What behaviors are related to ratings of social skills and/or social anxiety? Arkowitz, Lichtenstein, McGovern, & Hines (1975) found that out of ten behaviors coded in three situations, only the behaviors of mean response latency, mean number of words, and number of silences distinguished low-frequency daters from high-frequency daters. Minkin et al. (1976) found that the use of "conversational questions" and "positive conversational feedback" were perceived as enhancing one's impression in interaction. Rating the behaviors of "skilled" and "unskilled" psychiatric patients in initial encounter situations, Trower (1980) discovered that "skilled patients were found to speak, look, smile, gesture, and move their posture more than were unskilled patients; the skilled group also showed more variability in behavior in response to situation changes" (p. 327). Conger and Farrell (1981) demonstrated that subject talk time and gaze were negatively related to ratings of social skill. The number of subject smiles and gestures were positively related to ratings of social skill as well. An experiment by Dow, Glaser, and Biglan (1981) revealed that between 38 and 69 percent of the variance in social skill ratings was accounted for by the number of questions and silences used. St. Lawrence (1982) coded the behavior of mental health center outpatients in eight role-play situations. Although the subjects' amount of verbal praise and appreciation, eye contact, and response latencies were all significantly related to ratings of assertion, eye contact was by far the most significant predictor. Royce (1982) also found a significant effect for eye contact (coded as amount of downward gaze), as well as number of questions and gestures on the ratings of heterosocial skill.

A series of studies have indicated that latency of response is related negatively to third-party ratings of social skill and anxiety (McLaughlin, 1982; Fischetti, Curran, & Wessberg, 1977; Peterson, Fischetti, Curran, & Arland, 1981). Research in assertiveness as a socially skilled mode of behavior has found numerous significant correlates. Romano and Bellack (1980) found intonation, volume, posture, gestures, extraneous movements, restrained movements, and positive facial expressions to be significantly related to ratings of social skill in an assertion situation. Rose and Tyron (1979) designed assertion episodes varying systematically in extent of voice loudness, response latency, content compliance, gestures, and voice inflection. They found all of these to affect ratings of assertiveness significantly.

Kupke and his colleagues (Kupke, Hobbs, & Cheney, 1979; Kupke, Calhoun, & Hobbs, 1979) discovered through a series of experiments that personal attention behaviors (such as asking questions, using other personal pronouns such as "you") were perceived as enhancing the speaker's heterosocial attractiveness in a dating situation. Kelly, Urey, and Patterson (1980) also found questions, self-disclosure, and compliments directed to the other person significantly related to ratings of heterosocial conversational skill. Similarly, Scott and Edelstein (1981) trained confederates in both personal attention (other-enhancement strategy) and self-attention (self-enhancement strategy). Personal attention exerted a positive effect on social competence ratings, whereas self-attention was negatively related.

In addition, researchers have attempted to identify the behavioral correlates of empathy and interpersonal immediacy ratings (closeness, warmth, openness, and so on). In a review of several studies, Matarazzo and Wiens (1977) indicated that mean duration of utterance, total talk time, proportion of talk time, mean reaction time and frequency of interruption were associated significantly with ratings of empathy. Haase and Tepper (1972), through systematic variation of eye contact, trunk lean, distance, and body orientation, found that these behaviors all were significantly related to verbal empathy ratings. These results were replicated with the addition of a significant effect for facial expression (Tepper & Haase, 1978). Finally, Bayes (1972) found smiles, body and head movements, positive content about others, speech rate, positive content about self, hand gestures, and positive content about surroundings to be related significantly to ratings of interpersonal warmth.

Interaction management has been investigated in a molecular fashion, even though this line of research rarely relates the management behaviors to impressions of competence (e.g., Beattie, 1980; LaFrance, 1974; Thomas, Roger, & Bull, 1983; Wiemann & Knapp, 1975; McLaughlin & Cody, 1982). Pearce (1976) reviewed the work of Wiemann and others to identify the behaviors commonly utilized in turn yielding and turn taking. Turn yielding appears to be accompanied by intonation (falling pitch), paralanguage (drawl on final syllable), buffers (pause fillers), pitch/loudness (drop in conjunction with a pause filler), sentence completions, interrogatives (questions directed to other), gesticulations (hand gestures), auditor-directed gazes, head nods, interruptions, simultaneous talking, stutter starts, and reinforcers (short feedback cues). Duncan (1983) has speculated that many of these cues form a turn system, in which "turn signals" function to coordinate interaction. A turn signal is indicated by any of the following cues: (a) an intonation pattern toward the close of phonemic clauses; (b) a "sociocentric clause," such as "you see" or "you know;" (c) the end of a sentence or syntactic clause; (d) a drawl on the final syllable or the stressed syllable of a phonemic clause; (e) termination of a hand gesticulation or relaxation of a tensed hand position, such as a fist; and (f) decrease of paralinguistic pitch or loudness on a sociocentric sequence (p. 151). The occurrence of these cues is observed as "signaling" that a turn is being relinquished. Beattie (1980) argues for a more complex model of turn taking, in which singular cues take their meaning from a set of simultaneous behaviors. For example, Beattie (1980) reports that existing evidence does not actually support the importance of gaze by itself in affecting turn taking. However, in a "particular context, characterized by hesitation, and low levels of speaker gaze, when the single gaze cue does occur at the end of a paralinguistically complete speech segment, it does have a striking effect on the turntaking process" (p. 205). The everyday coordinated use of these behaviors generates a number of conversational consistencies; for example, (a) the majority of the time, only one party talks at a time; (b) speaker overlap is common, but such occurrences are brief; and (c) most turn transitions occur with no gap or minimal response latency (Sacks, Schegloff, & Jefferson, 1978).

Collectively, these findings suggest that positively reinforcing behaviors consistently produce impressions of conversational competence. Table 2.1 displays the results of a meta-analysis of the findings of 18 studies in which behavioral predictors of social skill ratings were observed. A meta-analysis is a procedure whereby the findings of several studies of the same variables are aggregated and the sources of error controlled for. In Table 2.1, the average correlation, standard deviation of the mean correlation, number of subjects and studies, and associated variability statistics are reported. The percentage of variation among studies attributable to sampling error reflects the degree to which the studies examined are comparable or whether some systematic variation is occurring. The chi-square column shows the results of tests of the significance of the between-study variation. In this analysis, Spitzberg and Dillard (1984) isolated 12 commonly studied behaviors as they related to third-party ratings of social skills. As can be seen by the column labeled "mean correlation of behavior with social skill," the average correlation between the behavioral predictors across studies ranges from a low of .18 to a high of .68. Most of the correlations found were not trivial and, in some cases, were substantial. These behaviors appear to bear a reliable relationship to ratings of social skill in the contexts studied in this meta-analysis.

The trait and molecular models may at first appear irreconcilable or at least inconsistent. In fact, the two models are more different in focus than in substance. It is likely that the production of molecular behaviors depends on certain internal psychological processes. Whether such processes reflect "per-

TABLE 2.1 Results of the Meta-Analysis Relating Verbal and Nonverbal Behaviors to Global Ratings of Social Skill

Behavior	Mean Correlation of Behavior with Social Skill (ρ)	Adjusted Standard Deviation of Rho ($\sigma\rho$)	No. of Subjects (N)	No. of Studies (K)	% of Between-Study Variance Attributable to Sampling Error	χ^2*
Nonverbal						
Latency	-.33	.00	526	9	100	4.31
Gaze	.35	.00	218	4	100	2.46
Eye contact	.24	.00	268	5	100	4.63
Smiles	.25	.00	189	9	100	2.79
Gestures	.45	.00	170	4	100	1.45
Head movements	.24	.00	110	3	100	1.38
Adaptors	-.18	.00	104	3	100	2.81
Volume	.31	.00	184	5	100	5.58
Talk time						
Nonpatients/in vivo	.68	.00	137	7	100	5.27
Nonpatients/role-play	.42	.04	289	6	91	6.59
Verbal						
Questions	.41	.00	338	8	100	7.05
Compliments	.41	.11	168	3	52	5.78
Minimal encourages	.22	.11	100	4	75	5.37

*df = k – 1; none of these values attained significance at the .05 level.

51

sonality dispositions" or merely motor skills (Argyle, 1969), information processing (Pavitt, 1982), or implementing skills (McFall, 1982) is still an empirical question. Eisler and Fredericksen (1980) assert that there are basic characteristics that may be considered requisite for the demonstration of social skill. These include a developed behavioral repertoire, awareness of social norms, the ability to select effective responses from among available alternatives, the ability to interpret feedback, and the ability to adapt behavior based upon feedback. Similar conceptualizations are offered by Cushman and Craig (1976), Meichenbaum, Butler, and Gruson (1981), and Sarason (1981). For Cushman and Craig (1976), listening, cueing, and negotiation skills are the essential components of competent communication. Meichenbaum et al. (1981) propose that interpersonal problem-solving skills, role-taking skills, and efficient information-processing skills facilitate social competence. Sarason (1981) recommends problem-solving skills, role taking, empathy, and nonimpulsive tendencies as skills underlying competent interaction.

To imply underlying cognitive and affective processes for behavior, however, is not to deny the validity of assessing the behavior that these traits produce. A behavioral definition of skills focuses on *behaviors* rather than on their generative psychological processes. The molecular or social skills approach emphasizes the observable nature of social behavior. Skills are tantamount to functional behaviors that are oriented toward achieving some effect. The trait or social competence approach, as we are using the terms, is concerned with the underlying cognitive abilities that presumably facilitate the production of socially competent behaviors. Although work related to the trait and molecular approaches to social skills has remained somewhat distinct and separate, these models are *not* inconsistent or mutually exclusive. Indeed, the dichotomy between cognitive and behavioral conceptualizations is artificial; the complementary nature of these two models would make their blending theoretically desirable (McFall, 1982; Wiemann & Kelly, 1981). Social competence/skills literature shares the concern of fundamental competence literature with the ability of people to achieve goals and produce effects. Consequently, both fundamental competence and social skills/competence emphasize the *effectiveness* of interaction as exemplified in functional outcomes. As Curran and Mariotto (1980) explain, "One generally accepted requirement of any definition of social skills inherent in a functional analysis of skills is the necessity for employing the consequence of a behavior, or a set of behaviors, as part of the ultimate criterion" (p. 9). The difference between the two arises with respect to focus. While fundamental competence is concerned with cognitive processes that lead to general adaptability and success, social competence entails the discovery of *specific* abilities and behaviors that lead to particular successes. This is exemplified by the abundance of assertiveness research from the social skills perspective. Assertiveness is a set of skills associated with expressing self-defined goals and resisting the undue influence of others. In addition, the interest in interaction *behaviors* related to social skills introduces the communication process. Social skills researchers study interaction (in the *manifestation* of skills) rather than imply it.

Another departure from fundamental competence constructs is reflected in the recognition of *context* implied in social skills. Skills must be assessed with respect to *application* in an actual task or situation. The criteria of social skills reside in the functions that behaviors fulfill; i.e., the outcomes that are produced. It is typical to assess social skills or social competence in terms of outcome measures such as heterosocial attractiveness, anxiety, dating frequency, or marital satisfaction. The importance of studying "skills in use" (Steffen & Redden, 1977) is indicated by the predominance of role playing as the methodology of choice among social skills researchers (Bellack, Hersen, & Lamparski, 1979). Role playing is adapted uniquely to applying a person's skills in context. The importance of context in the assessment of social skills is summarized by Eisler (1978), who maintains that "it is not only the observed behaviors which must be judged as relatively skilled or unskilled, but the interaction of those behaviors within a specific interpersonal context" (pp. 372-373).

Interpersonal Competence

Interpersonal competence is concerned with the ability of communicators to accomplish tasks successfully. The literature associated with interpersonal competence represents a wedding of concepts exhibited in both fundamental competence and social competence perspectives. Like fundamental competence, interpersonal competence concerns exerting control over the environment to achieve certain outcomes. Like social competence/skills, interpersonal competence focuses on certain abilities that enhance success in particular communication situations.

Crediting the original notion to Sullivan (1950), Foote and Cottrell (1955) coined the term "interpersonal competence." As an ability to perform particular kinds of tasks, interpersonal competence translated into personal characteristics of health, intelligence, empathy, autonomy, judgment, and creativity (Foote & Cottrell 1955; Stanton & Litwak, 1955). In this conceptualization, empathy and creativity entail role-taking ability and behavioral repertoires. Autonomy is a manifestation of self-concept, and judgment is reflected in making correct and productive decisions. The key feature for interpersonal competence, however, is the degree to which these abilities allow one to "control" the environment.

In an attempt to verify the elements of competence identified by Foote and Cottrell (1955), Farber (1962) surveyed 495 husbands who responded to 104 items "regarded intuitively as representing a domain of elements which could be described as competence in interpersonal relations" (p. 31). Factor analysis indicated support for the previously conceptualized factors of empathy, autonomy, and resourcefulness as well as for an unexpected dimension labeled "cooperativeness/mutual support." For theorists grouped in the interpersonal competence category, environmental control is generally constituted by the ability to achieve goals and produce desired effects on other people. Prototypical of this orientation is Weinstein (1969), who defines interpersonal competence as the ability to manipulate the responses of others. The ability to manipulate another depends, in turn, on the ability to take the role of the other and predict the consequences of behavior on the other person's definition of the situation. Consequently, identity management, empathy, and role taking are seen as skills essential to interpersonal competence because interpersonal control requires successfully affecting the way in which the other person defines the interaction situation. In addition, Weinstein indicates that interpersonal competence requires a large and diverse behavioral repertoire and the interpersonal resources needed to implement effective behavioral tactics.

Another conceptualization of competence consistent with the control orientation is proposed by Parks (1977b). Like Weinstein, Parks views competency as a function of communicators' abilities to specify and attain goals. Contrary to Weinstein (1969) and Foote and Cottrell (1955), however, Parks argues that competence is best seen as a characteristic of the *control process* whereby an individual interacts with the environment, rather than a characteristic of communicators per se. Thus, he identifies six phases involved in effective control: goal specification, information acquisition, prediction making, strategy selection, strategy implementation, and environmental testing. Differences in the content and structure of these phases account for a person's situational diversity in communication effectiveness. In short, competence is conceived as an environmental response rather than a cluster of personality traits.

In explicating the control orientation, Parks (1977b) maintains that value perspectives must not be confounded with the notion of effectiveness. Dimensions such as rewardingness, identity management, empathy, and self-disclosure, which are often identified as components of competence, should *not* be viewed as general characteristics of competence, according to Parks. Rather, they should be viewed as strategic factors that may or may not be relevant to effective control, depending upon the situation. Because these factors may situationally conflict with an effectiveness standard, Parks believes that it is useful to distinguish between these situation-bound strategic decisions and the more general process of effective control.

Several authors have circumscribed the notion of control such that interpersonal competence specifically involves the ability to solve interpersonal problems (see Gotlib & Asarnow, 1980; Platt & Spivack, 1972; Priestly, McGuire, Flegg, Hemsley, & Welham, 1978; Shure, 1980, 1981). Problem solving fits well into the interpersonal competence category because it emphasizes goal achievement and a strategic, "rational" orientation to interaction. Goldfried and D'Zurilla (1969), for example, developed a behavioral-analytic model for assessing competence in which competence was operationalized as an individual's effectiveness in responding to problematic situations.

Problematic situations are those "which, by virtue of their novelty or conflicting demands, present circumstances that involve the failure of previously effective responses. Such situations tend to be associated with a low likelihood of 'automatic' *effective* action, and thus require problem-solving behavior" (p. 159). The steps for assessing competence are quite similar to the phases of control outlined by Parks (1977): situational analysis, response enumeration, and response evaluation. Several researchers have adopted this behavior-analytic approach to competence assessment (Donahoe, 1978; Fisher-Beckfield, 1979; Fisher-Beckfield & McFall, 1981; Levenson & Gottman, 1978; Perri & Richards, 1979; Rose, Cayner, & Edelson, 1977; Steffen et al., 1979). Spivack, Platt, and Shure (1976) conceptualized a set of interpersonal cognitive problem-solving skills that parallel the behavioral-analytic model. These skills include awareness of potential interpersonal problems, ability to generate solutions, and ability to specify the means to implement those solutions.

Argyris (1968) also defined competence as the ability to correct interpersonal problems, but he added the qualification that they be solved *in such a way that the interpersonal relationship is productively maintained.* For Argyris (1962, 1965a, 1965b), competence involves a set of continua in which the positive behaviors are experimenting, openness, and owning up to one's behavior. Experimenting with ideas and feelings has to do with risk taking, that is, risking self-concept in order to stimulate new ideas and feelings. Openness to ideas and feelings means that a person expands the range of acceptable ideas and increases awareness of these ideas and feelings. "Owning" statements simply refer to being aware of and accepting responsibility for one's statements. A person can manifest any of these behaviors or can manifest behaviors that help someone else display such behavior. Thus, a person who owns, opens and risks or helps to own, open and risk is more likely to be interpersonally competent. These behavioral dimensions represent a person's ability to manage interpersonal relationships effectively (Argyris, 1968).

One salient feature of interpersonal competence constructs is strategic orientation. Strategies are formulated and implemented in order to achieve an objective or objectives: Goffman (1969) elaborates the defining conditions of strategic interaction, with certain aspects displaying qualities similar to those of the decision-making and problem-solving conceptualizations discussed earlier:

> Two or more parties must find themselves in a well-structured situation of mutual impingement where each party must make a move and where every possible move carries fateful implications for all of the parties. In this situation, each player must influence his own decisions by his knowing that the other players are likely to try to dope out his decision in advance, and may even appreciate that he knows this is likely. Courses of action or moves will then be made in light of one's thoughts about this other's thoughts about oneself. (pp. 100-101)

This illustrates one of the more overlooked features of "interpersonal" conceptualizations of competence. Specifically, Goffman (1969) is stressing the mutual interdependence of the "competent gamester" with another person, both having some control over outcomes of the interaction. Whereas Parks (1977b) and Argyris (1965a), stress the individual's ability to achieve desired outcomes, Goffman (1969) emphasizes that desired outcomes are strategically framed within an interdependent context.

Interpersonal competence constructs imply a strategic orientation to interaction, and this strategic orientation is very goal-oriented. Communication is seen as a means to the end of goal achievement, whether the goal is completely salient or only tacit. Though certain skills may facilitate goal achievement, interpersonal competence is not a skills construct per se. It is instead focused on the end product of interaction.

MESSAGE-FOCUSED APPROACHES

Fundamental competence constructs, social competence models, and interpersonal competence constructs generally reflect a greater interest in the effective accomplishment of outcomes than in elements of communication. Social skills models are more of a hybrid, combining a focus on specific behavior and its relation to the outcomes of competence impressions. We now turn to a consideration of linguistic competence and communicative competence, which are more concerned with issues of language and message behavior exclusively. This is followed by a brief summary of relational competence—another hybrid approach that equally embraces communication process and product.

Linguistic Competence

Linguistic competence pertains to the knowledge of rules underlying the use of language. Normal development within a culture necessitates at least a rudimentary knowledge of its language and linguistic forms (that is, how the linguistic symbols are put together to form normatively meaningful utterances). Linguistic theory in the Chomskian tradition is concerned with identifying the mental rules that underlie the use of language. As such, "linguistic theory is mentalistic since it is concerned with discovering mental reality underlying actual behavior" (Chomsky, 1965, p. 4). Because of factors such as memory limitations and variations in attention and interest, observed language behavior imperfectly corresponds to its underlying structure or mental representation. This idea led Chomsky (1965) to make a fundamental distinction between *competence* and *performance*. Whereas competence is knowledge of language, performance is the use of language in concrete situations. Because performance is not a true reflection of a person's competence, "linguistic theory is concerned primarily with an ideal speaker-listener, in a completely homogeneous speech community" (Chomsky, 1965, p. 3). This ideal speaker-listener situation essentially excludes empirical conditions (Was the utterance appropriate to the context? Was it understood by the listener? and so on). In short, *linguistic competence* is tantamount to knowledge relevant to the use of language. Differences in linguistic competence approaches are due principally to variations in the way this knowledge is conceptualized. The work of Chomsky (1965), Habermas (1970), and Jakobovitz (1970) is illustrative.

For Chomsky (1965), linguistic competence is described by a generative grammar. A generative grammar is a description of the ideal speaker-hearer's intrinsic competence, his or her intuitive knowledge of language. Very generally, this knowledge is intuitive in that a communicator may not be consciously aware of the structural rules he or she uses to generate and interpret language. This knowledge, according to Chomsky, is best represented as a set of rules that assigns structural descriptions to sentences. That is, language, in the form of sentences and deviant forms of sentences, is composed of certain structural elements (noun phrases, verbs, adjectives, and the like) that are combined in meaningful ways. The question relevant to linguistic competence is how individuals *know* to construct and interpret an almost infinite potential variety of these structural combinations in meaningful ways. To the extent that common, consistent patterns exist in these structural linguistic combinations, linguistic rules may be assumed to exist. If the entire set of rules for constructing and interpreting a given domain of sentences can be described, then the linguistic competence of an ideal speaker-hearer in this domain would be understood.

However, structural description of sentences would fail to represent a native speaker-hearer's knowledge of language if it described only the *surface structure* of sentences. Chomsky (1965) illustrates this with a set of sentences:

(8) (i) I persuaded a specialist to examine John.
    (ii) I persuaded John to be examined by a specialist.
(9) (i) I expected a specialist to examine John.
    (ii) I expected John to be examined by a specialist.(p. 22)

All of these sentences reveal identical structural descriptions on the surface (that is, noun phrase-verb-noun phrase sentence). While 9i and 9ii are virtually synonymous in meaning, 8i and 8ii are quite distinct in meaning. To say that the foregoing structural description "accounts" for these sentences equally well would be to overlook important distinctions. A *deep structure* must exist that allows a native speaker to intuit the finer distinctions among such structurally similar grammatical constructions. Thus, an appropriate account of these sentences requires that their deep structure be discovered. Chomsky assumes that this deep structure determines the semantic interpretation of sentences and that there must be "mapping rules" which serve to transform surface structures into deep structures.

The existence of structural mental rules for the construction and interpretation of sentences leads Chomsky (1965) into several speculative directions. First, these structural rules are assumed to be universal. The implication is that "all languages are cut to the same pattern" (p. 30), even though they do not correspond empirically on the surface. Such an assumption is reflected in Chomsky's (1965) belief that true progress in the field of linguistics will come about only when "certain features of given languages can be reduced to universal properties of language, and explained in terms of these deeper aspects of linguistic form" (p. 35). A related line of reasoning is that these "deeper aspects of linguistic form" are innate rather than learned. Chomsky argues that children learn language so rapidly and with such a relatively limited and degenerate sample of the entire domain of empirical possibilities that such learning must occur on a surface level, facilitated by extant innate linguistic principles. Such pre-existing principles for assimilating primary linguistic data (that is, language experiences) provide a framework for learning the surface aspects of language construction and interpretation.

The work of Habermas (1970) stands in contradistinction to Chomsky's. Habermas subscribes to the notion that linguistic competence entails knowledge not only of sentence structures but of communication *episodes* as well. Although Habermas's theory of communicative competence is concerned with a domain largely distinct from Chomsky's, the two still have much in common. For Habermas (1970), linguistic competence is insufficient to explain a person's capacity for using language:

> In order to participate in normal discourse, the speaker must have—in addition to his linguistic competence—basic qualifications of speech and of symbolic interaction (role behavior) at his disposal, which we may call communicative competence. Thus, communicative competence means the master of an ideal speech situation. (p. 138)

According to this definition, Habermas is not far from Chomsky's use of the term "linguistic competence." Indeed, Habermas (1970) claims to use the term "communicative competence" in a way similar to Chomsky's use of linguistic competence" (p. 147). The similarity, however, is more with the concept of the ideal speech situation than with the "corpus" of the theory. Basing the theory of communicative competence partly on ideas put forth by speech-act theorists (see Austin, 1971; Searle, 1971), Habermas argues that speech implies a level of content meaning and a level of pragmatic meaning. Pragmatic meaning concerns the way in which a statement refers to the speech situation and the role relationships contained within it. Habermas refers to the pragmatic level of meaning as involving dialogue constitutive universals. Dialogue constitutive universals are the universal pragmatic features of discourse that represent a class of expressions with "illocutionary force."

Illocutionary force refers to the linkage of utterances' meaning to the speech situation. For example, performatories such as promising, threatening, apologizing, and advising are neither true nor false as statements but are pragmatic in regard to their reference to behaviors and role relationships in the episode. They imply the performance of action (Austin, 1971), p. 13) and, by so doing, refer to an implicit relation of behavior in a situation. Another example of dialogue constitutive universals is the use of personal pronouns. As Habermas illustrates,

> The linguistic description can only make plausible why the sentence
>
> > I apparently am hungry
>
> deviates from
>
> > He apparently is hungry,
>
> if "I" is understood not only as one nominal pronoun among many, but as a reflexive specification of a speaker in a particular situation. (p. 139)

These examples, among others, imply a set of dialogue constitutive universals or linguistic expressions, "which serve to situate pragmatically the expressions generated by the linguistically competent speaker" (McCarthy, 1973, p. 137). Habermas (1970) therefore proposes to define communicative competence "by the ideal speaker's mastery of the dialogue constitutive universals irrespective of the actual restrictions under empirical conditions" (p. 141). Because the *performance* of these dialogue constitutives are contingent on the same empirical limitations as is a generative grammar, "communicative competence relates to an ideal speech situation in the same way that linguistic competence relates to the abstract system of linguistic rules" (Habermas, 1970, p. 140).

While this is a necessarily brief examination of only a small set of implications that can be drawn from Habermas's theory (see McCarthy, 1973; McGuire, 1977; Misgeld, 1977), it should help to locate the theory within the arena of constructs that seek to identify a communicator's knowledge of what Pearce (1976) refers to as constitutive rules. Constitutive rules in this sense specify what symbols "mean" (Pearce & Cronen, 1979) or how X counts for Y (Searle, 1971). In the theories of both Chomsky and Habermas, a grammar of speech is identified and the competence of a speaker is referenced by ideal mastery of this grammar.

A theory of competence that to a large extent encompasses the theories of both Chomsky and Habermas is outlined by Jakobovitz (1969, 1970). According to Jakobovitz, three forms of meaning (or inference) are necessary for a comprehensive theory of competence. *Linguistic meaning* involves lexical meanings, syntactic relations, and phonological actualization rules. Lexical meaning concerns include "syntactic manipulations such as subject-verb, verb-object, complement, relative clause, question, passive transformation, nominalization, tense, number, transitivity, and so on" (1970, p. 19). *Implicit meaning* refers to the denotative and connotative meanings of words. "Implicit references pertain to the semantic or conceptual implications of morphemes, words, and larger linguistic constructions" (1970, p. 19). Finally, *implicative meaning* reflects the relation between language and its speaker. Knowing the difference between a promise and a request; the linkage implied by words such as "therefore," "thus," "it follows that"; and how language can reflect the psychological state of its speaker all involve implicative meaning. This latter form of meaning corresponds fairly well with Habermas's conception of dialogue constitutive universals, while the former types of meaning are more closely allied with the domain of Chomsky's theory. Collectively, mastery of these three forms of meaning provides Jakobovitz with a model of competence.

The quality of communication (its breadth, scope, effectiveness) will be a function of the quality of inferences produced by the speaker and hearer on the three levels just outlined. Communicative competence is a reflection of the quality of the linguistic, implicit, and implicative inferences of which an individual is capable. (1970, p. 21)

Thus, Jakobovitz appears to combine the forms of knowledge with which Chomsky and Habermas are concerned. The result is a more comprehensive approach to competence. This approach, however, still conforms to the general nature of linguistic competence constructs. These constructs locate competence within the individual, as a form of tacit knowledge of linguistic/speech forms, regardless of an individual's actual behavior in a given context.

Communicative Competence

Communicative competence may be defined as the ability to adapt messages appropriately to the interaction context. As such, it is clearly broader in scope than linguistic competence. In fact, linguistic competence is usually considered a prerequisite for communicative competence. The specific differences between linguistic competence and communicative competence arise from the theoretical debate regarding Chomsky's (1965) distinction between *competence* and *performance*. While the debate consisted of several arguments (see Greene, 1977; Kaufer, 1979), two issues in particular help differentiate linguistic and communicative competence.

Hymes (1979) is one of the most influential and vociferous critics of the competence/performance distinction. He argues that Chomsky's use of the term "competence" is too narrow. For Hymes (1979), competence refers to the "abilities of individuals" (p. 41). Individual abilities relevant to communication clearly extend beyond knowledge of language. The ability to process information cognitively and the ability to explain and predict human behavior are just two examples that comprise more than grammar. Moreover, Hymes (1979) argues that knowledge by itself cannot account for the infinite potential of linguistic forms. As a consequence, a person's competence should refer to the *ability to perform* as well as to the *knowledge of how to perform*.

The second argument against the competence/performance distinction notes that linguistic competence, the "ideal speaker-hearer's knowledge of language," ignores the concept of context. To a large extent, the argument is one of practical utility. As Hymes (1971) states,

> We have to account for the fact that a normal child acquires knowledge of sentences, not only as grammatical but also as appropriate….There are rules of use without which the rules of grammar would be useless. (p. 10)

The relevance of contextual factors, factors that specify how speech behavior is appropriate to a given context, is clear in a number of examples. Geest, Gerstel, Appel, and Tervoort (1973) provide illustrations of "sentences to which no linguist cares to pay attention, and for which he consequently does not give any rules" (p. 14). For example, a mother interacting with an infant can say "Thank you, Mommy" to stimulate in the infant a courtesy response that mirrors the mother's statement. The message "May I?" may mean "May I take a cigarette?" or "May I open the door for you?" But these interpretations take on their correct meaning only when placed in context. It is this contextual information that is foregone by the distinction between competence and performance. Competence, for Chomsky, pertains to the "ideal" speaker-hearer, irrespective of actual contextual conditions.

The introduction of context for usage into the conceptualization of competence represents a major break with the competence/performance distinction. Once contextual factors are implied, so is the concept of appropriateness or acceptability. But Chomsky (1965) and linguistic competence theorists are uninterested in the notion of appropriateness because it falls within the domain of performance. At a minimum, proponents of communicative competence call for the break from linguistic competence constructs by arguing for consideration of knowledge of what is appropriate in a given context rather than what is grammatical. Some theorists in this school maintain the competence/performance distinction but choose to view competence as knowledge of appropriate communication behavior in a given context and view performance as the actual production of that communicative behavior (see McCroskey, 1982b;

Paulston, 1974). Most theorists tend to follow Hymes's (1971, 1972b) position, however, and view communicative competence as inclusive of both knowledge and performance (see Black, 1979; Briere, 1979; Ervin-Tripp, 1973; Sankoff, 1974).

While many have acknowledged appropriateness as the fundamental criterion of communicative competence, the precise meaning of the term remains somewhat unclear. Fillmore's (1979) distinction between "knowing that" and "knowing how" suggests the difference between "knowing linguistic forms and knowing when to use them" (p. 92). However, the explicit nature of knowing how is not elaborated. The basis for judgment of a behavior's appropriateness in a given situation is not clear. One approach has been to identify the rules of a given situation. While not directly concerned with the competence construct, the most comprehensive treatment of communication rules is provided by Shimanoff (1980): *"A rule is a followable prescription that indicates what behavior is obligated, preferred, or prohibited in certain contexts"* (p. 57). According to Shimanoff, the existence of a communication rule is indicated by several types of evidence, the most relevant of which is the criterion that rule-generated behavior is criticizable. Rule-based behavior is criticizable if it can (a) be judged as appropriate or inappropriate, (b) be responded to with negative sanctions, or (c) be recognized as creating a repair of behavioral deviations (p. 115). The point here is that criticizable behavior implies the notion of appropriateness, which, in turn, is the critical indicator of communicative competence. "Appropriateness, then, appears to be the single criterion with the power to discriminate the phenomenon of communication competence from other communicative phenomena" (Backlund, 1977, p. 15). A communicator's sense of appropriateness provides the basis for judging what behavior is called for in a given context. The communicator's audience will be a very important influence on his or her sense of appropriateness.

The idea that communicators possess a range of behaviors from which to choose suggests the notion of behavioral repertoire. Once imbued with a conception of what is appropriate and inappropriate in a situation (that is, what the rules are), a communicator still faces the task of selecting a behavior to perform from the range of behaviors at his or her command.

The idea that communicators possess a set or range of behaviors that can be implemented in given contexts complements the criterion of appropriateness; it simultaneously specifies the definition of competence as "knowledge." This conceptualization is exemplified by the symposium of the Speech Communication Association's National Project on Speech Communication Competencies. According to their perspective,

> Competence is characterized by four principal features: (1) the exercise of competence depends upon an available repertoire of experiences; (2) it requires that the individual make critical choices from that repertoire; (3) it is revealed when suitable behaviors are brought to bear in performing desired tasks; and (4) it is sustained when individuals are able to evaluate their performance behaviors objectively—thereby enriching their repertoires of experience. (Allen & Brown, 1976, p. 248)

The suggestion has been forwarded that repertoires actually develop for both behaviors and situations (Johnson, 1979, p. 18). Hymes (1972) speaks of a communicative repertoire as including three considerations. First there is the set of communicative means (behaviors) available and their associated meanings. Second, there is the set of contexts and their associated meanings in which these means may be expressed. Third, there are the relations among these means and contexts (pp. xxxiv-xxxv). Thus, when the criteria of appropriateness and behavioral repertoire are used in conjunction, it becomes clearer how a person's knowledge of appropriate communicative behavior in a given context is manifested. A person's knowledge is indicated by the range of his or her behavioral and contextual repertoire and accurate comprehension of the rules relating these behaviors and contexts.

In sum, communication competence refers to the ability to demonstrate appropriate communication in a given context. While some authors have interpreted ability to mean knowledge of what is appropriate, many have construed ability to include skill (that is, performance of what is appropriate) as well. Communicative competence is distinguished from linguistic competence in two important ways. First, while linguistic competence is concerned with what is grammatical, communicative competence is concerned with what is situationally appropriate. Thus, while linguistic competence entails knowledge of grammatical rules, communicative competence implies knowledge of cultural, social, and interpersonal rules for acceptability of behavior. Second, because it embraces the assumption of contextuality, communicative competence recognizes that dimensions other than knowledge about language necessarily affect the demonstration of competent communication behavior.

Relational Competence

The various approaches to competence in communicating reviewed thus far emphasize appropriateness or effectiveness in communicating. Fundamental competence constructs, social competence constructs, and interpersonal competence constructs tend to focus on identifiable outcomes (such as social adjustment, skill performance, and goal achievement) with a corresponding deemphasis of the linkage between process and outcome. Linguistic and communicative competence constructs, on the other hand, generally focus on the appropriateness of messages, either grammatically or contextually, with a corresponding deemphasis of the functional outcomes of the communication observed. The social skills molecular model emphasizes the relation between specific behaviors and impressions of social skillfulness, which usually entails notions of appropriateness and effectiveness. While the appropriateness-effectiveness dichotomy is an oversimplification of the vast number of specific differences among these authors, it still serves a useful heuristic purpose. Many authors do not specifically or clearly differentiate appropriateness and effectiveness (McCroskey, 1981; Wiemann & Backlund, 1980), while others make this a major theoretical issue (Parks, 1977b). There is, however, another camp, which recognizes the distinctions between appropriateness and effectiveness and simultaneously argues for the necessity of *both* criteria for a comprehensive conceptualization of competent interaction. The category of constructs associated with this camp will be referred to as relational competence. Given the dual criteria of appropriateness and effectiveness, relational competence does not focus exclusively on the communication process or communication outcomes; rather, like the social skills model, it displays an explicit focus on the linkage between the two. But un-like the social skills model, relational competence constructs are not normative. The social skills approach attempts to iden-tify the normatively or socially accepted behaviors in certain common situations. Relational competence approaches avoid normative judgments (except to the extent that such judgments are internalized by the interactants), focusing instead on the perception of competence by the participants in a given con-versation and relationship. While the assumptions of relational competence are detailed in Chapter 4, some of the fundamen-tal characteristics are summarized here.

One of the most essential features of relational competence is a recognition of the reciprocal and interdependent nature of human interaction. This inherent interdependence leads to the premise that a person can be interpersonally competent *only* in the context of a relationship. Thus, to the ability to achieve objectives and the ability to adapt to varied situations, Bochner and Kelly (1974) add the component of the ability to collabo-rate effectively with others as central to competence. The mutual satisfaction of interactants is consequently a typical criterion of relationally competent communication (see O'Mal-ley, 1977; Pearce, 1976; Ruben, 1976; Wiemann & Kelly, 1981). Competent communication is considered a coordinated process in which individuals achieve goals in a prosocial fash-ion. That is, personal effectiveness accrues in such a way that the attendant strategies and outcomes are perceived to be be-nign or positive by the other interactant(s). As Brandt (1979) succinctly summarized, the conceptualization of relational competence suggests "a perspective in which the importance of goal-achievement, communication skills, *and* sensitivity to both situations and other persons are equally stressed" (p. 225).

Several authors have attempted to identify behavioral skill components that an individual needs in order to maximize the potential for mutual satisfaction. For example, Fitts (1970) iden-tified the behavioral components of involvement, responsi-bility, freedom, empathy, openness, caring, and acceptance. Pearce (1976) similarly prescribed the skills of reflexive capa-bility (that is, awareness of strategic choices), empathy, ability to articulate meanings at a high level of abstraction, ability to cope with linguistic structure, ability to use appropriate meanings and messages, ability to negotiate, and ability to be creative. Ruben (1976) recommended the behaviors of display of respect, interaction posture, orientation to knowledge, empathy, self-oriented role behavior, interaction management, and tolerance for ambiguity. Likewise, Wiemann and Backlund (1980) identified the skills of empathy (including affiliation and support), behavioral flexibility, and interaction management as fundamental skills of competence.

Underlying the varied skills is the general perspective labeled "other orientation." This perspective implies that a person is considered competent to the extent that the other communicators present are attended to appropriately. In general, other-orientation skills allow a communicator to be "supportive of the faces and lines" of fellow interactants (Wiemann, 1977, p. 197). Feingold's (1977) research specifically demonstrated that effective communicators are perceived as other-oriented to the extent that they are perceived (a) as able to adapt communication appropriately, (b) as committed to their message, and (c) as empathic listeners. It is important to note that being other-oriented does not exclude the possibility of being effective. As Wiemann (1977) indicates, "The competent communicator is the person who can have his way in the relationship while maintaining a mutually acceptable definition of that relationship" (p. 198). A person who is other-oriented may be able to manifest attentive, concerned, and empathic communication and still be able to manage the conversation(s) in personally desirable ways. In fact, other-orientation skills may facilitate the perception of cues that allow an instrumental management of the conversation. In addition, a person who is perceived as being other-oriented may be in a better position to attain personal objectives because the perceiver (or conversational other) is gratified by the conversation and is more willing to be managed.

Rather than focus on generic skills, Bennis and his colleagues (1968) maintained that the criteria for satisfying and effective relationships depend upon the primary *function* of the relationship. Emotional-expressive relationships are formed to fulfill themselves, as in love, marriage, and friendship, and comfirmatory relationships are oriented to the co-creation and maintenance of self and contextual "reality." Change-influence relationships focus their interaction on altering the other person (his or her attitude or behavior, for example), while instrumental relationships are motivated by the drive to accomplish a goal or task. Each relationship type is hypothesized to be characterized by a predominant mode of interaction and consequent outcomes indicating the degree of success in the relationship. As a result, emotional-expressive relationships are characterized by reciprocity of feelings; confirmatory relationships, by information about the self or situation; change-influence relationships, by information about desired goals and the progress made toward the goals; instrumental relationships, by task-related information. Given distinct relationship types, Bennis et al. (1968) suggest distinct criteria for evaluating these relationships. Emotional-expressive relationships are successful in that they achieve mutual satisfaction; confirmatory relationships are successful if they result in confirmation or consensus; change-influence relationships are successful to the extent that they accomplish the desired change; and instrumental relationships are successful if productivity and creativity result.

SUMMARY

Competence theories generally attempt to explain how and why people adequately function with one another. All approaches to the study of competence are ultimately concerned with the ability of humans to behave successfully and/or properly. Clearly, there are several distinct orientations in the literature that bear on the conceptualization of competence. Although the approaches exhibit commonality and overlap, there are at least six distinguishable categories for classifying competence constructs.

Fundamental competence, social competence, and interpersonal competence are all concerned with the *effective* achievement of *outcomes*. Fundamental competence describes the general ability to *control* the environment through *adapta-*

tion. Interpersonal competence is more circumscribed in that it pertains to specific processes and abilities that yield effective *goal achievement.* Likewise, social skills/competence identifies specific dimensions that facilitate effective social interaction; these dimensions reflect underlying psychological traits. Fundamental, social, and interpersonal competence constructs are chiefly concerned with explaining effective outcomes.

Linguistic competence and communication competence are message-focused rather than outcome-focused. That is, they attempt to explain message behavior. Linguistic competence refers to knowledge about language (for example, grammatical knowledge) that enables its usage. Communication competence is less atomistic than linguistic competence; it deals with the ability to engage in *appropriate* communication behavior in a given context. For some scholars, that ability refers to relevant knowledge of communication rules, situations, and strategies. For others, communication competence also entails the skilled demonstration of appropriate communication behavior.

Finally, relational competence and the molecular social skills models represent hybrid approaches that examine the relationship between molecular behaviors and outcomes such as the perception of appropriateness and effectiveness, or social skillfulness. Specifically, these approaches address the links between communication processes and functional outcomes. A model of relational competence is explicated in Chapter 4. But first, we would like to consider some issues that are generally problematic to the conceptualization and measurement of competence in communicating.

3

COMPETENCE IN COMMUNICATING

A Critique of Issues

THE PURPOSE OF THIS chapter is to present a critical analysis of some key assumptions that underlie most efforts to study communication competence. Our aim is not to boast any panacea for thorny conceptual problems. Instead, we offer an ussue-oriented analysis that we hope will enhance theoretical power and heurism. Four generic issues serve to organize the discussion: (a) the development of theory, (b) the consciousness of communicators, (c) the contextuality of communication, and (d) the locus of competence measurement.

THEORY DEVELOPMENT

Problems in studying communication competence are both conceptual and methodological. It has been argued that advances in the measurement of competence have far exceeded our theoretical gains (Larson et al., 1978) and consequently that most scholarly pitfalls are conceptual. However, it is difficult to separate conceptualizations from operationalizations. As will become apparent, problems of conceptualization and measurement are inextricably related.

At a general level, the most significant indictment of inquiry into the phenomenon of communication competence is the dearth of theory. Perhaps it is because competence is typically viewed from a pragmatic/pedagogical perspective that theoretical development has been stifled. Thinking of competence in a strictly *prescriptive* fashion may have inhibited us from reckoning with it theoretically—as an empirical phenomenon worthy of explanation and prediction in its own right. To the extent that the purpose of theory is to explain and predict phenomena, it is desirable to develop *theories* of competence to assist in understanding and producing competent communication.

Another factor which may have limited the development of competence theories is the sheer breadth of the competence issue. Because competence is as broad as the domain of communication, a comprehensive theory of competence would be tantamount to a grand theory of communication. In the way it is commonly used, the term "competence" refers to the *ability* to interact appropriately and/or effectively. A theory of competence therefore, would seek to explain how people perform and perceive communicative behaviors. What cognitive, affective, and motor capacities are involved in the production of behavior and the coordination of complex sequences of interactive behaviors? What evaluative dimensions and cues do people use to assess appropriateness and effectiveness? These are broad and expansive questions. It is clear that these questions require an integration of research in at least the areas of social psychology, psycholinguistics, and communication science. A theory of competence is not solely a communication or a psychological issue. A comprehensive explanation of competence in communicating necessitates a consideration of both psychological and communicative domains. The development of an adequate theory of competence will not be a rapid occurrence. Nevertheless, the task of seeking acceptable theoretical models is vital to the ultimate goals of understanding and predicting communicative behavior.

That theory building efforts have been neglected is evidenced (and perpetuated) by the variable-analytic nature of research on competence. Indeed, most research seems to have been aimed at developing measurement devices. There is a painful paucity of research aimed at constructing or testing theoretical explanations of competent and incompetent interaction. Compounding this lack of theory is the lack of systematic integration of accumulated knowledge. Scholarly efforts are diffuse and uncoordinated. New information is seldom related to extant theories of communication. For example, probably the most common approach to explaining communication competence is through the construct of component skills. Unfortunately, component skill models tend to oversimplify the complexities of the communicative encounter. To say that empathy and interaction management are positively related is easy. To explain exactly what the processes of empathy and interaction management entail is far more difficult. To say that the skill of listening is positively related to competence assumes that a skilled listener *wants* to use that skill, is in a context that facilitates the use of that skill, and that other relevant skills (articulation, role taking, and so on) are also utilized effectively. Such assumptions are not automatically tenable even in "common" everyday interaction, much less in more problematic situations. Clearly, greater specificity is needed before most skills approaches can be considered "theories" of competent interaction.

The problem of inadequate theorizing is certainly not unique to the area of competence; nor is the problem inherent. The future looks optimistic to the extent that scholars increasingly attend to issues of conceptualization and theory (see Pearce & Cronen, 1980; Wiemann, 1977).

THE CONSCIOUSNESS ISSUE

Intentionality is a central issue when it comes to conceptualizing communication (Bowers & Bradac, 1982). This issue is typically reflected in such questions as: To what extent do communicators exert conscious forethought, planning, and monitoring of their behavior? Historically, many communication scholars have chosen to restrict their domain of interest to *conscious* and *intentional* interaction. Likewise, many approaches to communication competence have assumed strategic awareness and intentionality on the part of successful communicators. Skill constructs, for example, which provide the conceptual foundation for many competence conceptualizations, are often defined as abilities consciously directed toward the accomplishment of a particular goal. Thus, in teaching a skill such as assertiveness, it is assumed that a person learns to be aware of when to use the skill, how to use it, and what objectives are likely to accrue to its use. Strategic competence constructs use terms such as "problem solving," "goal achievement," and "objectives," all of which suggest a high degree of consciousness. Conceptualizations of interpersonal competence (see Bochner & Kelly, 1974; Parks, 1977b; Weinstein, 1969) often imply a high degree of strategic orientation; that is, individuals are competent because they are able to formulate and successfully implement strategies designed to achieve planned or conscious goals.

The assumption of full cognizance on the part of communicators is becoming increasingly tenuous (Berger & Douglas, 1982; Roloff, 1980). Much human behavior is role-governed and ritualistic. Standardized and recurring episode types are scripted and the corresponding behaviors become habitual (Langer, 1978). Consequently, individuals often engage in "mindless" interaction that entails low levels of attention and awareness. Indeed, it has been argued that individuals can be expected to be highly aware of their behavior under only certain circumstances:

> (1) in novel situations where, by definition, no appropriate script exists, (2) where external factors prevent completion of a script, (3) when scripted behavior becomes effortful because substantially more of the behavior is required than is usual, (4) when a discrepant outcome is experienced, or (5) where multiple scripts come into conflict so that involvement in any one script is suspended. (Berger & Douglas, 1982, p. 46)

Not only does the degree of consciousness vary, but contextual stimuli can alter the *focus* of one's consciousness as well. Goffman (1967) has depicted several forms of "alienation" that commonly detract from a person's spontaneous involvement in interaction. Proper attention may be distracted because of *external preoccupation* with matters unrelated to the current communication context or because of *interaction consciousness* in which there is an undue concern with the interaction qua interaction. Similarly, one may become overly *self-conscious*, owing to such states as embarrassment or anxiety, or overly *other-conscious* by focusing on imputed characteristics such as affectation, insincerity, and immodesty. Such forms of misinvolvement, according to Goffman (1967), are quite common and affect the quality of social interaction.

It is simply becoming unrealistic to develop theories of human interaction that are based on the presumption that people always or typically are highly conscious of their communicative behavior and strategic decisions. Likewise, there may be little reason to endow models of competence with an exceedingly high level of awareness. Reward attainment, for instance, need not be related to any particular intentional desire. As Thorngate (1967) has illustrated, several interaction management skills are habitualized because of internal gratification reactions. As a result, higher-order thought processes are not requisite to competent interaction in many familiar encounters and are brought into play chiefly during novel episodes.

A more realistic approach would be to conceive of the awareness of human behavior as existing on a continuum (see Toulmin, 1974). Just as communication functions are differentially salient to communicators in diverse situations, so too are the tools of communication—strategies and tactics. Moreover, strong evidence indicates that humans differ dispositionally with respect to their cross-situational levels of self-awareness (see Roloff, 1980). Given the diversity of human awareness during interaction, Berger (1980) asks: "Do higher levels of self-consciousness produce more competent communication in everyday interaction situations?" (p. 96). More specifically, the question emerges: Does the degree of an individual's awareness affect the quality of communication? There are at least four lines of research which suggest that varying degrees of perceptual awareness and sensitivity may be linked to differences in communicator competence. This research centers on the constructs of objective self-awareness, self-consciousness, self-monitoring, and interaction involvement

Objective Self-Awareness

According to Duval and Wicklund (1972), there are two mutually exclusive states of self-awareness. *Objective self-awareness* occurs when one's attention is focused internally, upon the self. In other words, objective self-awareness exists when one is the object of his or her own consciousness. Alternatively, *subjective self-awareness* is the result of one's attention being externally focused on the environment.

A characteristic of objectively self-aware individuals is that they are particularly sensitive to self-relevant information in their environments (Hull & Levy, 1979). Consequently, they are concerned with the self-image they present to others. In short, objectively self-aware people strategically control their behavior to create desirable impressions on others. Furthermore, they "observe socially appropriate standards for conduct more closely" (Schlenker, 1980, p. 73). Given their concern for self-presentation and social rules, objectively self-aware people may be more tactful and adaptable as communicators. It can be argued, therefore, that they are typically perceived to be more competent in their interactions than their subjectively self-aware counterparts.

On the other hand, extreme levels of self-focused attention may produce anxiety and diminish the spontaneity of interaction, thereby eroding competence impressions. Unfortunately, there is a lack of research regarding the effects of self-awareness on *interpersonal* behavior. As Fenigstein (1979) indicates, "Although self-awareness has been shown to have consequences for many realms of behavior, virtually all of these behaviors have been nonsocial, involving little interaction with others" (p. 76). There is a clear need to explore the influence of self-awareness on communication.

Self-Consciousness

In addition to self-awareness that is contextually stimulated, there are enduring individual differences in self-attention. Fenigstein and colleagues (Fenigstein, Scheier, & Buss, 1975) have conceptualized self-consciousness as a multifaceted personality trait that has been found to have both private and public dimensions. *Privately self-conscious* persons are preoccupied with their own thoughts and feelings. Consequently, Berger and Douglas (1982) speculate that

> Those people who are highly private self-conscious can be expected to have a restricted knowledge of social expectations and are, therefore, potentially disposed to exhibit behavior that violates or more nearly violates public standards. (p. 47)

Public self-consciousness. Public self-consciousness occurs when one is aware of oneself, or of the self as a social object. The result of public self-consciousness is an increased concern with public presentation and the evaluations of self by others. Like objective self-awareness, public self-consciousness may enhance or deter communication competence. Because they are more sensitive to feedback (Fenigstein, 1979) and may have a greater concern with reducing uncertainty (Berger & Douglas, 1982), publicly self-conscious communicators may possess social knowledge requisite for effective interaction. However, it is not clear under what conditions such knowledge and concomitant self-evaluation may be distracting and disruptive to the flow of interaction. "Again, because of the relative youth of the self-consciousness research, it is difficult to talk about these links to communicative conduct with any degree of certainty" (Berger & Bradac, 1982, p. 47).

Self-Monitoring

Self-monitoring is a construct related to awareness that was developed by Snyder (1974). Persons who are high self-monitors are particularly sensitive to the situational appropriateness of their social behavior and consequently focus on the self-presentation and expression of conversational others. They utilize the behavioral cues of others to guide their own self-presentation (Snyder, 1979a, 1979b). This results in high self-monitors being attentive, other-oriented, and adaptable to diverse communication situations, and it gives them the ability to manage effectively the impressions of others by presenting themselves in desired ways. Given these characteristics, which stem from being situationally rather than dispositionally guided, it can be argued that the high self-monitor is likely to be a highly competent communicator (Berger & Douglas, 1982; Spitzberg & Cupach, 1981). However, the empirical evidence regarding the link between self-monitoring and communicator competence is inconclusive (Spitzberg & Cupach, 1981). This may be due to measurement validity problems (see Briggs, Cheek, & Buss, 1980; Gabrenya & Arkin, 1980), or because self-monitoring is a necessary but not sufficient characteristic of competence, or because it facilitates competent performance only in certain contexts.

Self-monitoring appears to be very similar to public self-consciousness, but the two constructs are distinguishable. The exhibited empirical relationship between public self-consciousness and self-monitoring has been small (Fenigstein, 1979; Scheier & Carver, 1977). Fenigstein (1979) explains: "Although the self-monitor must obviously attend to his or her own behavior, the orientation is primarily outward toward situational requirements, as opposed to the self-conscious person, whose attention is primarily self-directed" (p. 76). Thus, self-focused attention may be a contributory, but not sufficient, ingredient of self-monitoring. Publicly self-conscious persons may or may not be high self-monitors.

Interaction Involvement

A fourth construct related to awareness in conversational encounters is interaction involvement: "the extent to which an individual partakes of a social environment" (Cegala, 1981, p. 112). Cegala (1981) maintains that interaction involvement entails the demonstration of responsiveness, perceptiveness, and attentiveness by communicators and thus reflects a critical component of communicative competence. Research by Cegala and his colleagues (Cegala, Savage, Brunner, & Conrad, 1982) has demonstrated a negative relationship between the responsiveness dimension of involvement and the variables of social anxiety and interpersonal communication apprehension. As expected, several communication competence factors (behavioral flexibility, interaction management, affiliation and support, empathy, and social relaxation) were positively correlated with involvement, especially the perceptiveness dimension. The relationship between self-consciousness and involvement was equivocal: Perceptiveness was positively related to private self-consciousness for males and public self-consciousness for females. This, of course, clouds the issue of how competence and consciousness are related. In addition, despite conceptual similarity, dimensions of interaction involvement and self-monitoring did not display significant empirical relationships (Cegala et al., 1982, p. 234). These latter two anomalous findings illustrate the relatively unexplored nature of the relationships between facets of consciousness and communication competence. They also indicate the need to discover and investigate such potential relationships and perhaps the difficulty of validly measuring distinct aspects of communicator awareness/consciousness.

Some Implications

That individuals differ with respect to their degrees of awareness when communicating seems clear. If and how such differences substantially affect communication competence seems less obvious at this point. We do believe, however, that the relevant study of competence should not be limited to eposides in which comminicators display relatively high levels of awareness and planning. We concur with Lofland (1976), who maintains that

actions have strategic consequences in, upon, and on a situation regardless of whether anyone in that situation consciously intends those consequences. "Unthinking," "mindless," "habitual," "routine" action does not necessarily lack strategic *significance* (consequences or import) simply because the person performing it does not consciously perceive or intend strategic significance. (p. 53)

The effect of this position is to expand the circumference of interest potentially to include all interaction, since all interaction is potentially strategic in impact. To assume that competent interaction occurs when individuals intend to produce certain effects and strategically accomplish those effects is to limit the occurrence of identifiable interpersonally competent interaction to a potentially small amount of all communicative interaction. It may be naive to assume that consistent high awareness is the most competent state of affairs; constant high awareness might paradoxically lead to inefficient communication under certain circumstances.

By way of elaborating this paradox, we might speculate on the implication for teaching communication competence. The purpose of most basic communication textbooks is to impart general knowledge and develop awareness of communicators so that they can analyze their communicative relationships and apply relevant principles and skills. What is sometimes overlooked is that such monitoring and analyzing can be taken to an inimical extreme. A communicator can become extremely self-aware and obsessed with analyzing every detail of a communication encounter or relationship. Such a communicator can become obsessed to the point of distraction and incompetence. Take the example of the mate who insists on explaining *every* utterance of a relational partner—much to the displeasure of that partner. In such cases, the overly attentive/analytical individual spends too much time *analyzing* communication and not enough time doing it (and enjoying it). This situation might reflect a cognitive tendency that is related to (but distinct from) awareness, but it would seem to merit exploration. After all, don't we often teach students of public speaking to *avoid* analyzing their performance during a speech in order to reduce anxiety?

One fruitful avenue for study is in the area of memory and knowledge heuristics. If communicative behaviors, routines, sequences, and even episodes can be overlearned, then it is reasonable to assume that the overlearning involves the "storage" of these events and forms in a level of knowledge that is available to "inform" behavior yet that does not interfere substantially with our conscious cognitive activities. That is, in relatively familiar episodes (such as greeting rituals), communication behaviors may be recalled on the basis of extant knowledge schemas regarding the episode, the person, or both. Research by Planalp (1983) found that people possess a fairly resilient memory for behaviors enacted in a student-professor episode, apparently because the subjects had internalized a cognitive schema regarding the rights and obligations of students and professors. Because the subjects, in this case college students, had clear concepts of student-professor relations, they were able to recall behavior not because it was remembered precisely but because the behavior "fit" into a recognizable pattern of an episode prototype. Similarly, in everyday episodes, people may be able to call forth behavior not on the basis of a complex and extensive cognitive search of behavior but on the basis of simply applying behaviors that have been used (or observed) in a *type* of episode. If a person had to execute a comprehensive mental search for all of the possible behaviors and statements that could be made in a given situation, the demands on his or her cognitive processing could be debilitating. Instead, it is more efficient to apply familiar episodes and behavioral sequences that both are immediately available and require that few highly conscious choices be made. Research into how such cognitive schemas are formed, how stable they are, and how their efficient use can be facilitated is a high priority in understanding how someone "knows" what to do in a communicative situation.

Given the potentially complex relationships between awareness and competence, a number of additional questions arise. It is not simply a matter of whether one is "conscious" when communicating. It is more important to ask: (a) What is the relative degree of awareness? (b) Where is attention focused? and (c) What are the effects of various levels and forms of awareness on communication? For example, Langer and colleagues (Langer, 1979; Langer & Imber, 1979) have been investigating the role of "mindlessness" in interaction. Mindlessness refers to the overlearning of a task or sequence of behaviors to the point that there is no longer conscious awareness of the performance. Langer (1979) suggests that much presumably thoughtful social behavior is indeed mindless. Mindless social behavior can be very efficient to the extent that it is functional because it requires little cognitive effort. It is possible that competent interaction routines are overlearned and efficiently performed with a modicum of cognitive investment. However, Langer (1979) indicates concern about mindlessness in the face of apparent or implied failure:

> Putting in writing what you have said informally a hundred times before and giving a formal talk that you have practiced repeatedly and given repeatedly are just two of the countless instances where people think they should think before or while they act. Our data suggest that such attention to responses that were previously overlearned and unattended to will result in poorer performance. The unexpected experience of this poorer performance may have severe consequences for individuals and may lead them inappropriately to infer incompetence. (pp. 306-307)

Beyond the question of how one's *actual* consciousness affects communication behavior, it is of pragmatic interest to investigate how communicators manage impressions of awareness and involvement. For instance, effective communication sometimes requires that a person be highly self-aware and strategic. However, appearing strategic can violate the obligation to be spontaneously involved in interaction (Goffman, 1967) and can create a climate of defensiveness (Gibb, 1961). How do communicators effectively deal with this paradox? Other questions relevant to the study of communication competance include: Under what conditions is involvement more or less important or salient to communicators? What verbal and nonverbal cues are associated with attributions of awareness and involvement? How are these attributions related to the impression of competence? These questions (and others) need to be answered if we are to achieve a comprehensive understanding of communication competence. Scholars have begun to clarify the nature of self-consciousness and its general impact on behavior. A next important step is to discover how consciousness constructs relate to communication and judgments of competence.

THE CONTEXT ISSUE: TRAIT VERSUS STATE

Another issue that underlies conceptions of competence concerns whether competence is defined as a *trait* or a *state*. Most extant competence measures reflect a trait orientation. That is, competence is viewed as a function of an individual's self-reported tendency to perform certain communicative behaviors across communication situations. Recently, some researchers have attempted to recast competence assessment methods into context-specific forms (see Cupach & Spitzberg, 1981; Ruben, 1976). These "event-focused" approaches assume that competence is reflected in a particular communication episode rather than in behavioral tendencies across events or contexts. Such efforts raise the question: Is competence in communicating best conceptualized (and therefore assessed) as an event or as a tendency?

In order to elucidate this issue, it is useful to make a distinction between competence *conceived* as a state or trait and competence *measured* as a state or trait (that is, conceptualization versus operationalization). Assessment methods can be divided into *situational* and *dispositional* forms. These terms correspond roughly to state and trait conceptualizations. We hesitate to embrace the terms "trait" and "state," because the distinction between them is often arbitrary and ambiguous (Allen & Potkay, 1981), especially when one considers their operationalization. To measure a state, questionnaire items must tap perceptions of a particular place, time, and activity. Trait measures, on the other hand, usually span place, time, and activity to reflect a proclivity or tendency across contexts. These measurement strategies correspond to the terms "situational" and "dispositional." Dispositional measures refer to behavioral tendencies over several communication events to provide a summative measure of a person's communicative predisposition(s). Dispositional measures might include Likert-type items such as "I do not mind meeting strangers" and "I pay attention to my conversations," suggesting that the respondent tends (or will tend) to behave in accordance with the item content. Even when the items are focused on a particular person or role (such as supervisor or spouse) or a particular context (such as organizational or marital), if the items and response formats refer to general tendencies, the measure is dispositional. In short, dispositional (trait) measures of competence are *tendency-focused.*

A situational measure references a particular communication event or episode. Items such as "s/he was awkward in the conversation" and "I interrupted too much in the conversation" incorporate implicit respondent conceptions of relationship and place. What is "awkward" or "too much" is judged according to the relationship and the situation that frame the conversation. Hence, situational measures of competence are *event-focused.*

Given the distinction between situational and dispositional measures, it is now appropriate briefly to review the ways in which these measures have been utilized in communication research. This review will serve to support two points: (a) that most approaches to competence are dispositional and (b) that where situational approaches are implied, measurement strategies are inconsistent with situational assumptions.

Dispositional Competence Constructs

Since its origins are in psychiatry and social psychology, it is not surprising that early renditions of interpersonal competence ventured trait-oriented views. Foote and Cottrell (1955) stressed that "interpersonal competence is neither a trait nor a state" (p. 49). However, their definition of competence as the capability "to meet and deal with a changing world, to formulate ends and implement them" (p. 49) is translated into six trait constructs: health, intelligence, empathy, autonomy, judgment, and creativity. Years later, Weinstein (1969) defined interpersonal competence as "the ability to accomplish interpersonal tasks" (p. 755). this ability, he argued, is fostered by the constellation of personality factors of high empathy, self-esteem, Machiavellianism, internal locus of control, and low need for approval, rigidity, alienation, and failure avoidance. Fitts (1970) typified the dispositional approach to competence, defining it as "the ability to establish and maintain mutually satisfying relationships with a variety of people across diverse situations" (p. 61).

Numerous studies have been conducted from a trait perspective. Although cast in the marital context, Farber's (1962) measurement study assessed competence across communication and psychological events. Spouses were asked to rate how frequently their partners engaged in certain types of behavior or perception. The resulting factors revealed traits similar to those of Foote and Cottrell (such as physical energy, expressiveness, sensitivity, and leadership). Bienvenu (1971) was one of the first competence researchers to emphasize communication, although he still relied on a dispositional instrument in which students were asked to rate how likely they were to engage in certain behaviors presumed to be competent. Competent behaviors were cross-situational tendencies to listen, empathize, understand, and express feelings.

Several communication studies and measurement attempts have relied on trait-oriented approaches. Macklin and Rossiter (1976) developed a measure of psychological health (that is, self-actualization) in interpersonal communication. The dispositional items represented expressiveness, self-disclosure, and understanding. Phelps and Snavely (1980) modified four instruments (those of Bienvenu, 1971; Holland & Baird, 1968; Macklin & Rossiter, 1976; Weimann, 1977) to form an aggregate tendency-focused self-report questionnaire. Their factor analysis revealed traits similar to those forming the original scales, including empathy, self-disclosure, social anxiety, listening, and health. The resulting instrument has since been modified and utilized in interpersonal and organizational settings, but still in a dispositional format (Spitzberg, 1982b; Walters & Snavely, 1981). The majority of items that "loaded" in the Phelps and Snavely (1980) factor analysis originated in Wiemann's measure of communicative competence. A self-report dispositional form of Wiemann's (1977) instrument has been used in studies of androgyny and communicator style (Brunner & Phelps, 1980; Jones & Brunner, 1981).

Even recently, several competence constructs have been developed utilizing dispositional operationalizations. Communicative adaptability, a cometence-relevant construct, is composed of five dispositional factors: social confirmation, social composure, articulation, social adaptability, and wit (Duran, Zakahi, & Parrish, 1981). Berryman-Fink and Pederson (1981) developed an innovative measure referencing the skills of empathy, descriptiveness, owning, and self-disclosure. These skills were assessed by summing the appropriateness of responses to a set of hypothetical interpersonal situations. While specific situations were used, the procedure of summing scores has the effect of creating a cross-situational tendency measure. Monge, Bachman, Dillard, and Eisenberg (1982) constructed a superior-subordinate organizational competence measure tapping the factors of encoding (for example, can deal with others effectively; generally says the right thing at the right time) and decoding (for example, pays attention to what other people say to him or her; usually responds to messages...quickly). Despite the intent to focus this measure on a particular context, the instrument clearly represents a dispositional assessment of an individual's competence.

Situational Competence Constructs

The idea that competence is manifested in a specific communicative encounter, and not necessarily across encounters, has been late in developing. Only a handful of efforts have been made to conceptualize *and* measure communicative competence in an event-specific manner.

A landmark investigation of communicative competence in initial dyadic interactions was conducted by Wiemann (1977). He examined competence in an interview setting, with an observer-rating measure representing the a priori factors of affiliation/support, social relaxation, empathy, behavioral flexibility, and interaction management. Although this measure was applied to a specific conversational encounter, it should be noted that some of the items represented cross-situational tendencies in their content (S finds it easy to get along with others; S can adapt to changing situations; S ignores other people's feelings; and the like). Thus, Wiemann's instrument requires that cross-situational and cross-relational inferences be made, even though interactants are rated on the basis of a single encounter.

Bochner and Yerby (1977) utilized an eight-item instrument to assess group and individual competence consisting of statements that reflected openness and acceptance/flexibility (for example, I see him as a relaxed, easygoing person). However, this measure was applied in a group after a series of meetings. The measure is appropriate for an event-focused assessment but was not applied as such in the Bochner and Yerby investigation.

In 1979, Brandt conceptualized social competence as a function of "goal achievement, communication skills, *and* sensitivity to both situations and other persons" (p. 225). He assessed social competence in video taped acquaintance encounters with rating scales representing the factors of communication effectiveness, social attractiveness, and task attractiveness. While the research effort displays considerable context specificity, it nevertheless applied a normative rather than idiosyncratic rating procedure. Raters were asked to use the criterion of 100 as indicating "the average level of _____ (a given stylistic attribute) displayed by most people in an initial interaction situation" (p. 231). Even the items for measuring communication effectiveness required raters to make tendency inferences (for example, This person is an effective communicator; It is easy for this person to communicate on a one-to-one basis with strangers; This person does not communicate effectively with others in an initial interaction). The effect of these measurement strategies is to apply a dispositional judgment criterion to a specific dyadic communication event.

Indictments of Trait Approaches

Consistant with the growing dissatisfaction with psychological traits in general, dispositional approaches to communication competence have met with criticism. The chief indictment centers on the assumption that communication is contextual. To the extent that communication is constrained by context, so, too, is communication *competence*. Detractors of the trait approach point out that people are "differentially competent when dealing with different topics, with different people in different situations" (Larson et al., 1978, p. 19). It is this assumption of contextuality that has led to statements such as Hecht's (1978c), that trait approaches to the measurement of communication competence are "empirically and theoretically counterproductive" (p. 352).

A heavy reliance on skills constructs undoubtedly has contributed to the adherence to trait-oriented accounts of communication competence—and not without attendant problems. For example, interaction management is presumed to be a cometence skill and is expected to be positively related to competent interaction. While this association may be generally accurate, the perspective ignores important considerations, such as what the person *wants* to do in terms of interaction management. Does the conversational other give the person an opportunity to manage the flow of interaction competently? Does the context or topic mitigate this skill? These factors are often ignored when skills are made the primary or only explanatory mechanism.

This overreliance on skills constructs is perhaps most problematic when adaptability (that is, behavioral flexibility) is viewed as a critical competence. The very notion of adaptability implies that different behaviors and skills are applied indifferent contexts and situations. However, adaptability itself is viewed as a skill. Thus, the *skill* of adaptability is supposed to be context-independent (that is, unique across contexts). Such conceptual dilemmas have not been addressed by proponents of trait constructs (such as Duran et al., 1981; Hart, Carlson, & Eadie, 1980; Neal & Hughey, 1979), although other approaches may offer more realistic information-processing interpretations (Hale & Deli, 1976).

Inattention to the role of context leads to the consideration of two interralated conceptual problems. Certain skills models operate under the dubious assumption that certain skills domains are universal assets for competence (see Argyle, 1969;

Cushman & Craig, 1976; Wiemann, 1977). Some models, for example, have assumed that social sensitivity is a universally required skill for competent interaction. It is not difficult, however, to imagine situations in which extreme social sensitivity is damaging or stultifying to the process of interaction and/or the interactants involved. Too much social sensitivity (empathy or role taking) in a task group setting can lead to indecisiveness and difficulty in achieving task solutions, due to excessive attention and concern for competing positions (Steiner, 1955). Such exceptions have led several researchers and theorists to apologize for the general inability to find universally essential social skills (Arkowitz, 1977; Barlow, Abel, Blanchard, Bristow, & Young, 1977; Dow et al., 1981; Gambrill, 1977; Koffman, Getter, & Chinsky, 1978). Representative of this school of thought is Eisler (1978), who admits that, "at present, there are no generally agreed upon definitions of social skills which apply to all interpersonal situations" (p. 370). To some extent, this conclusion should be expected from the simple assumption that communication is contextual. It would seem to be realistic to accept that competence is not a characteristic that inheres in skill or behavior and instead is an interpersonal impression that is based, in part, on behavior but is also based on the prior relational history of the communicators and other contextual stimuli. Under this assumption, certain skills could be viewed as *likely* to lead to heightened impressions of competence, but hey would not be viewed as the sine qua non of interactional competence.

Related to this criticism is the general inattention to the relational context that most competence constructs reveal. Presumably, social and cultural norms are easier to identify and are thus more parsimonious for a theory of competence. However, interpersonal encounters, especially where the interactants have an established relational history, are likely to operate according to idiosyncratic rules instead of social norms (Knapp, 1978; Knapp, Ellis, & Williams, 1980; Miller & Steinberg, 1975). As Weinstein (1966) indicates, the "rules of polite intercourse are most likely to be violated in relationships to which commitment is the strongest" (p. 398). That is, social norms may be violated completely if the relational partners have established new or unique rules. Research by Gottman (1979) on marital interaction suggests

> differences in individual modes of responding as a function of marital satisfaction....However, in interaction with strangers, distressed and nondistressed spouses cannot be distinguished. This suggests that individual social competence should not be conceptualized as a trait, but, rather, as a relationship-specific construct. (p. 211)

Furthermore, inappropriate behavior is often undertaken by the interactant for a specific reason. Assertive behavior, for example, often is perceived by another as aggressive and inappropriate. To the asserter, however, such behavior is the only reasonable and appropriate response to the situaion. Stated differently, communication can be *socially* appropriate yet quite inappropriate to the specific interpersonal context, and vice versa.

Recasting the Trait-State Dichotomy

Like most dichotomies, the trait-state distinction tends to produce rather extreme, polarized positions. Although we have outlined some weaknesses inhering in the trait approach to competence, it should be pointed out emphatically that this is not to deny the relevance or importance of trait variables in explaining competence. Rather, the point is that the phenomenon of competence qua competence is better conceptualized as a situation-specific occurrence, reflected in the attributions of communicators, which in turn are based on the observation of behaviors in context, relational history and perception, and perceived traits of self and other(s). Competence *as a trait* ultimately must boil down to an individual effectively communicating across contexts—with different people, in different environments, with diverse goals and topics. This consistency of performance is really tantamount to general communicative adaptability and behavioral flexibility. However, such flexibility can never *guarantee*, a priori, that communication in a given episode will be competent; hence the need for situational measures of competence.

What seems useful is to recognize that states and traits are not mutually exclusive. This suggests a distinction between *competence as trait* (that is, general flexibility) and *competence-related traits*. There are several ways in which competence-related traits could enhance or contribute to situation-specific explanations of competence. First, traits contribute to situational competence insofar as they enhance the general *propensity* of an individual to be perceived as competent in a given episode. Variables such as cognitive complexity (a dispositional cognitive capacity) and rhetorical sensitivity (a general attitude toward encoding messages) are likely to *facilitate* the performance of competent communication. Moreover, certain traits may contribute to competence attributions in such a way that one's partner may come to perceive competence on the basis of specific situated behaviors *and* the perception of one's personality dispositions. An example would be that a person is perceived to be competent because he or she is perceived to be generally trustworthy and also is perceived as having displayed appropriate and effective behaviors in a given context. Finally, it is likely that traits interact with situations; in other words, certain dispositional characteristics may lead to competence in some situations but not in others. For example, a high self-monitor may *use* self-monitoring abilities in novel or enigmatic contexts where the bases for appropriate behavior are ambiguous. In ritualized or highly familiar situations, the high self-monitor is likely already to know how to behave and would be less likely to invoke self-monitoring tendencies. Similarly, it can be argued that Machiavellian individuals use their strategic and manipulative skills only in situations in which clear objectives are to be gained. In situations in which there are few salient rewards other than phatic interaction or relational maintenance, the high Machiavellian person may be just as spontaneous and nonstrategic as a low Machiavellian person. In the future, more sophisticated approaches to communication competence should address the issue of how traits and situations interface to enhance competence. We now turn to an issue that parallels the trait-state distinction: where the essence of competence is captured empirically.

THE LOCUS OF MEASUREMENT ISSUE

The locus of measurement issue is concerned with where competence resides. This issue is reflected in two critical questions: (a) Who should rate competence (third-party observers or interactants)? and (b) What should be rated (behaviors or cognitions)? Answers to these questions determine whether one's view of competence is clear and encompassing or myopic and restricted.

Several researchers have utilized third-party observers to rate the competence of interactants. As our discussion of contextuality suggests, the judgment of competence made by a third-party observer lacks the relationship-specific knowledge that would inform such judgments for the interactants. Communicators possess a distinct perceptual position as well as personal and relational data to rely upon in assessing the conversational competence of self and other. An interactant is the only person who knows whether his or her conversational objectives were achieved, and the conversational partner is in the best position to know whether such goals were obtained via appropriate interaction. In Judith Guest's novel *Ordinary People*, Conrad Jarrett has been tormented by the loss of a brother, for which he blamed himself, frustrated by an intolerable family atmosphere and recently released from a mental hospital where he tried to recover from his attempted suicide and was virtually isolated from his high school peer network. Not surprisingly, his social relations and interpersonal interactions are strained and generally dissatisfying. Here is someone who is *generally* incompetent in communicating. Despite this, he is capable of developing an appropriate and effective relationship (entailing satisfying interactions) with his new girlfriend, Jeanine. An outside observer, even one who knows him, might find his interaction with Jeanine somewhat stilted and awkward. But Jeanine comes (eventually) to understand his problems and to accept and enjoy interacting with him. While this example is fictional, we do not believe it to be unrealistic. The most "competent" among us occasionally experiences an interaction with someone that seems awkward, strained, and dissatisfying. Furthermore, the same statements (such as an off-color joke) made in the presence of two different people can result in very different reactions. The point is that the interactants themselves are in the best position to know whether their interaction is appropriate and effective. The issue here is whether competence is better assessed at the actor's level of meaning or at society's level of meaning (as exemplified by presumably normative third-party ratings). To some extent, this issue can be recast as the semantic distinction between interpersonal and social competence. The actor's level of meaning is intrinsic to the *interpersonal* relationship, whereas a third party almost necessarily invokes his or her own sense of *social* or normative criterial in the judgment of competence. A distinction between social and interpersonal (relational) competence based on the level of idiosyncratic relational knowledge with which such judgments are made seems to have utility.

Another significant issue pertains to what elements researchers should focus on. Wiemann and Backlund (1980) indicate that most competence perspectives may be classified as cognitive or behavioral. The literature on social skills, for example, is replete with purely behavioral conceptualizations and operationalizations of skills. A skill is considered present if the subject is capable of producing behavior representative of that skill. The underlying cognitive and affective processes are ignored for the most part (Morrison & Bellack, 1981). Indeed, the method of choice in the study of social skills is behavioral role playing. Unfortunately, research has yet to support the generalizability of role-played behaviors to actual situations (Bellack et al., 1979; Farrell, Mariotto, Cooper, Curran, & Wallander, 1979; Shepard, 1977). Moreover, by only observing the behaviors produced, valuable cognitive and affective information is ignored under the assumption that it adds nothing to the behavioral model. The psychological precursors that lead to the display of effective behavior and the cognitive/affective outcomes associated with the attribution of competence are not accounted for.

Just as the social skills approach has been largely limited to behaviors, communication scholars typically have relied on psychological measures. As has been indicated, the vast majority of communication competence measures reflect self-perceived dispositions. Only infrequently have such perceptions been related to overt communicative behaviors. Although a cognitive approach seems necessary to the explanation of competent communication, it does not seem to be sufficient. Indeed, it is a contradiction to speak of *communication* competence without reference to communicative behaviors. At a conceptual level, communication and interpersonal approaches to competence should emphasize the interdependency of cognitive and behavioral dimensions.

Thus, just as social skills researchers overemphasize behavioral explanations of competence, communication researchers overemphasize cognitive and affective explanations. Research increasingly suggests the need to integrate these two approaches. In particular, several studies have found that specific conversational behaviors (amount of eye contact, nonfluencies, volume, posture, and so on) do not differentiate self-reported skilled and unskilled interactants. Nevertheless, the global social skill ratings of third-party observers do appear to discriminate these same groups statistically (Arkowitz et al., 1975; Glasgow & Arkowitz, 1975; Greenwald, 1977). Additionally, dispositional measures have revealed insignificant to small associations with situational criteria of competence (see Cupach & Spitzberg, 1983). Thus, neither specific behaviors nor self-reported tendencies are very powerful predictors of competent interaction. However, it appears to be obvious (in a molar sense) to interactants when social incompetence and competence are encountered in actual conversations. From a therapeutic standpoint, the evidence suggests that successful intervention for social skill deficits requires cognitive as well as behavioral modification (Trower, 1981). These findings suggest a need to embrace simultaneously both cognitive and behavioral perspectives when assessing competence. If we are interested in *communication competence*, it seems a fallacy to focus on only behaviors (communication) or only attributions (competence).

SUMMARY

There are numerous critical issues pertaining to the conceptualization and measurement of communication competence. The issues chosen for elaboration here necessarily reflect selectivity. Our intentions have been to identify some weaknesses and to suggest some implications and directions that we hope will generate academic debate and lead to progress in our understanding of the concept of competence in communicating. In conclusion, we maintained the following: (a) that more theory development is necessary for an adequate understanding of competence-related phenomena, (b) that we should investigate the ways in which consciousness affects communication competence, (c) that we should recognize the contextuality of communication in our conceptualization and measurement of competence, and (d) that the measurement of competence should include the attributions of interactants and that both cognitive and behavioral components are essential to a comprehensive explanation of communication competence.

4

MODEL OF RELATIONAL COMPETENCE

THE NOTION OF COMMUNICATION competence has been defined in many diverse ways. The various approaches, although exhibiting substantial overlap, often focus on different critical concepts. Some approaches are cognitive in their orientation, while others are behavioral. Some concentrate on messages, and others focus on outcomes. But as we have argued, cognition and behavior are related inextricably; process cannot be fully understood without linkage to outcomes. Perhaps the most serious criticism of our knowledge of competence is the general lack of coherent conceptualization and theory. As Larson et al. (1978) indicate, conceptual problems in the study of communication competence seem to outweigh by far the methodological problems.

What follows is an effort to construct a fresh, integrative approach to the conceptualization of competence in communicating. Specifically, offered here is an elaboration of the relational competence construct. We do not claim that this is the only viable approach to competence, but we do maintain that relational competence constitutes a useful and parsimonious framework for studying competence. First, seven critical interrelated assumptions of the relational competence approach are

laid out. The assumptions are not necessarily unique to relational competence—other approaches embrace some of them.
In fact, the assumptions derive from diverse conceptual and
empirical literature. The convergence of these assumptions
contributes to our "gestalt" of competence in communicating.

Second, we present a component model of relational competence. The elements of motivation, knowledge, and skill are
seen as interacting with communicative situations to constitute
the process of competence which leads to functional outcomes.

ASSUMPTIONS OF THE MODEL

Competence Is Perceived Appropriateness and Effectiveness

Relational competence can be defined conceptually as the
extent to which objectives functionally related to communication are fulfilled through cooperative interaction appropriate to
the interpersonal context. Therefore, relationally competent
communication is conceptualized as a function of perceived
appropriateness and *effectiveness*. To facilitate a full understanding of these two notions, we provide the following short
review of their respective literatures.

Appropriateness is often conceptualized in terms of social
sanctions. For example, Bellack and Hersen (1978) define social skills as "interpersonal behaviors which are normally and/
or socially sanctioned" (p. 169). Trenholm and Rose (1981)
specified that "in order to act and speak appropriately, individuals must recognize that different situations give rise to different sets of rules; compliance and noncompliance separate
those who 'belong' from those who do not 'fit in'" (p. 13).

Other theorists conceptualize appropriateness in terms of
its characteristics. For example, Getter and Nowinski (1981) define inappropriate behaviors as follows: "An inappropriate response to a situation is one which is unnecessarily abrasive,
intense, or bizarre. It is also likely to result in negative conse-

quences which could have been averted, without sacrifice of the goal, by more appropriate actions" (p. 303). Similarly, Numbers and Chapman (1982) operationalized social inappropriateness in terms of the avoidance, hostility, and/or oddness of a communicative response. Several theorists have conceptualized appropriateness as a molar impression of competent communication (Allen and Wood, 1978; Black, 1979; Hymes, 1972b; Sankoff, 1974). Wiemann and Backlund (1980), however, elaborate the construct:

> Appropriateness generally refers to the ability of an interactant to meet the basic contextual requirements of the situation—to be effective in a general sense....These contextual requirements include: (1) The verbal context, that is, making sense in terms of wording, of statements, and of topic; (2) the relationship context, that is, the structuring, type and style of messages so that they are consonant with the particular relationship at hand; and (3) the environmental context, that is, the consideration of constraints imposed on message making by the symbolic and physical environments. (p. 191)

Similarly, for Larson and his colleagues (Larson, 1978; Larson et al., 1978), communication is appropriate if it involves logical consistency among acts, meets the informational requirements of the act, and does not violate the social norms of the interactants involved. Thus the fundamental criteria of appropriateness are that the interactants perceive that they understand the content of the encounter and have not had their norms or rules violated too extensively. It is conceivable that a skillful communicator could violate another's rules in the process of initiating new rules for the context at hand. This creative management of meaning (Pearce & Cronen, 1980) is simply another way of avoiding rule violation. For example, a professor interested in establishing a friendship with a student often must first violate the student's rules for the professor-student context. By acting like a social friend instead of a professor, new rules are developed in the process of violating (or at least modifying) existing rules.

Effectiveness appears to be a common criterion by which communication is judged. Typically, effectiveness is conceptualized as the achievement of interactant goals or objectives, or as the satisfaction of interactant needs, desires, or intentions (Breen et al., 1977; Foote and Cottrell, 1955; Fitts, 1970; Pearce, 1976; Weinstein, 1969). Argyris (1965a, 1968), Goldfried and D'Zurilla (1969), and Spivack, Platt, & Shure (1976) view competence specifically as the ability to resolve interpersonal problems. Parks (1977b) conceptualizes competence as a function of the interactant's skill at exerting influence on the environment. In a detailed analysis of relationship types, Bennis and his colleagues (Bennis, Berlew, Schein, & Steele, 1968) indicate that effectiveness depends upon the primary functions being fulfilled. Thus, the criteria for good relationships, contingent upon the type of relationship, are mutual satisfaction, confirmation, consensus, desired change, productivity, and creativity. When applied to communication encounters rather than relationship types, a functional approach suggests that effective communication "is instrumental in the attainment of reward(s), whether the rewards are explicit objectives or tacit functions" (Cupach & Spitzberg, 1981, p. 5). Fulfillment of communicator objectives, in turn, results in satisfaction as a positively related affective response (Hecht, 1978a; Ruesch, 1972). However, there may be situations that can be satisfying without the fulfillment of specific objectives. To avoid confusing satisfaction and effectiveness, Thayer (1968) conceptualizes three aspects of efficacy:

> One's effectiveness as a communicator depends first upon the implicit facilitators and inhibitors (the "circumstances") which establish consequences as possible, inevitable, or impossible; then and only then upon his competence accurately to discern which type of situation he is in; and then and only then (a) upon his ability to compensate for those situations in which certain communicative intentions or goals are impossible, and (b) upon his tactical competence to succeed in those situations in which it is possible to achieve his purpose to some degree. (p. 151)

This perspective illustrates that several cognitive processes precede the actual accomplishment of a goal, which, in turn, would result in satisfaction.

Together, these diverse views of effectiveness indicate that it can be conceptualized as successful adaptation to or resolution of interpersonally problematic situations and the achievement of intended or desirable results through communication. Effective communication is likely to result in molar impressions of satisfaction.

Aside from the conceptual rationale for viewing competence as appropriate and effective communication, there are empirical reasons. From an initial pool of 200 items, Kohn and Rosman (1972) developed a 90-item Social Competence Scale for children. Their factor analysis revealed two basic dimensions represented by both positive and negative items. Items representative of the first factor included "Child gets others interested in what he's doing," "Child is able to express his own desires or opinions in a group," "Child fails to secure cooperation when he has to direct activities," and "Child is at a loss without other children directing him or organizing activities for him." These items clearly reflect a child's degree of effectiveness in influencing the outcome of interpersonal relations. Items on the second factor included the following: "Child cooperates with rules and regulations," "Child responds with immediate compliance to teacher's directions," "Child makes transition from one activity to the next easily," "Child disrupts activities of others," and "Child quarrels with other children." These items portray a child's capacity for dealing with people in an appropriate manner. The authors interpret these factors as reflecting

the major adaptive demands which a preschool setting makes on a child: (a) how to use the opportunities for learning, for pleasurable play activities, and for interaction with peers; and (b) how to live within the norms, rules, and limits, so that an orderly group process can develop and be maintained. (p. 443)

The use of opportunities for learning and pleasure and the adherence to norms and rules collectively provide evidence of appropriateness and effectiveness dimensions in the perception of interpersonal behavior.

That these dimensions are not exclusive to children's behavior is indicated by a series of three studies of relational competence. Spitzberg and Phelps (1982) conducted two of these studies using a 26-item semantic differential instrument tapping the two dimensions of appropriateness (such as proper-improper, appropriate-inappropriate, awkward-smooth) and effectiveness (such as satisfying-dissatisfying, effective-ineffective, successful-unsuccessful). In one study, subjects were requested to recall a recent extended conversation and assess the conversation according to the semantic differential items and two competence rating instruments: one that indicates the perceived competence of the other person's communication (for example, s/he was trustworthy, s/he was cooperative, s/he was awkward) and one that refers to self's communication competence. The semantic differential scale revealed two factors of appropriateness and effectiveness, both of which were related substantially and positively to the measures of self and other's competence. In the second study, the same instruments were used in reference to actual interactions (either a problem-solving or a get-acquainted interaction induced by the researchers). In this study, the semantic differential items reflecting appropriateness and effectiveness were virtually unidimensional (that is, they were perceived by subjects as identical concepts). Again, the perception of appropriateness/effectiveness was related positively and highly to the perception of self's and other's competence in communicating. Finally, in a study by Spitzberg and Canary (1983), the concepts of appropriateness and effectiveness were translated into 40 (Likert-type) items each, in an attempt to provide more detailed behavioral referents for the dimensions. Thus, appropriateness was measured by the degree to which the other person was perceived to have said rude, unexpected, or disruptive remarks or to have disrupted the flow of the conversation. Effectiveness referred to the degree to which self objectives and rewards were obtained and the degree to which the conversation was productive or useful. Again, both measures related substantially and positively to the perception of self and other's competence in an actual get-acquainted interaction. Thus, both theory and research indicate that competence is related to the perception of appropriateness *and* effectiveness.

In our view, competence is best viewed as a construct concerned with quality of communication. The competence of a performance refers not only to the ability to perform but also to the ability to perform a task *more or less excellently*. To rely on either appropriateness or effectiveness alone as a criterion of competent interaction allows for communication of questionable quality. A person resorting to destructive tactics such as threats, force, and trickery in a conflict situation may be effective, but such a style of communication is hardly what most interactants would consider a competent performance. The other person in the same conflict situation may react passively, careful not to violate any contextual rules or to be incomprehensible. However, this other person accomplishes nothing in the conflict other than giving in to the aggressive partner. Neither of the hypothetical communicators appears to provide prototypes of competent interaction. Instead, we propose as a prototype the person who accomplishes personal objectives through communication in a way that is appropriate to the interpersonal context. Such interaction is optimal in the sense that it functions productively for the communicator *and* the relationship in which the behavior is enacted. It is in this way that we can speak of "relational" competence.

The crux of this assumption is that *both* appropriateness and effectiveness are necessary and integral to the definition of relational competence. An individual can behave appropriately but be ineffective; likewise, one can be effective yet inappropriate. To illustrate the point, let us consider the use of deception in different contexts. Suppose Jack, a deft communicator, attempts to convince Holly, his intimate partner, to do something she does not want to do. In using deception, Jack may be effective in gaining compliance, but it may be inappropriate to the extent that lying violates the implicit ethical rules established within their interpersonal relationship. In another instance, Jack may be playing poker with some friends. Don, a poker partner, engages in bluffing behavior that Jack immediately recognizes and capitalizes upon. Jack wins the poker hand; Don has behaved appropriately but ineffectively. Now say that Jack skillfully bluffs his poker partners. He has acted appropriately, effectively, and hence competently (Hayano, 1980). Certainly, his partners may be disgruntled, not only in losing but also in Jack's skill at deception. Nevertheless, Jack's partners recognize that deception does not violate the established rules of the game (as cheating would). Indeed, it is part of the game—it is expected and appropriate. It is important to note, however, that appropriateness and effectiveness are not generally independent of each other. "The likelihood of achieving one's goals is markedly enhanced if the individual grasps and makes use of generally accepted social norms and expectations" (Liberman, 1982, p. 66). Thus, while appropriateness and effectiveness can be independent, they are likely to be correlated in most communicative episodes.

Finally, since appropriateness and effectiveness are perceptual phenomena, they are susceptible to change over time. For example, immediately after a conflict, a dyad's members may emerge with perceptions of each other's incompetence. But after some time has elapsed, they may recognize that certain valuable issues were resolved in the conflict in the best conceivable way. In relative terms, the members may come to perceive each other's conflict management in that episode as competent.

Competence Is Contextual

That communication is context bound is widely recognized. The intrinsically ambiguous nature of messages renders them uninterpretable when divorced from situations and relationships. Norms, rules, expectations, and conventions endemic to a particular situation govern the unfolding of communication behavior during a conversational episode. Increasingly, scholars have called for formal conceptualizations of communication situations in order adequately to account for communication phenomena (Baxter, 1980; Bochner, 1978; Hewes, 1978). The "interactional" school of social psychology has generated considerable work in the last decade to identify dimensions of situations and to develop situational taxonomies (for reviews, see Argyle, Furnham, & Graham, 1981; Forgas, 1979, 1982; Furnham & Argyle, 1981). This interest has recently spilled into the discipline of communication (see Baxter, 1980; Cody & McLaughlin, 1980; Cupach & Hazleton, 1982). Empirical research indicates that situational variables significantly influence the selection of communication strategies (see Lustig & King, 1980; McLaughlin, Cody, & Robey, 1980; Miller, Boster, Roloff, & Seibold, 1977; Roloff & Barnicott, 1978), the evaluative judgments made about communicators (Liska, 1978), and the affective judgments made about conversations (Hecht, 1978b).

Because the appropriateness of a given behavior can be judged accurately only according to the mutually defined standards of a specific relationship and context, the second assumption of the relational competence construct becomes clear: Competence is contextual (Garrison & Powell, 1977; Garrison, Sullivan, & Pate, 1976; Gottman, 1979; Helper, 1970; Pearce & Cronen, 1980; Powell, 1979; Rathjen, 1980). Behaviors that are normatively sanctioned in general may not be so in a particular relationship. Behaviors that are socially *proscribed* in one situation may be relationally *prescribed* in another. The notion that interpersonal relationships engender idiosyncratic rule systems suggests the importance of viewing appropriateness as a context-specific phenomenon (Knapp et al., 1980), requiring correspondent operationalization. In essence, this assumption implies that "competence lies in the relational system and as such must be evaluated from an interpersonal perspective" (Prutting, 1982, p. 129).

It is critical to note that this assumption does not deny that certain behaviors may be *typically* or *normatively* perceived as communicatively competent; it simply indicates the importance of discovering these norms anew in each contextual episode. The standards for effectiveness are also influenced by situation. In order to achieve objectives, communicators must follow rules that indicate relevant and efficacious strategies and tactics. Strategies and tactics are enacted to fulfill objectives relevant to the situation. As objectives change, strategies to achieve the objectives must often change. Moreover, even when objectives remain constant but other aspects of context change, strategies must often change as well. For instance, the use of ingratiation may be an effective technique for eliciting a favor from a neighbor but may be totally ineffective when used with one's spouse. Ingratiation might be effective and acceptable for both spouses in a relationship, but the *styles* of ingratiation may be different. That is, one spouse may need to ingratiate with tangible rewards (such as money or duties performed), whereas the other spouse needs to use verbal ingratiation (compliments, stroking, or the like).

That situational exigencies and constraints determine the appropriateness and effectiveness of communication behavior explains why behavioral flexibility skills (and underlying cognitive processes such as empathy, role taking, and problem-solving skills) are so widely and consistently cited as indicators of competence. Behavioral flexibility implies a large and diverse

strategic repertoire of behavior, the ability to select and implement behaviors appropriate to the situation, and the creativity
to enact routines to cope with novel or unexpected communication situations. In short, the hallmark of behavioral flexibility
is the adaptation of communication to situations. This behavioral flexibility in turn relies on the individual's ability to dis-
cern the relevant characteristics of the situation that "correspond" to the person's available repertoire of behavior. "It is
thus a mark of competent interaction that actors have not only
a well-developed discriminative facility but also a highly developed capacity for what Piaget calls 'accommodation' of
familiar patterns of thought and action to the ever-changing
particularities of immediate situations" (Athay & Darley, 1981,
p. 297). A person must not only possess the ability to enact
the behaviors appropriate to a situation but also be able to *rec-*
ognize what the situational parameters of appropriateness are.

One obvious implication of the contextual assumption is
that relational competence is *not* a cross-situational trait. Instead, individuals are typically more competent in dealing with
certain kinds of situations and less competent in dealing with
others (Larson et al., 1978; Powell, 1979; Wiemann & Backlund, 1980). This does *not* deny the relevance of personality
constructs. Indeed, stable traits such as cognitive complexity,
self-esteem, tolerance for ambiguity, Machiavellianism, rhetorical sensitivity, and the like influence relational competence in
at least two ways. First, traits that generally affect receptive and
expressive capacities of communicators can facilitate or inhibit
their *propensity* for being competent *across* situations. For example, rhetorical sensitivity and cognitive complexity may be
traits that allow communicators to make appropriate and effective message choices. Of course, there is no *guarantee*. Highly
cognitively complex and sensitive individuals can be incompetent. Ultimately, the judgment of competence in a particular
situation must rest with the knowledge, motivation, skills, and
outcomes exhibited in a particular situation. Situational knowledge, motivation, and skills mediate the influence of personality traits.

Second, personality variables can interact with situational
variables to produce competent communication. Given the
high task orientation of Machiavellians (Christie & Geis, 1970),
for example, we might speculate that they would be more likely
to be viewed as enacting competent strategies in most task/in-

strumental situations, whereas they may be perceived as less competent in situations emphasizing identity-management objectives. Thus, the high Machiavellian is likely to be perceived as more competent in certain kinds of situations in which his or her personality would facilitate appropriate and effective behavior.

Another implication of the contextual assumption is that judgments of competence can change within and during an interactional episode. Because situations are negotiated tacitly and constructed by communicators during interaction, definitions of situations are subject to change (Ginsburg, 1980). In essence, the situation may shift during a single episode (Heise, 1977). Consequently, competence in an episode can also change unless knowledge, motivation, and skill commensurate with the change in situation are present.

In summary, while some communicators have traits that allow them to display competence across more situations than other communicators, traits alone are insufficient for predicting and judging competence *in situ,* because the requirements for appropriate and effective communication vary with situations.

Competence Is a Matter of Degree

A third assumption of the relational competence construct is that judgments of appropriateness and effectiveness are arrayed along a continuum, not a dichotomy. There is no "minimal condition" threshold whereupon a person or conversation "becomes" competent (Shatz, 1977, p. 33). Instead, the perception of competence is a graduated phenomenon in which behaviors, affective responses, and cognitions are enmeshed within an unfolding dynamic process of conversation. This dynamic process leads to impressions of a person or conversation as more or less appropriate and effective. For example, in a conversation with Kim, Pat may tell an off-color joke impugning Jews. Kim, being Jewish, may be insulted. But the remark must be judged within an episodic frame of reference. Several judgmental conclusions are open to Kim, including: (a) that remark was insensitive and rude, and therefore, the conversation was *very* inappropriate; (b) *except* for that one remark, the conversation was smooth, comfortable, and appropriate; (c) although I did not appreciate the remark, I can understand how it seemed appropriate at the time; (d) the conversation was *generally* appropriate; and so on. The example illustrates that judgments of communication are complex and multidimensional. In any given episode, a person can key on certain specific remarks, the conversation as a whole, or even segments of the conversation. These various bits of the conversation can be weighted differentially. Although the example regards appropriateness, judgments of effectiveness are graduated similarly. Conversants typically achieve a degree of their objectives, not all or none.

Consistent with the continuum assumption is the fact that communication performance can vary from episode to episode (within similar contexts), from situation to situation (between contexts), and even within a particular episode. Moreover, given the developmental and evolutionary nature of situational definitions, the *criteria* for appropriateness and effectiveness can fluctuate, necessitating relative versus absolute judgments. A continuum approach also recognizes that in a given situation, there may be more than one optimal set of outcomes. Moreover, a "negative" outcome involving some dissatisfaction may still reflect competence if that outcome is *relatively* better than its alternatives.

Competence Is Both Molar and Molecular

This complex perceptual process further legitimates a fourth assumption. Interpersonal judgments of competence are based on both molar and molecular perceptions. This is similar to a holistic-atomistic distinction in pedagogy (Friedrich, 1981). For example, a single faux pas can be so noticeably inappropriate and awkward that it creates an impression of considerable incompetence. By comparison, a mundane ritualized greeting followed by extended phatic communication may result in impressions of competence, even if specific behaviors are not salient in this judgment. To assess the competence of a conversational episode and its interactants accurately, both specific "molecular" behaviors (for example, s/he asked me questions) *and* abstract "molar" impressions (for example, s/he was trustworthy) need to be considered. This provides a more complete picture of communication competence. Molecular behaviors provide specific communicative indicants of competence and provide a reference point for skill enhancement. Molar impressions provide evaluative outcome criteria.

To focus on *only* molar impressions *or* specific behaviors is to fall prey to the unfortunate distinction between cognitive and behavioral approaches to competence. We concur with Wiemann and Kelly (1981):

> The cognitive-behavioral dichotomy in the study of communica-
> tive competence is spurious. It is just as inappropriate to focus
> only on behavior with no concern for how the person "got that
> way" as it is to study only "ideal" communication structure with
> no regard for the fact that the real world in which humans inter-
> act is far from ideal. An alternative is to treat competence as
> both cognitive and behavioral. (p. 290)

Some scholars studying *social skills* have also recently recognized the desirability of blending cognitive and behavioral (molar and molecular) approaches (see Bellack, 1979, 1983; Hops, 1983; McFall, 1982).

Research is not entirely clear on how molar and molecular cues are utilized by observers and interactants. The elements on which raters focus in making judgments of competence may vary with time, target, and topic. Research suggests, for example, that judgments of current conversations tend to focus on microscopic behaviors while evaluations of recalled conversations focus more on global judgments (Hecht, 1978b). Research by Planalp (1983) revealed that knowledge of specific verbal behaviors enacted in a conversation provided a more potent predictor of conversational memory than did general evaluative dimensions. That is, when assessing a conversation, subjects are more likely to remember remarks that are consistent with *expectations* for specific comments in that relational context than they are to remember comments that are consistent with general dominance-submissiveness evaluations. This result suggests that people do attend to specific behaviors in certain conversations, and they organize these behavioral perceptions according to "relational schemata" that correspond to the situation. Other research, however, found that even after five minutes, subjects are able to remember only about 10 percent of the actual content of a preceding conversation (Stafford & Daly, 1983). Significantly, subjects in this experiment remembered *noncontent* information (53 percent) more often than content-based information (47 percent). The most common noncontent reproductions were general themes of the conversation (23.5 percent), evaluations (13.6 percent), elaborations (8.7 percent), and descriptions (6.0 percent). Thus, people remembered specific conversational content as well as general inferential evaluations and molar impressions from a conversation that had occurred only five minutes prior to the recall instruction. It appears that people process both specific actions and general inferences, both of which contribute to their "impression" of a conversation and the conversants involved. Although specific conversational behaviors contribute to generalized impressions of competence, *other* criteria that interactants may use to construct general impressions are not fully understood.

Competent Communication Is Functional

A fifth assumption of the relational competence construct is that communication is functional. As obvious as this assumption may be, its complexities rarely are realized in conceptualizations of competence. To say that communication is functional is to say that messages "do" rather than simply "are." People accomplish ends through communication, intentionally and unintentionally. Messages are functionally related to communication effects, however transient and seemingly intangible. Consequently, to view communication as functional is to view the *process* as related to and productive of functional *outcomes*.

Although the functions of communication are not well understood at present, several reasonable functional representations have been proffered (see Allen & Brown, 1976; Bennis et al., 1968; Dance & Larson, 1972; Larson et al., 1978; Brown et al., 1977). Perhaps the most generic and par- simonious approach is that of Clark and Delia (1979). They construct a tripartite schema of "objectives" that are served by communication. Communication affects individual goals (instrumental objective), relational status or goals (interpersonal objective), and one's sense of self (identity objective). These objectives, in turn, suggest functional outcomes. Instrumentally effective communication, because it results in the fulfillment of positive expectations, should be self-satisfying. Interpersonally successful communication, because it brings about relational rewards or congruence of relationship definition, should result in relationship satisfaction and perceptual congruence. Effective identity-related communication, because it maintains, repairs, or enhances self-concept, should result in perceived confirmation.

Another useful functional approach is presented by the National Project on Speech Communication Competencies (Allen & Brown, 1976). The conference report of this body identifies five functional classes of communicative behavior: controlling, feeling, informing, ritualizing, and imagining. Communication behaviors act to affect, alter, or accomplish goals of controlling, feeling, informing, ritualizing, and imagining. Specifically, when applied to children's communication behavior, each of these functions normally is fulfilled by certain behaviors. Controlling acts function to influence behavior (of others). Feeling acts are those that function to express feelings and attitudes as an affective response. Informing acts function to offer or solicit information. Acts that function primarily to maintain interpersonal relationships and to facilitate communication are ritualizing in nature. Finally, imagining acts are behaviors that portray the participants in imaginary or fictional roles and situations. While other functions may exist at different levels of abstraction (informative, regulative, phatic, and so on), the point is that identifiable functions indicate identifiable criterion outcomes of competent interaction. Thus, given the contextual nature of competence judgments, a given behavioral sequence can be assessed as competent only if it is related to functional outcomes of competence.

Competence Is an Interdependent Process

An assumption related to the first and last assumptions is now implied. The assessment of competence requires that both (all) interactants involved be at least referenced. If the relational context is a vital consideration, then all participants to that relationship need to be considered. Relational competence assumes that "competence lies in the relational system. Consequently, judgments of competence can only validly be made in terms of systemic effectiveness, appropriateness and satisfaction" (Wiemann & Kelly, 1981, p. 289). An individual is competent *only* in the context of a relationship. Thus, as Wiemann (1977) argues, one may be personally effective in achieving goals but "may be incompetent in an interpersonal sense if such effectiveness precludes the possibility of others accomplishing their goals" (p. 196).

Further, since the judgment of functional outcomes requires that all of the interactants' perceptions be assessed, it is important that all participants' functional fulfillment be included as well. "The interpersonal component of competence must be assessed by both self-reports and observer-reports, since each contributes a unique perspective on role performance" (Blechman, 1981, p. 230). Two illustrations help justify this assumption. First, presume that person A is asked to rate A's own competence in a conversation with B. Conceivably, A would perceive self to have been competent only if B had also been a competent conversationalist. The fact that self-rated competence has revealed a substantial positive relationship to ratings of other's competence supports this expectation (Spitzberg, 1982c). Indeed, research suggests that while individuals have a tendency to rate themselves as uniformly higher in conversational skills than do peers (Jansen, Robb, & Bonk, 1973; Phillips, 1949), the two sets of ratings are significantly related to each other. This is valuable information, because it indicates the interdependency of competent interaction. Thus, both participants need to be referenced (that is, rated). Second, presume now that both A and B are asked to rate self and other in their conversation. It is entirely possible that in a given instance A may view A as having been fairly competent and B as fairly incompetent, while B could come out of the episode with oppositely valenced impressions. To ignore either interactant's perceptions in this case would be to bias the researcher's conclusions and any theoretical conclusions drawn. Therefore, it becomes essential that both (or all) interactants would rate self and other(s) involved. To date, our research indicates that A's rating of B's competence is a more powerful predictor of A's satisfaction, self-perceived confirmation, and self-perceived appropriateness, while A's ratings of A's own competence is more predictive of A's self-perceived effectiveness (Spitzberg, 1982c; Spitzberg & Canary, 1983). This suggests that self and other ratings interact to affect conversational outcomes. Conceptually, it may make more sense to have B make molecular and molar ratings of A and have A rate A's outcomes if A's competence is the focus of interest, since A may be less attentive to his or her own communication behaviors. B, on the other hand, is perceptually focused on A and can provide such ratings with potentially greater objectivity.

Competence Is an Interpersonal Impression

Throughout the elaboration of the assumptions, one basic belief has guided the development of the construct of relational competence. Competence is not something intrinsic to a person's nature or behavior; it is an impression that a person has of self or other. This impression is based on the behavioral minutae of a given episode and the history of the relationship that contextualizes the behavioral choreography enacted within it. Competence is not enduring; it is ever-changing. To assess it at any one point in time is to ask at least one individual's impressions of both his or her own competence in a given conversational episode and his or her impressions of other's competence.

McFall (1982) succinctly summarizes the ramifications of viewing competence as an evaluative impression of performance:

> First, competence does not actually reside in the performance; it is an *evaluation* of the performance by someone. Its evaluative nature is reflected in the fact that alternative terms, such as adequate, effective or good, could be substituted without seriously changing the meaning. Second, the fact that *someone* is making the evaluation means that it is subject to error, bias, and judgmental inferences; different judges using the same criteria may evaluate the same performance differently. Third, since the evaluation always must be made with reference to some set of implicit or explicit *criteria*, the evaluation cannot be understood or validated without knowing the criteria being employed; thus, the same performance may be judged to be competent by one standard and incompetent by another. (pp. 13-14)

This assumption represents a major definitional and theoretical move outside of traditional skill- and trait-based approaches to competence. An assumption underlying skills approaches, for example, seems to be that social skills permit the performance of competent behavior. The implication is that the behavior is competent—that competence is a feature inherent in the behavior itself.

In contrast, to assume that competence is an interpersonal impression is to identify the perceptual process as the crucial feature of competence. This is not to ignore the importance of objective behaviors, but it is to argue that behavior is not the most productive place to look for competence. Ultimately, both "locations" of competence are vital to a theoretical model. It is important to discover what interactants perceive to be competent, how they derive such perceptions, how contexts affect these perceptions and how interactants produce communicative behaviors that are subsequently perceived to be competent. In developing such a model, we choose to retain the notion of skills when referring to interactant behavior and of competence when referring to the impressions of this behavior. How does this conception affect the traditional idea of a "competent communicator"? A communicator is competent if he or she is perceived to be competent by self and/or others. There are likely to be several skills that increase the probability that the impression of competence will be produced. But the skills and behaviors themselves are not intrinsically competent; they provide no guarantee that another will perceive the performance as competent.

The assumption that competence is an interpersonal impression is derived from several of the prior assumptions. Specifically, the assumption that competence is appropriate and effective interaction introduces two evaluative standards. Behavior is not objectively appropriate or effective. These subjective standards are learned and developed in cultural, social, and relational process. Despite some general consistencies, different interactants perceive different behaviors as appropriate and effective in different contexts. This assertion reveals another basis for assuming that competence is an impression. If it is possible for a given behavior to be perceived as competent in one context and incompetent in another, then the ability to perform the behavior does not seem to be the source of competence. In short, a person can possess numerous communicative skills, can perform a considerable repertoire of behavior, can recognize differences in contextual types, and still may not be viewed as competent by self or others in a given encounter. That is, personal characteristics cannot guarantee that an impression of competence will be produced in another person in a given episode of interaction.

If there is no guarantee, then what good does it do to study competence? The suggestion that personal characteristics provide no certainty in being viewed as competent does not imply that personal characteristics are irrelevant or unimportant. The model that follows is an attempt to integrate personal characteristics, context, and perceptual processes. The intent is to identify those personal characteristics that produce the highest *probability* of leading to impressions of competence in self and other. At the same time, these personal characteristics need to be cast at a level general enough both to integrate existing research and to be relevant to most communicative encounters.

A COMPONENT MODEL OF RELATIONAL COMPETENCE

Competence is neither purely psychological nor entirely behavioral. An integrative model, therefore, would include both realms. Such a model consists of four personal components or eight dyadic components (motivation, knowledge, skills, and criterion outcomes) and a complex contextual component. An interactant is not likely to communicate competently if he or she is anxious or unmotivated. Even if the interactant wants to interact, he or she may not know exactly what to say or how to say it. Further, being motivated to act competently and knowing what to say does not guarantee the requisite behavioral sequences (Ring, Braginsky, & Braginsky, 1966; Ring, Braginsky, Levine, & Braginsky, 1967; Ring & Wallston, 1968).

Finally, a person may be very motivated, knowledgeable, and skillful according to self-report indices, yet unless criterion outcomes are enhanced through the interaction, the components cannot be assumed to have been enacted competently. When extended to a dyadic situation, it is assumed that A's perception of B's competence is related to A's functional outcomes (such as communication satisfaction). Further, although there are likely to be systematic differences and exceptions, A's self-rated competence should be related positively to B's rating of A's competence and B's functional outcomes. This expectation presumes a certain degree of perceptual similarity and has been partially supported by research (Spitzberg, 1982c). While this perspective has not been elaborated before, several theorists have suggested these, or similar, components (see Gutkin, 1981; Knapp, 1978). Speaking about an organizational setting, Clinard (1979) identified three factors of skill development:

1. Knowledge (a cognitive understanding of the skill, what it comprises, how and when to use it, what to avoid, etc.).

2. Practice (experiences, experiments, role playing and actual skill development).

3. Valueing (appreciation of the skill, an awareness of the need for it and the potential benefits of its use). (p. 35)

Konsky and Murdock (1980) argue that

competency has two dimensions—knowledge and skills. *Knowledge* includes our awareness and understanding of the numerous variables which affect human relationships. *Skills* involve the ability to pragmatically apply, consciously or even unconsciously, our knowledge. (p. 86)

Elsewhere, they note the importance of being sensitive to self, other's, and relational goals (p. 90), which roughly represents a communicator's motivation. Wiemann and Backlund (1980) touch upon the same three components when they write:

Communicative competence focuses on the individual's ability and skill, which necessarily includes both knowledge of the social communicative rules and the wherewithal to perform in an appropriate manner. (p. 188)

The most direct recognition of these components is by Havighurst (1957):

A person's competence in filling the common social roles is due to (a) his skill in these roles, (b) his motivation to perform well in these roles, and (c) his knowledge of the behavior which is expected by society of people in these roles. (p. 339)

While each of these authors sketched the general components of competence, none of them sought to specify the various theoretical constructs entailed by these components. The following sections attempt to make an initial foray into the theoretical potential of the motivation, knowledge, skills, and outcome components.

Motivation

The most basic reaction to any interpersonal encounter is one of approach-avoidance (Mehrabian & Russell, 1974; Zajonc, 1980). This is similar to what Kelley (1950) referred to as the cold-warm impression in interpersonal perception. In a sequential conceptualization, this general affective response is likely to be the first or initial process in determining the competence of an interactant's impression management. It is also likely to affect the rest of the interaction episode by generating expectancies that serve to guide self's behavior (Ickes, Patterson, Rajecki, & Tanford, 1982; Trower, 1982). This basic motivational component can reference at least the factors of context, other, and self-objectives. A person can be motivated to approach or avoid a given context or a particular person. A person can also be motivated to approach or avoid an encounter because of simple reward contingencies or desired "goals." These approach and avoidance judgments are presumably contextual and changeable within the conversational episode itself. For example, for a student, a professor's request to "see me in my office after class" may initially set up several negative avoidance reactions in the student's mind. However, once involved in the interaction, the student may find that the meeting is actually for praise of his or her work in the course.

Three constructs that seem particularly relevant to the motivation component are altercentrism, anxiety, and involvement.

These constructs are each conceptualized as states or traits that prompt approach or avoidance in communicative encounters. Altercentrism, or other orientation, is a tendency to be interested in, attentive to, and adaptive to other in conversational interaction (Feingold, 1977; Hart & Burks, 1972; Hart et al., 1980; Knapp, 1978; Lange, 1980; Spitzberg, 1982a). Altercentric communication is referenced by such perceptual cues as attentiveness, cooperativeness, politeness, concern, and interest. Behaviorally, altercentrism typically is indicated by such cues as topic support (Derber, 1979), head nods, eye contact, direct and open orientation, questions, and use of positively reinforcing remarks (Norton & Pettegrew, 1979). Altercentric communication overlaps with immediacy cues. Nonverbal immediacy refers to behaviors that signal approach, availability for communication, arousal or sensory stimulation, and/or interpersonal warmth and closeness (Andersen, 1983). While the exact nature of this overlap is unclear, it is fairly clear that signs of immediacy often reflect other-oriented attitudes.

Social anxiety is an avoidance motivation wherein a person's history of reward contingencies has been negative in a given social situation or contextual form (McCroskey, 1977; Spitzberg, 1981b). Anxiety is referenced by such factors as undue perspiration, shakiness, postural rigidity, vocal smoothness, self and object adaptors, and minimal response tendencies (Morganstern & Wheeless, 1980; Zuroff and Schwarz, 1978). Social anxiety can be viewed as a dispositional apprehension of communicative contexts (Leary, 1983a, 1983b; McCroskey, 1977; Richardson & Tasto, 1976) or as a state of anxiety in a specific conversation (Cupach & Spitzberg, 1983; Spitzberg & Hecht, 1984).

Involvement concerns the degree to which the individual perceives the topic, situation, or other to involve his or her conception of self and self-reward. Indicators of such involvement might be the number of compliance-gaining or resisting tactics used, topical persistence, and self-perceived ego involvement in the topic. Involvement and altercentric cues should be related positively to impressions of competence, although it is easy to visualize a person as overly motivated to the point of distraction (thus indicating a possible curvilinear relationship at the upper ranges of motivational perceptions). The example of a shy high school boy on his first date comes to mind. In his eagerness to make a good impression and show interest in his date, he finds himself asking dozens of mundane questions or stumbling awkwardly in attempting to demonstrate his knowledge and expertise on every topic that arises. In the former case, he shifts the responsibility to the other person for sustaining boring topics by simply hanging on every word of his date. In the latter case, he finds himself trapped into appearing egocentric and/or nervous by his desire to be oriented toward his date's presumed positive expectations.

The importance of traitlike motivation in influencing interaction is summarized by Williams (1979):

> Higher motivational levels of competence are associated with greater breadth and clarity of perception, increased attention span, and greater receptivity to relevant stimuli. This allows for a better ordering of alternative pathways and choices, greater insight into situations, and an extended future perspective. Higher motivational levels are associated with greater cognitive complexity, the ability to engage in creative or divergent thinking, and the behavior productivity that would be expected to characterize the highly competent personality. (p. 184)

Motivation not only serves to facilitate actual performance, then, but, over the long term, also acts to stimulate other attributes, such as social perception and cognitive complexity, that can enhance the competence of a person's interaction.

The basis for an individual's motivation in a given conversational encounter has often been conceptualized from a social learning perspective. Derived originally from a behaviorist reinforcement perspective, social learning emphasizes the cognitive processes of modeling and expectancy, as well as the behavioral processes of reinforcement and contingency history. A person experiences numerous types of people and situations, each of which results in differential reinforcement values. When a new or relatively novel situation is encountered, the individual selects a response to that situation according to certain factors. There is the degree to which the situation and interactants involved are similar to situations or situation types encountered before. These prior situations have a reinforcement value associated with them, according to the competence with which the person coped with them. This value will then define a degree of motivation (approach or avoidance) for this new situation, provided that the old situations are perceived to be similar enough to assimilate the reinforcement potential. If the situation encountered is truly novel, then other sources of motivation are available. The other interactant(s) provide reinforcement values as well as the situation, and there may be salient goals or objectives a person wants to accomplish in the situation. The degree of motivation, however, ultimately is mediated by a person's *ability* to cope with the situation in addition to the actual reinforcement value of the situation.

The idea of ability and reinforcement interacting to affect motivation is explained by social learning theory in terms of behavior-outcome expectancies (Mischel, 1973) and self-efficacy and behavioral efficacy beliefs (Bandura, 1977; Saltzer, 1982). Behavior-outcome expectancies are contingency rules that represent

"if—, then—" relations between behavioral alternatives and probable outcomes anticipated with regard to particular behavioral possibilities in particular situations. In any given situation, the person will generate the response pattern which he expects is most likely to lead to the most subjectively valuable outcomes (consequences) in that situation. (Mischel, 1973, p. 270)

However, the person must believe that he or she is capable of producing this response pattern (self-efficacy belief) and that the behaviors it entails will actually result in the valued outcomes (behavioral efficacy beliefs). These beliefs in turn depend on the interactant's prior experience with enacting such behavior. Given little or no prior experience in producing such behaviors, the individual may still be capable of enacting the behaviors through a process of modeling. Through modeling, an individual imagines self reenacting or enacting behavior as another person (real or ideal) was observed (or is imagined) to have performed. It may be conjectured that modeling itself is a process facilitated by such cognitive abilities as cognitive complexity and role taking. These abilities would enhance an individual's capacities to expand and refine his or her *knowledge* of communicative strategies and behavioral repertoires.

Knowledge

Once a person has "decided" to approach an interpersonal encounter, the requisite lines of interaction must be anticipated, schemas searched for familiar routines, and cues and appropriate rule analogues retrieved and assessed (Athay & Darley, 1981). The implementation of a skill presumes some rudimentary knowledge or model of how to perform it. Consequently, knowledge also consists of repertoires of behavioral patterns, tactics, and strategies that constitute a given individual's social heuristic for enacting dialogue. In short, knowledge in this model consists of the possession of, or ability creatively to acquire, the requisite cognitive information necessary to implement conversationally competent behaviors in an interpersonal context. In this sense, knowledge is similar to Snyder's self-monitoring construct (Ickes & Barnes, 1977; Snyder, 1974, 1979a, 1979b; Snyder & Cantor, 1980). Self-monitoring represents the proclivity of an individual to monitor a social environment for cues that could inform the appropriate adaptation of interaction to that context. Specifically, self-monitoring is characterized along five conceptual dimensions:

(1) concern with social appropriateness of one's self-presentation...(2) attention to social comparison information as cues to situationally appropriate expressive self-presentation...(3) the ability to control and modify one's self-presentation and expressive behavior...(4) the use of this ability in particular situations...(5) the extent to which one's expressive behavior and self-presentation are tailored and molded to particular situations. (Snyder, 1979a, p. 184)

Clearly, the self-monitoring construct encompasses more than knowledge, although knowledge is a predominant component in its conceptualization. The role of knowledge in the self-monitoring construct is evident in a study by Snyder and Cantor (1980) in which high self-monitors were found to be "particularly knowledgeable about individuals who are prototypes of a wide variety of trait domains" (p. 222). In other words, high self-monitors possess a rich and complex base of knowledge about person types. This form of knowledge presumably informs one's subsequent interaction with others. Despite the apparent relevance of the self-monitoring construct and its generally supportive validity evidence (see Brandt, Miller, & Hocking, 1980; Brockner & Eckenrode, 1979; Ickes & Barnes, 1977; Rarick et al., 1979; Snyder, 1974, 1979b; Snyder & Tanke, 1976; Snyder & Swann, 1976, 1978; Tunnell, 1980; Zanna, Olson, & Fazio, 1980), it is not substantially related to the negotiation of intimacy in dyadic interactions (Davis, 1978), measures of nonverbal expressiveness (Cunningham, 1977; Friedman, Prince, Riggio, & DiMatteo, 1980), adaptability (Dabbs, Evans, Hopper, & Purvis, 1980), or ratings of conversational competence (Spitzberg, 1982c; Spitzberg & Cupach, 1981). The inconsistent results suggest that the construct of self-monitoring is neither purely a knowledge-based concept nor consistently related to competent interaction. Factor analytic studies support the conclusion that, at least, the self-monitoring measure is multidimensional and not a pure measure of social perceptual attentiveness or knowledge per se (Briggs et al., 1980; Gabrenya & Arkin, 1980; Tobey & Tunnell, 1981). Consequently, the construct is appealing as a knowledge-facilitating trait, even though extant measures appear to be poor operationalizations.

Alternative ways of conceptualizing and operationalizing knowledge appear to be more relevant to competence in communicating. One relatively recent development is the concept of human information processing as it relates to interaction. Shatz (1977) proposes that human skills are integrally related to the way in which information is processed. It is assumed that any complex task can be viewed as a composite of subtasks, each requiring certain possible techniques (that is, skills) for task accomplishment and each technique in turn with an outcome value (degree of task success, appropriateness, certainty, and so on). Each technique in turn requires a certain amount of resources (such as time and effort) to implement. Thus, certain techniques will be utilized rather than others because their "demands" on the person and their outcome values for the person vary. A person may fail to manifest a certain skill either because its outcome value is low *or* because it requires too many personal resources. Applied to knowledge in interaction, this model suggests that people may possess a certain repertoire or knowledge of skills yet elicit these skills differentially depending upon the effort required to reproduce them and their outcome values and probabilities.

An alternative (though not exclusive) information-processing approach is proffered by Pavitt and Haight (Haight & Pavitt, 1982; Pavitt, 1982, 1983; Pavitt & Haight, 1982). Basically, a hierarchical person memory model is proposed to describe and explain the process of impression formation relevant to perceiving someone as a competent communicator. The person memory model is composed of four levels: the focal concept of the competent communicator (level one), trait adjectives and inferences (level two), behavioral generalizations (level three), and memories of specific communicative events (level four). A person possesses a prototype of a communicatively competent individual (level one). This prototype is "defined" by positive and negative trait adjectives (enthusiastic, open-minded, interesting, argumentative, hostile, boring, and so on), behavioral generalizations (for example, listens well, uses voice expressively, understands, is relaxed, speaks frequently, tells jokes and stories), and specific events in which these behaviors (and inferences) have been encountered. The degree to which A (focal concept) is perceived to be competent by B is contingent on the degree to which A's behaviors correspond to B's "competent communicator" prototype (and its subordinate concepts).

The practical implication of this person memory model for a conceptualization of competence is at least twofold. First, it suggests how people process information about people in regard to competence. How do people "know" others as competent or incompetent? How do these types of impressions come about? Second, the person memory model applied to competence is really a specific case of the more general model of object-based information processing. During interaction, individuals must recall information regarding the management of the interaction itself. Particular situations and persons may require different conversational strategies. There are certain things that simply "are not said" in certain situations and in front of certain people. But how is such a rule "known" or remembered? Apparently, a given individual may be perceived as a focal concept and thereby attributed with certain personality inferences and evaluations, associated with certain types of behaviors, and recalled from actual prior encounters. The resulting impression informs future interaction with this person.

A somewhat related type of knowledge is referred to as "script" knowledge. Scripts are sequences or routines of events involving an individual as an interactant or observer which are stored in memory (Abelson, 1981; Schank & Abelson, 1977). Scripts represent "ways" in which certain things are done or are assumed to be done. As a dramaturgical metaphor, scripts are cognitive representations of how interactants are supposed to relate, that is, the script that is "supposed" to be performed. Scripts may be derived, consciously or unconsciously, from actual interaction, modeling, or media. An interesting example is found in a set of experiments conducted by Wilson and Capitman (1982). These researchers had subjects read one of two stories (supposedly for recall purposes): the experimental boy-meets-girl (that is, the sociable story) or a brief excerpt from Mark Twain's *Life on the Mississippi* as a control condition with no reference to social interaction at all. Subsequently, in a waiting-room interaction with a female confederate, the boy-meets-girl script subjects were rated (blindly) as friendlier and were observed to smile more, talk more, lean closer, and gaze more than the control-condition subjects. The authors interpret the findings in terms of the "friendly" script availability that the experimental subjects possessed.

A very different approach to knowledge is presented in the behavioral-analytic and problem-solving approaches to competent interaction. Whereas the person memory model concerns declarative knowledge (knowledge of...knowledge that...), the problem-solving approach concerns procedural knowledge (knowledge how...). The behavioral-analytic approach is a competence assessment strategy involving several stages. First, a sample of problematic interpersonal situations is solicited. Second, these situations are abstracted, and the most frequently mentioned situations are used in a second sample to elicit possible responses to the situations. Third, these responses are abstracted and rated in terms of effectiveness in coping with the situation. Finally, the target sample is presented with the situations and randomly ordered effective and ineffective responses to the situations. The subjects are asked to rate the responses in terms of effectiveness or likelihood of usage. The more discrepant their ratings are from normative ratings, the more "incompetent" the subjects are in their knowledge of effective interaction strategies. This approach has been used productively in a number of studies (Donahoe, 1978; Fisher-Beckfield, 1979; Goldfried & D'Zurilla, 1969; Martinez-Diaz & Edelstein, 1980) and represents a flexible approach to assessing knowledge.

A related approach is the problem-solving therapy of Spivack et al. (1976; Shure, 1980, 1981, 1982). The problem-solving therapy involves training children to think in means-ends forms, to examine alternatives, and to develop plans and methods to achieve goals.

> A series of studies have shown that means-ends thinking skills significantly distinguish normals from the diagnostically disturbed or behaviorally troubled beginning at about age 9, while a spontaneous tendency to weigh pros and cons of an act emerges as significant to behavior during the adolescent years. (Shure, 1981, p. 159)

Such knowledge constitutes procedural knowledge of how to analyze a problematic situation in such a way that the most adaptive response can be made.

Knowledge, like motivation, is cast appropriately at the intrapersonal level. However, several indicators might be adduced to represent a person's knowledge indirectly. Perceptually, rule knowledge exists on at least three levels—linguistic, social, and interpersonal. Linguistic rule knowledge involves cognizance of syntactic and grammatical relations. Social rule knowledge concerns an understanding of culturally normative contextual standards of appropriateness. Interpersonal rule knowledge applies to familiarity with the idiosyncratic rule systems of a given relationship. Knowledge in these three areas should lead to an ability to differentiate various persons and situations cognitively in terms of their implicit standards of appropriateness and effectiveness. Therefore, three related cognitive/affective processes should also be indicative of rule knowledge: cognitive complexity, role-taking skills, and empathy. Cognitive complexity refers to the number of a person's schemas or constructs for evaluating and understanding stimuli. A cognitively complex individual is likely to possess appropriateness and effectiveness constructs for interpreting social episodes (Bruch et al., 1981; Hale, 1980; Hale & Delia,

1976; O'Keefe & Delia, 1979). Role taking is an ability cognitively to decenter or reconstruct the perceptual set of an other. Empathy is similar to role taking but involves the affective reconstruction of an other's emotional state (Spitzberg, 1980). Role taking and empathy allow an individual better to assess other people's judgments of appropriateness in a given context (Lane, 1981; Marsh et al., 1981). Behaviorally, knowledge might be referenced by an individual's awareness (or usage) of knowledge acquisition strategies (for example, invoking the norm of reciprocity via self-disclosure, interrogation, or deviation testing; Berger, Gardner, Parks, Schulman, & Miller, 1976). Other indicators might be self-perceived range of appropriate strategies and behaviors in given contexts (Argyle et al., 1981; Price & Bouffard, 1974; Thomas & Bookwalter, 1982). Collectively, these indices of knowledge and its acquisition should be positively related to competent impression management.

Additionally, research from a variety of areas has demonstrated the importance of relationship-specific knowledge to competent communication. Kent, Davis, and Shapiro (1981) have found that mutually acquainted dyads constructed conversations in a smoother fashion without the use of meta-instructions (that is, questions) than did stranger dyads. In fact, the unconstrained conversational turns of the strangers were easier to "reconstruct" in proper sequence by third parties than were those of mutual acquaintances. This indicates that acquaintances do develop idiosyncratic understanding that informs their conversational interaction. Honeycutt et al. (1983) found that dyad members with greater relational knowledge generally were more accurate in predicting their partners' communicative messages and that intimate partners did seem to share a more idiosyncratic communication system than did initial acquaintances. Orlofsky (1976) found that intimate dyads characterized by openness and empathy did indeed "share a greater degree of mutual knowledge and understanding with their partners" than did medium- or low- intimacy-status dyads (p. 73). This finding is qualified by the results of Robinson and Price's (1980) observational study of satisfied and dissatisfied marital couples. Their research compared the *observed* exchange of pleasurable and displeasurable behaviors to the couple's *perceived* exchange of these behaviors. The investigators found that spouses in dissatisfied couples "underesti-mated the rate of pleasurable behavior by approximately 50%" (p. 118). This finding is significant, because it suggests that couples' knowledge of each other varies not only according to what actually occurs between partners but also according to the quality of the affective bonds between partners.

The assumption is made that knowledge can be treated as separate from motivation. This is intuitively reasonable. For example, a person may desperately want a higher dating frequency yet be ignorant of the initial conversation ritual that could lead to a more satisfying level of dating. Empirically, this assumption is borne out as well. For example, communication apprehension has been found to be unrelated to knowledge of compliance-gaining strategies (Lustig & King, 1980), and as-sertiveness has been found to be unrelated to knowledge of assertive responses (Alden & Cappe, 1981). Such findings suggest that the components of knowledge and motivation can be treated as relatively independent (that is, additive) con-tributors to competent impression management.

Skill

An individual may be motivated to interact competently, and may also know what needs to be done, yet find it difficult actually to enact the desired behavioral sequences. Such diffi-culties would not indicate a motivation or knowledge deficit, but a skill deficit instead. Research has found that subjects self-defined as socially anxious often are not perceived as unskilled by third-party observers (Clark & Arkowitz, 1975; Glasgow & Arkowitz, 1975; Kelly, 1982). A similar finding is that of Curran, Wallander, and Fischetti (1980), who found that high-anxiety/high-skill subjects judged their own social skills to be lower than did third-party judges, whereas high-anxiety/low-skill sub-ject ratings corresponded with those of the judges. Garland (1981) found that after listening skills training, married couples were capable of listening actively but did not actually utilize these skills in interaction. These findings indicate that motivation (such as anxiety) may be somewhat independent of skills. Still other research has failed to find a relationship among self-perceived anxiety, nonverbal cue sensitivity, and the skill of communicative adaptability (Christensen et al.,

1980). Two studies, moreover, have found that low assertive subjects differ from high assertive subjects in negative self-evaluation and knowledge of assertive responses but not in actual enactment of assertive responses (Alden & Cappe, 1981; Schwartz & Gottman, 1976). These findings suggest that knowledge and skills may be independent, lending legitimacy to Bandura's (1982) statement that "people often do not behave optimally, even though they know full well what to do" (p. 122). The relative independence of knowledge, motivation, and skills is implied by the apparently common experience, "I *knew* what I *wanted* to say, but I just couldn't seem to *actually say it.*" Just such a possibility was investigated by Bellack, Hersen, and Turner (1978) in their comparison of subjects' *knowledge* of appropriate assertive responses in a structured interview (SI) and their use of these role-playing encounters.

> The results for the comparisons of those two situations with the SI were not entirely consistent. It appears, however, that subjects generally "talked a better game than they played." With one exception, interview performance matched or was more socially skillful than enacted behavior on every measure. (p. 674)

After completing four studies of heterosocial avoidance, Twentyman, Boland, and McFall (1981) concluded that "there is little correlation between a man's willingness to initiate interaction with women and his skill in carrying out such [interactions]" (p. 543). In speculating why some interpersonally skillful men avoid heterosocial interaction, the authors suggest that "such men are uncertain about their heterosocial competence; they are less knowledgeable about interpreting social cues and thus are less able to feel confident about judging their effect on others" (p. 544). These authors imply a curious relationship among motivation, knowledge, and skill. While each *can be* and sometimes *is* unrelated to the other components, each can also influence the others.

Findings from a variety of research projects, therefore, suggest that constructs reflecting motivation, knowledge, and skills are conceptually separable and often empirically unique. It is important not to carry this assumption too far, however. In some contexts, wanting to communicate leads to repetitive knowledge acquisition encounters which, in turn, lead to the

(text continues on page 136)

TABLE 4.1   **Selected Behaviorally Focused Items from Self-Report Competence and Related Measures**

Bienvenu (1917)

Do you pretend you are listening to others when actually you are not really listening?

Do your words come out the way you would like them to in conversations?

Do you find yourself being inattentive while in conversation with others?

Is it difficult for you to admit that you are wrong when you recognize that you are wrong about something?

Do you have a tendency to change the subject when your feelings are brought into a discussion?

Do you fail to express disagreement with others because you are afraid they will get angry?

Is it difficult to accept constructive criticism from others?

When a problem arises between you and another person are you able to discuss it together in a calm manner?

Do other persons have a tendency to put words in your mouth when you are trying to explain something?

Is it difficult for you to confide in people?

Duran, Zakahi, & Parrish (1981)

My voice sounds nervous when I talk with others.

When (I am) talking, my posture seems rigid and tense.

I sometimes use words incorrectly.

At times, I don't use appropriate verb tense.

When speaking, I have problems with grammar.

I often make jokes when in tense situations.

When someone makes a negative comment about me, I respond with a witty comeback.

Eadie & Paulson (1983)

X's use of language was adapted to what Y was saying.

. . . X has a large vocabulary.

X's use of language in this situation was smooth and efficient.

X used language in a way that was appropriate for this situation.

Elder, Wallace, & Harris (1980)

Appears quite jittery and tense in social situations.

Seldom touches when expressing tenderness.

Times statements somewhat poorly.

Makes few or no hand gestures when speaking.

At times, shakes head negatively when conversing.

At times, speaks of matters of low personal importance (such as weather).

At times, leans forward when talking.

At times, speaks at moderately intimate levels (as when discussing likes and dislikes).

Often says "I'm sorry" when appropriate.

(continued)

TABLE 4.1 Continued

Gillingham, Griffiths, & Care (1977)

Able to look the other person in the eye/unable to look the other person in the eye.

Unable to cope with the other person/able to cope with the other person.

Talks confidently/talks with hesitation.

Looks at ease/looks restless.

Lacking in self-confidence/full of self-confidence.

Facial expression strained/facial expression natural.

Relaxed/tense.

A strain to talk to/easy to talk to.

Active in conversation/passive in conversation.

Fails to maintain a spontaneous flow of conversation/maintains a spontaneous flow of conversation.

Initiates topics of conversation/follows the other person.

Holland & Baird (1968)

I find it easy to talk with all kinds of people.

I find it easy to play many roles—student, leader, follower, church-goer, athlete, traveler, and so on.

People seek me out to tell me about their troubles.

If I want to, I can be a very persuasive person.

Kelly & Chase (1978)

Tends to be supportive of other people; he/she seems to want to "help."

Is an open person; reveals his/her inner self to others when appropriate.

Is able to express ideas clearly.

Is able to receive new information that is contrary to his/her values.

Is a very good listener.

Is not afraid to show affection.

Is easily embarrassed.

Is rather shy.

Is rather quiet.

Lowe & Cautela (1978)

Has eye contact when speaking.

Reacts with more anger than a situation calls for.

Is aggressive when s/he takes issue with someone.

Initiates contact and conversation with others.

Puts himself/herself down.

Makes other people laugh (with jokes, funny stories, and so on).

Interrupts others.

TABLE 4.1 Continued

Tries to work out problems with others by talking to them.

Gives the impression that s/he's an expert on everything.

Seems impatient for others to finish their remarks.

Shows appreciation when someone does something for him/her.

Says little in conversations s/he has.

Talks negatively about others when they are not present.

Reveals personal information and feelings to those with whom s/he is close.

Insults others.

Threatens others verbally or physically.

Rejects or criticizes other people before knowing much about them.

Talks repeatedly about his/her problems and worries.

Asks others how they've been, what they've been up to, and so on.

Laughs at other people's jokes and funny stories.

Gets into arguments.

Listens when spoken to.

Remembers and discusses topics previously discussed with others.

Shows interest in what another is saying (with appropriate facial movement, comments, and questions, for example).

Gives unsolicited advice.

Directs rather than requests people to do something.

Makes embarrassing comments.

Directs conversation with other people toward topics the other person is interested in.

Makes fun of others.

Blames others for his/her problems.

Asks questions when talking with others.

Admits to mistakes or errors s/he makes.

Gives polite feedback to others.

Speaks in a monotone.

Is able to recognize when people are troubled.

Tells people what s/he thinks they want to hear.

Refuses to change his/her opinions or beliefs.

Compliments others on their clothes, hairstyle, and so on.

Complains.

Perceives insults or criticism when none were intended.

Makes facial gestures (such as shaking his/her head) or sounds (such as sighs) which indicate disapproval of others.

Seems bored when interacting with others.

Talks too much about himself/herself.

Discusses a variety of topics with others.

Explains things in too much detail.

Mentions people's names when talking to them.

(continued)

TABLE 4.1 Continued

Macklin & Rossiter (1976)

Do you talk with others about unpleasant things?

When (you are) listening to another person speak, does your attention often drift to sounds other than those of his/her voice?

Do you find it difficult to determine the feelings of others by their facial and bodily gestures?

In conversation, do you often attempt to conceal many of your thoughts and feelings from others?

Do you talk about yourself to people in your daily encounters?

Do you hesitate to talk at social affairs because you're afraid that people will criticize you if you say the wrong things?

Pavitt (1982)

Listens well.

Argues to prove s/he is right.

Lets others know s/he understands them.

Relaxed and comfortable when speaking.

Speaks very frequently.

Uses picturesque language.

Tells jokes and stories.

Actively uses facial expressions.

Phillips (1949)

It was an interesting topic.

Other people had worthwhile ideas.

Others had good knowledge of the subject.

All had pleasant voices.

They included me in the conversation.

Other people were interested in what I had to say.

I liked most or all of the topics brought up.

It was easy to introduce subjects into the conversation.

They were good listeners.

Couldn't find a common topic.

The talked about themselves too much.

They gossiped too much.

The conversation became an argument and put us all in a poor mood.

They were not frank and sincere.

They did not do their share in making conversation.

They excluded me from the conversation.

They had unpleasant voices.

TABLE 4.1 Continued

Spitzberg & Hecht (1984)

Spoke fluently and smoothly.

Knew when it was her/his turn to speak.

Looked at me while I was talking.

Indicated support for what I was saying with head nods, "um-hmms," and/or approving comments.

Complimented me.

Referred to me (for example, used the word "you") frequently.

Smiled/laughed several times.

Used many gestures while talking.

Stood/sat fairly close to each other.

Arms/legs were crossed.

Stood in front of each other and faced each other directly.

Rarely looked in each other's eyes.

Smiled very much.

Made many physical gestures.

Walters & Snavely (1981)

Appears nervous when talking with others.

Tries to see things from others' perspectives.

Often appears intimidated by other people.

Readily understands the feelings of others.

Adjusts own conversation to make others feel comfortable.

Focuses his/her attention on others in conversations.

Shares personal aspirations with others.

Is a good role-player.

Is versatile in adapting to different situations.

Wiemann (1977)

S's personal relations are cold and distant.

S ignores other people's feelings.

S generally knows how others feel.

S lets others know she understands them.

S listens to what people say to her.

S is supportive of others.

People can go to S with their problems.

S likes to use her voice and body expressively.

S is relaxed and comfortable when speaking.

"learning" of behavioral skills. This is, to some extent, what is involved in social skills training. Moreover, in a study by Eisler, Fredericksen, and Peterson (1978), highly assertive individuals both expected more positive outcomes from their interactions and "appeared to be more aware of the socially appropriate value of assertive responses" (p. 425) than unassertive individuals. In this instance, subjects who were more socially skilled (that is, assertive) were apparently also more knowledgeable about interaction and more confident of achieving positive results (that is, more motivated).

Although numerous skills measures have been developed, it is possible that collectively they tap common domains. Some of the behaviors that subjects consistently report and recall as related significantly to competence in interaction are displayed in Table 4.1. These are relatively molecular behaviors that people systematically associate with competent interaction. The research cannot substantiate that individuals actually use and attend to these behaviors in making their judgments in actual interaction. Instead, it is possible that these behaviors simply reflect common social stereotypes (schemas) about what behaviors are consistently reinforcing in interaction. Close scrutiny of extant factor analytic studies of competence in interaction consistently reveal four broad dimensions: other-oriented behaviors, social anxiety, expressiveness, and interaction management (Bayes, 1972; Duran et al., 1981; Farber, 1962; Flint, Hick, Horan, Irvine, & Kukuk, 1980; Mehrabian & Ksionzky, 1972; Phelps & Snavely, 1980; Steffen et al., 1979; Wiemann, 1977). Behaviors representing the former two already have been considered. Expressiveness behaviors (vividness of facial expressions, vocal modulation, gesturing, postural shifts, and the like) may be reflective of involvement (just as other-orientation skills logically reflect altercentrism). However, interaction management appears to be a set of skills that may only partly reflect underlying knowledge or motivation. The intentionality or awareness of microscopic nonverbal behaviors involved in turn taking, greeting rituals, and leave-taking management has not been demonstrated. The complex interactions of audible breath inhalations, pause synchronizations, eye-contact initiation and avoidance, tone maintenance, and body orientations are not well understood at present (Mayo & La France, 1978). It seems clear, however, that they are related to interaction management. At a more abstract level, interaction management can be tapped by such evaluations as "the conversation went smoothly," "there were few interruptions," and "the conversation was awkward." At a more precise behavioral level, interaction management can be assessed through measurement of talk overlaps, response durations (McLaughlin & Cody, 1982), fluency, and even topic shifts (Derber, 1981). Available evidence indicates a positive linear relationship between these skills and competent impression management (Wiemann, 1977).

Based on our analysis thus far, a partial set of behavioral indicators for the skills component of the model of relational competence can be summarized (see Table 4.2). The behaviors and indicators listed reveal some overlap, which simply suggests that the skills are not entirely independent. It also reflects an unavoidable ambiguity in assessing the function of behavior. A given behavior (such as asking a question or establishing eye contact) can serve multiple functions simultaneously. The classification of behaviors in Table 4.2, therefore, is meant to be one likely set of functions served by the behaviors listed. Empirically, the prediction would be that each component set of behaviors would manifest a higher correlation among behaviors within the set than between the sets (although some correlation between each pair of components is expected).

Outcomes

The number of outcomes is likely to be as high as, if not higher than, the number of functions of communication. However, several outcomes have been investigated sufficiently to warrant extended analysis here. Among the outcomes that are expected to provide criteria of competent interaction are communication satisfaction, feeling good, interpersonal attraction, interpersonal solidarity, relational satisfaction, relational trust, negotiation and conflict satisfaction, and certain forms of intimacy. These outcomes can be viewed as episodic or relational,

TABLE 4.2   **Potential Behavioral Features of Competence Skills**

I. Interaction Management
   A. Verbal
   1. Topic initiation and maintenance (Derber, 1979)
   2. Open-ended questions (Garner, 1980)
   3. Use of questions (Minkin et al., 1976)
   4. Sentence completions (Pearce, 1976)
   5. Reinforcers (Pearce, 1976)
   B. Nonverbal
   1. Intonation, falling pitch (Pearce, 1976)
   2. Paralanguage, drawl on last syllable (Pearce, 1976)
   3. Buffers, pause fillers (Pearce, 1976)
   4. Gesticulations (Pearce, 1976)
   5. Gaze (Pearce, 1976)
   6. Response latency (Arkowitz, Lichtenstein, McGovern, & Hines, 1975;
      McLaughlin & Cody, 1982)
   7. Head nods (Pearce, 1976)
   8. Interruptions (Greenwald, 1977)
   9. Stutter starts (Pearce, 1976)

II. Social Relaxation (Anxiety)
   1. Touching/manipulating objects (Morganstern & Wheeless, 1980)
   2. Fidgeting feet and legs (Morganstern & Wheeless, 1980)
   3. Crossed arms/legs (Morganstern & Wheeless, 1980)
   4. Eye contact avoidance (Morganstern & Wheeless, 1980)
   5. Rapid speaking (Morganstern & Wheeless, 1980)
   6. Self-manipulation (Morganstern & Wheeless, 1980)
   7. Loud speaking (Morganstern & Wheeless, 1980)
   8. Self-grooming (Morganstern & Wheeless, 1980)
   9. Abrupt head movements (Morganstern & Wheeless, 1980)
   10. Postural swaying (Morganstern & Wheeless, 1980)
   11. Arm posture rigidity (Zuroff & Schwarz, 1978)
   12. Speech blockage (Zuroff & Schwarz, 1978)
   13. Speech nonfluencies (Zuroff & Schwarz, 1978)
   14. Topically irrelevant responses (Zuroff & Schwarz, 1978)
   15. Tense voice (Zuroff & Schwarz, 1978)

III. Expressiveness
   A. Verbal
   1. Affective self-references (Crowley & Ivey, 1976)
   2. Expressing feelings (Rose, Cayner, & Edelson, 1977; Kelly, Urey, &
      Patterson, 1980)
   3. Expressing opinions (Rose et al., 1977)
   4. Persistence (Rose et al., 1977)
   5. Giving clarification (Rose et al., 1977)
   6. Request for change (Foy, Massey, Duer, Ross, & Wooten, 1979)
   7. Humor (Robinson & Price, 1980)
   8. Owning up to (Argyris, 1965a)
   9. Openness (Argyris, 1965a; Brandt, 1979)
   10. Experimenting (Argyris, 1965a)

TABLE 4.2 Continued

B. Nonverbal
   1. Talk time (Greenwald, 1977; Lavin & Kupke, 1980; Trower, 1980)
   2. Appropriate affect (Barlow, Able, Blanchard, Bristow, & Young, 1977; Rose et al., 1977)
   3. Appropriate volume (Romano & Bellack, 1980; Rose et al., 1977)
   4. Role behavior (Ruben, 1976)
   5. Laugh/smile (Barlow et al., 1977; Robinson & Price, 1980)
   6. Impression leaving (Brandt, 1979)
   7. Animated (Brandt, 1979)
   8. Gesturing (Romano & Bellack, 1980; Trower, 1980)
   9. Vocal range (Barlow et al., 1977; Romano & Bellack, 1980)
   10. Facial expressiveness (Barlow et al., 1977; Romano & Bellack, 1980)

IV. Altercentrism (Other Orientation)
   A. Verbal
      1. Identifying feelings (Romano & Bellack, 1980; Rose et al., 1977)
      2. Seeking clarification (Rose et al., 1977)
      3. Disqualification (Bavelas & Smith, 1982)
      4. Interaction posture (Ruben, 1976)
      5. Orientation to knowledge (Ruben, 1976)
      6. Empathy (Ruben, 1976)
      7. Agreement (Minkin et al., 1976)
      8. Compliance/compromise (Robinson & Price, 1980; Romano & Bellack, 1980)
      9. Helping alter own, open, experiment (Argyris, 1965a)
      10. Questions (Dow, Glaser, & Biglan, 1980; Kelly et al., 1980)
      11. Compliments (Dow et al., 1980; Kelly et al., 1980)
      12. Personal attention (Kupke, Calhoun, & Hobbs, 1979; Kupke, Hobbs, & Cheney, 1979)
      13. Minimal response (McLaughlin & Cody, 1982)
      14. Approval (Minkin et al., 1976; Robinson & Price, 1980)
      15. Affective partner references (Crowley & Ivey, 1976)

   B. Nonverbal
      1. Head nods (Greenwald, 1977)
      2. Eye contact (Barlow et al., 1977; Cherulnik, Neely, Flanagan, & Zachau, 1978; Foy et al., 1979; Trower, 1980)
      3. Role behavior (Ruben, 1976)
      4. Attending (Robinson & Price, 1980)
      5. Positive physical interaction (Robinson & Price, 1980)
      6. Concern (Robinson & Price, 1980)
      7. Pleasantness of facial expression (Wiemann, 1977)
      8. Immediacy (Spitzberg & Hecht, in press)
      9. Reciprocity of affect displays (Wiemann, 1977)
      10. Attentiveness (Norton & Pettegrew, 1979)

depending on their stimulus, that is, whether the competent interaction is viewed in a given conversational context or over the history of the relationship.

Communication satisfaction represents an affective reaction to the fulfillment of positively valenced expectations (Hecht, 1978d). It reflects a desirable emotional feeling regarding a conversational episode. To date, communication satisfaction has provided statistically significant classification of cultural memberships (Ribeau & Hecht, 1979), relationship types, and recency of conversations (Hecht, 1978b) on the basis of the communication used in these contexts. Communication satisfaction has also revealed substantial positive relationships to ratings of other's competence and self-rated competence (Cupach, 1982a; Cupach & Spitzberg, 1981; Duran, Zakahi, & Mumper, 1982; Spitzberg, 1982a, 1982b, 1982c). Other research indicates a significant relationship between communication satisfaction and a similar construct of feeling good (Spitzberg, 1982c). The state of feeling good reflects a "peak experience" of affective reaction to a conversation (Prisbell, 1979, 1980). As such, competent communication, since it enhances the achievement of objectives, should result in a good feeling about the conversation in most instances. Research has supported this prediction as well (Cupach & Spitzberg, 1983). Satisfaction has been utilized as a criterion of quality communication in organizational (Baird & Bradley, 1978; Crino & White, 1981), casual (McLaughlin & Cody, 1982), conflictive (Cupach, 1982a), health care (Jain, 1973; Lane, 1983) and marital (Allen & Thompson, 1983) contexts, suggesting that it provides a broad-based, generalizable outcome of competent interaction.

Perceived confirmation is an impression that one's self-concept has been validated and reinforced in a conversation (Cissna, 1976; Cissna & Keating, 1979; Sieburg, 1973; Sieburg & Larson, 1971). It is related closely to the concept of disqualification (Bavelas & Smith, 1982). Disqualification concerns the directness, clarity, and responsiveness of a message. A disqualified message is one that is ambiguous in regard to its content meaning, who is sending it, who is receiving it, and/or its context (Bavelas, 1983). The greater this ambiguity, the more the message deviates from an ideal of directness and relevance to prior messages. The greater this deviation, the more disconfirming the message is likely to be, because it fails to recognize essential features of the situation and other interactants involved. Since competent communication is perceived to be appropriate, it should not significantly violate other's sense of contextual self. Further, effective communication is reinforcing and gratifying to people's need for efficacy (Bandura, 1977; Broucek, 1979; Harter, 1978; Ruesch, 1972; White, 1959). Consequently, competent communication should be confirming (Wilmot, 1979). This expectation has been supported strongly by extant research on relational competence (Spitzberg, 1982c).

A person who is satisfying and confirming to talk with is also likely to be seen as more attractive than one who is dissatisfying and disconfirming. This is virtually axiomatic and has been indirectly supported by research in interpersonal attraction and competence (Glasgow & Arkowitz, 1975; Greenwald, 1977; Kupke, Hobbs, & Cheney, 1979; Scott & Edelstein, 1981). Thus, competent interaction should lead to increased perceptions of other's attractiveness (McCroskey & McCain, 1974). However, attraction and competence are not isomorphic, and research on relational competence has revealed a moderate positive relationship between attraction and rating of other's competence (Cupach & Spitzberg, 1983).

Finally, since competent communication is defined as appropriate and effective interaction, it makes sense that competence leads to impressions of an episode as appropriate and effective. Research has supported this assumption and has indirectly indicated the validity of defining competence in this manner (Spitzberg, 1982a; Spitzberg & Canary, 1983).

These episodic outcomes are criteria of competence in given episodes. However, an implication of the model is that over the course of a relationship, the extent to which the interactant's typical interaction is competent influences his or her relational outcomes. In short, if a dyad's average or normal conversational episode tends to be very competent (over a given period of time), the dyad's relationship satisfaction (Crino & White, 1981; Kirkpatrick, 1977; McArthur, 1978; Mettetal & Gottman, 1980; Robinson & Price, 1980; Sharpley & Cross, 1982; Snyder, 1979; Spanier, 1976; Spanier & Thompson, 1982), trust (Larzelere & Huston, 1980), and even intimacy (Schaefer & Olson, 1981) are expected to be high as well. The reasoning is similar to the rationale for the episodic outcomes, with the added assumption that these gratifications and perceptions accumulate over time to create a more generalized, less transient impression regarding the relationship.

As mentioned before, numerous other outcomes can be identified (for example, conflict outcomes, Smith, 1981; task effectiveness, Hale, 1980; communication fidelity, Powers & Lowry, 1980). Outcomes serve to validate measures and conceptions of competence. While there may be a good a priori reason to expect a given conversational behavior (for example, the personal attention behavior of referring to "you") to be competent, it cannot be presumed to be in a given episode unless such behaviors have actually been related to functional outcomes in that episode. It is conceivable that an altercentric person would feel better *not* receiving such altercentric behavior (Derber, 1979). If so, the only way to be certain of the behavior's competence is to relate perceived outcomes to the behavior. It is in this sense that competence is an impression, not an intrinsic characteristic of the behavior itself. "*Competence* is used as a general evaluative term referring to the quality or adequacy of a person's overall performance in a particular task" (McFall, 1982, p. 12). This evaluation is a judgment made by a person or persons in regard to a communicative performance. Accordingly, "the ultimate criterion for evaluating performance is its outcome or effect" (McFall, 1982, p. 17). The perception of a competent performance, therefore, is contingent upon the perceived outcomes of the performance. A fundamental assumption made by Athay and Darley (1981) is that "the outcomes of a social interactional sequence should more closely match the dictates of the instrumental needs of highly competent participants than those of less competent actors" (p. 306). Applied to our perspective, this means that a person *perceived* as competent will be perceived as having effectively achieved outcomes in a manner appropriate to the interpersonal relationships.

Context

The study of contexts is a relatively recent phenomenon in behavioral science. Contexts have been conceptualized under numerous rubrics and theoretical approaches. Consequently, it is not surprising that the term "context" itself is enigmatic. Forgas (1979), in tracing the evolution of scientific thought about contexts, notes that there has been a substantial shift or expansion in the way contexts are viewed. The traditional view approached "situations" as objective environments, whereas there is now a move toward viewing situations in terms of the subjective perceptions of the inhabitants and in terms of culturally stereotyped patterns of interaction. Forgas (1979), for instance, prefers the notion of "social episodes," defined "as cognitive representations of stereotypical interaction sequences, which are representative of a given cultural environment" (p. 15). Thus, for Forgas (1979), episodes are perceived units of ongoing behavior, and these perceptions are influenced by cultural stereotypes which are the norms and rules that govern social interactions. Brown and Fraser (1979) classify the scene and the participants as the major components of any situation. Scene includes the setting (bystanders, locale, and time) and purpose (type of activity and topic of interaction). Factors relevant to the participants include their dispositional (for example, personality, physical) and temporary (for example, mood, attitude) features, their social class, their interpersonal relationships (such as, liking, knowledge), and their social role relations (such as status, power). Argyle et al. (1981) define a social situation as "the features of the behaviour system, for the duration of a social encounter" (p. 3). In analyzing social situations, Argyle (1981) proposes nine relevant situational features: goals and goal structure, rules, roles, repertoire, sequences of behavior, cultural stereotypes for situation, environmental setting, language and speech, and skills and difficulties. Baxter (1980) defines social situations primarily in terms of three classes: types of activities, types of settings, and types of relationships.

These researchers reveal a number of manageable features of contexts. In an attempt to elaborate a comprehensive analytic schema for contexts, Thomas and Bookwalter (1982) derive six relevant features from the literature (see Table 4.3). These features are arranged as a sequence of questions a person might ask in analyzing any given communicative context,

TABLE 4.3   Elaborated Set of Contextual Questions and Dimensions
             (main questions adapted from Thomas & Bookwalter, 1982)

A. What culture is this? Evaluative dimensions (Osgood, May, & Miron, 1975;
   Triandis, 1978)
   1. Association-dissociation
   2. Superordination-subordination
   3. Intimacy-formality
   4. Overt-covert behavior

B. Where is this? That is, how is the setting perceived? (Mehrabian & Russell, 1974;
   Mehrabian, 1980)
   1. Evaluation: good, nice, usual vs. bad, awful, unusual
   2. Potency: powerful, big, coercive vs. powerless, weak, equal
   3. Activity: fast, young, noisy vs. slow, old, quiet

C. What kind (that is, type) of situation is this? (Argyle, Furnham, & Graham, 1981)
   1. Formal social events
   2. Intimate encounters with close friends or relations
   3. Casual encounters with acquaintances
   4. Formal encounters in shops and offices
   5. Asymmetrical social skills occasions
   6. Negotiation and conflict
   7. Group discussion
D. How do I see myself in relation to the people around me? (Wish, 1979; Wish &
   Kaplan, 1977; Wish, D'Andrade, & Goodnow, 1980)
   1. Cooperative vs. competitive
   2. Intense vs. superficial
   3. Task-oriented vs. non-task-oriented
   4. Dominant vs. equal
   5. Impersonal/formal vs. personal/informal

E. What is the purpose of my communication? (Allen & Brown, 1976; Clark & Delia,
   1979)
   1. Behavioral
      a. Controlling
      b. Feeling
      c. Informing
      d. Imagining
      e. Ritualizing
   2. Psychological
      a. Identity
      b. Interpersonal
      c. Instrumental

F. Do I see myself as able to enact the appropriate behavior? (Bandura, 1977)

which we adapt in interpretation below (see also Spitzberg & Lane, 1983). First, "What culture is this?" Although cultures vary considerably in their communicative norms, they apparently share a small number of affective dimensions for interpreting meaning. That is, research indicates that there are universal dimensions of meaning. Osgood, May, and Miron (1975) found that the meanings of terms in almost 25 cultures reflected three basic affective dimensions: evaluation (nice-awful, good-bad, happy-sad), potency (big-little, powerful-powerless, strong-weak), and activity (hot-cold, fast-slow, sharp-dull, young-old, noisy-quiet, alive-dead). Triandis (1978) hypothesized a slightly larger but similar set of cross-cultural dimensions (association-dissociation, superordination-subordination, intimacy-formality, overt-covert behavior).

The second question pertaining to contexts is "Where is this?" This question concerns the environmental setting or place. While there may be an almost infinite number of settings, there again may be a small number of dimensions along which settings are perceived. Mehrabian and Russell (1974), for example, had subjects evaluate 40 physical settings (four per subject) along 66 paired semantic differential items. A nine-factor representation of the settings resulted (examples of paired items appear in parentheses): pleasant (attractive-unattractive, uncomfortable-comfortable, cheerful-gloomy), bright and colorful (colorful-drab, bright-dull), organized (neat-messy, orderly-chaotic), ventilated (stale odor-fresh odor, drafty-stuffy), elegant (ornate-plain, unfashionable-fashionable), impressive (ordinary-distinctive, impressive-unimpressive), large (narrow-wide, cramped-roomy), modern (modern-old-fashioned, old-new), and functional (functional-nonfunctional, useful-useless). Even this set of factors, it was found, was correlated highly to the three basic affective states of evaluation, potency and activity. Evaluation, especially, related substantially to each factor (R ranged from .23 to .83). These and other results later led Mehrabian (1980) to posit the three emotions of pleasure (that is, evaluation), dominance (potency), and arousal (activity and alertness) as the fundamental affective modes of response to any set of stimuli.

A third analytic question is "What kind (that is, type) of situation is this?" Many efforts have been made to construct a typology or taxonomy of situation types. Thus far, no one is claiming to have a comprehensive typology. Argyle et al. (1981), however, found that over a series of studies a seven-category representation was fairly inclusive. Situations, as defined by a diverse sampling of subjects, tended to fall within one of the following classes: formal social events, intimate encounters with close friends or relations, casual encounters with acquaintances, formal encounters in shops and offices, asymmetrical social skills occasions (such as teaching, training), negotiation and conflict, and group discussions. Note that these situations actually combine relationships, tasks, and settings to form types. Over a series of studies, the researchers found that these situations symmetrically generated distinctive perceptions of goals, rules, skills, language use, and difficulties. Ruesch and Prestwood (1950) identified five a priori categories of social situations: domestic, social and recreational, occupational, operative and service, and community. Price and Blashfield (1975) found 12 clusters of "behavior setting" which resemble situation types: youth performance, religious, women's organizational, elementary school, high school, adult, men's organizational, local business, large membership, high school performance, family-oriented, and government. In a series of studies on such settings, Price and colleagues (Price, 1974; Price & Bouffard, 1974) have had subjects rate the appropriateness of various behaviors (such as run, talk, kiss) across the situations (such as class, date, bus). Not surprisingly, consistent differences were found, indicating that individuals do possess shared notions of situational appropriateness.

A fourth question regarding contexts is "How do I see myself in relation to the people around me?" Wish and his colleagues have conducted several studies that consistently reveal five basic dimensions of situations relevant to interactant relationships (Wish, 1979; Wish, D'Andrade, & Goodnow, 1980; Wish & Kaplan, 1977). Generally, a person is viewed, or views himself or herself, in terms of the following relational characteristics: cooperative versus competitive, intense versus superficial, task-oriented versus non-task-oriented, dominant versus equal, and impersonal/formal versus personal/formal. Knapp et al. (1980) had people rate relationship terms (lover, best friend, friend, pal, colleague, acquaintance, and so on) according to a variety of communication characteristics (such as uniqueness, depth, breadth, difficulty, flexibility, smoothness, and spontaneity of the interaction). These ratings revealed three basic factors reflecting the degree to which interaction was personalized, synchronized, and difficult. As the intimacy of the relationship increased, so did the perceived personalness and synchrony. Difficulty was perceived across relationship types. Again, as features of the perceived context vary, so do perceptions of communication behavior.

A fifth contextual analysis question is "What is the purpose of my communication?" This question concerns the function and goal aspects of communication dealt with under the functional assumption in the early part of this chapter. Interaction activity can serve a variety of psychological goals (such as identity, interpersonal, instrumental) and behavioral content functions (such as controlling, feeling, informing, imagining, ritualizing). The appropriateness of behavior obviously relies on the objective of that behavior in any given situation.

Finally, assuming an interactant has analyzed all of the foregoing contextual factors (culture, setting, situation type, relationships, and purpose), there is still another question remaining: "Do I see myself as able to enact the appropriate behavior?" At first glance, this question appears further removed from the notion of context than the other questions. Upon reconsideration, however, it is a very salient feature of contexts as perceived by interactants. This question corresponds roughly to Argyle et al.'s (1981) situational component of difficulties and skills. Forgas (1983b) found a dimension of episode perception common to several samples, which he labeled "don't know how to behave—know how to behave" (see, for example, p. 178). This dimension also corresponds somewhat with a social anxiety dimension found in numerous situational evaluation studies. Not knowing the appropriate behavior to perform is one potential cause of situational anxiety (Argyle et al., 1981).

Given the varied features included in the concept of context, is there a systematic way of incorporating it into a model of relational competence impression formation? At least one approach appears very promising. Throughout the discussion of the context-analytic questions, the three dimensions of evaluation, potency, and activity repeatedly surfaced. So ubiquitous are these dimensions in the study of needs (Schutz, 1966), language (Goldberg, 1981), and affect (Mehrabian, 1980; Osgood, 1970) that they may provide a general framework for contextual impression formation. One such framework has been elaborated by Heise (1977) and Smith-Lovin (1979). Heise proposes an affect control theory of context construal. According to affect control theory, any individual's feelings toward an object (such as a person, situation, or activity) can be plotted along the dimensions of evaluation, potency, and activity (EPA). These feelings have two facets: a stable underlying fundamental sentiment and a transient state that sometimes deviates from the underlying sentiment. For example, a person may have a stable sentiment of positive evaluation regarding a mother interacting with her infant. However, the transient evaluation may become negative if the mother is interpreted as spoiling the infant. Affect control theory predicts that people will actively adjust their behavior and/or construal of events to confirm their fundamental sentiments. Thus, a person will have a set of fundamental affective evaluations for the various features of a context. To the extent that the context actually encountered stimulates transient feelings congruent with the fundamental sentiments, the actor will behave so as to maintain this definition of the situation. However, to the extent that the context encountered evokes affective responses that deviate from the fundamental sentiments, the actor will attempt to restore the context to a congruent state. This restorative action presumably could involve changing the fundamental sentiments by changing one's definition of the situation (for example, the mother is not actually spoiling the child but is only being loving toward it), by attending to other features of the context itself, or by exiting the context.

The implications of this theory are extended by Smith-Lovin (1979). Since both persons and contexts are assessed in terms of the EPA dimensions, it becomes a simple logical step to conceive of a person-context congruence prediction. Smith-Lovin speculates that

> if an actor engages in an act that is not in keeping with the pace or tempo of the surrounding social environment , he or she may lose evaluation (i.e., other's opinion of the actor may be lowered). Engaging in very active expressive behaviors (for example, dancing or playing) in a very quiet place (for example, a church or library) might lower others' evaluation of the actor, as might quiet and withdrawn behavior in a place where lively ex-

pressive behavior is usual. Conversely, behavior appropriate to
the setting may enhance evaluation. (p. 41)

Applied to competence impressions, this congruence
hypothesis predicts that a person's perceived competence is
positively related to the degree of EPA congruence of the person's communicative behavior with the context within which
the behavior is enacted. Of course, the valence of the incongru-
ence needs to be considered as well. For example, if a person
initially has a very negative evaluation of a context or person,
and the encounter deviates substantially (that is, actually is
perceived to be positive), then the opposite prediction would
seem reasonable. A perceived congruence variable of this type
could be inserted as a compatible feature of the relational competence model. Thus, the more motivated, knowledgeable,
and skilled A is (or is perceived to be) and the more congruent
A's communicative behavior is (or is perceived to be) with positively valenced evaluations, the more relationally competent A
is (or is perceived to be) in the encounter being assessed. Of
course, as particular features of a given context become salient, the EPA dimensions might be expanded or altered to provide another set of dimensions to assess congruence. For example, in studying compliance-gaining situations, Cody, Woelfel, and Jordan (1983) proposed seven relevant factors: personal benefits, situation apprehension, resistance to persuasion, rights, intimacy, dominance, and relational consequences. Each of these factors could be viewed as an evaluative dimension and used to formulate a congruence variable.
The generality of the approach, therefore, appears very promising. However, there is still a scarcity of research to test the
contextual congruence hypothesis, and thus, this component
of the model must be considered highly speculative at this
point.

A related approach to the interface between competence
and context is presented by French, Rodgers, and Cobb (1974).
Instead of viewing context along a set of affective dimensions,
these authors envision a concept of personal adjustment, in
which an individual's adjustment is a direct function of person-
environment "fit." This fit depends on the supplies that a person is capable of producing in meeting the demands placed

upon him or her. Two types of demands are motives and role requirements. A person's motives to attain certain objectives make demands on the person's performance. A lonely person faces the demand of establishing new interpersonal relationships. A competitive person faces the demand of finding situations in which he or she can achieve victory or some other measure of success. Similarly, other persons in any given situation define role requirements differently. A person not surprised by a surprise birthday party may still perceive the demand of acting as if he or she is surprised. A "meet the new son-in-law" episode carries with it certain implicit role requirements for appropriate behavior. A person's abilities to meet these two types of demands constitute the notion of supplies. Thus, the adjustment of an individual is represented by the equation $F = E - P$, in which F is the person's fit, E is the environmental supply, and P is the person's need for fit. This fit, in turn, can be of an objective or subjective nature. A person may objectively need food and water in an environment devoid of any, yet subjectively be in a state of delusion regarding this deficit. Since most social needs and situations seem less objective than physiological and physical stimuli, the subjective model appears more relevant. In the equation $F = E - P$, positive values represent excessive abilities and negative values represent insufficient abilities. Negative values indicate lack of adjustment and are likely to be associated with psychological strain and the performance of coping and defensive behavior.

One intriguing possibility suggested by French et al. (1974) is that demands and supplies may end up being incompatible. For example, the needs for affiliation and privacy are both important yet somewhat incompatible motives (Altman et al., 1981). A person faced with too much opportunity to affiliate may be faced with too little opportunity for privacy as a result. The example makes it clear that aspects of both the individual and the context need to be included in a model of competence.

WHY RELATIONAL?

The preceding model of relational competence is essentially a model of the individual, contextual, and relational factors that are likely to affect impressions of competence in communicating. The emphasis thus far has been on the individual and contextual factors. The issues of how the process of interaction and the nature of the relationship between interactants influence impressions of competence are extremely important yet not well understood. The question arises, then: In what way is this model relational?

There are many approaches to relational communication. One approach is associated with the pragmatic or interactional view of communication. This approach typically assumes that to study relational communication, one must first code specific interactional data and then interpret those data in terms of interaction sequences and patterns over time. While this approach has yielded important insights into the patterning of interpersonal interaction, it is only one way of getting at relationship. To study behavior to the exclusion of perceptions of the relationship clearly does not comport with a model concerned with impression formation. Consequently, we choose to view relationship as a confluence of behavior and perception. To us, it is at least as important to know how people view the behavior of self and other in terms of relational definitions as it is to know what behavior is actually performed. Both approaches tap the communicator's relationship, but at different levels of abstraction and meaning. The model of relational competence is relational in the sense that it is sensitive to the implicit perceptions of the relationship held by the interactants. The operational procedures used to measure relational competence are episode-specific, meaning that interactants are asked to assess their self and other competence in a particular episode. In so doing, the appropriateness and effectiveness of behaviors and the specific process in which these behaviors are enacted are contextualized by the relational definitions the interactants possess at the time. The judgment of self and other competence has in fact been found to have a small but statistically reliable positive association to perceived intimacy of the relationship and to interpersonal solidarity. Such effects suggest that relational perceptions do influence competence judgments.

Another way in which the model is relational is that it is dyadic in nature. The possibility exists of obtaining and crossing self and other perceptions for all interactants involved in an episode. That is, person A's perceptions of A's and B's motivation, knowledge, skills, context, and outcomes can be related to B's perception of the same phenomena. In a study by Spitzberg and Hecht (1984), it was found that A's perceptions of A's motivation and of B's skills were the most important predictors of A's own satisfaction with the conversation, although B's perception of A's skills was also significantly related to A's satisfaction. In a similar vein, it has been found repeatedly that A's perceptions of B's competence is a more powerful predictor of A's communication satisfaction than is A's perception of his or her own competence.

These findings reveal the importance of referencing both or all of the interactants involved. They also support the importance of communicator's perceptions of the interaction to the goals and outcomes of the communicators. The study of actual communicative behavior is vital and should be pursued vigorously. There is nothing in the model of relational competence to preclude the inclusion of microscopically coded behavior. In fact, the skills component can be viewed as interactant perceptions of behavior performed, as third-party ratings or codings of behavior performed, or as both. The question of which view is most predictive is an empirical question and is likely to depend upon the type of outcome variable being studied.

SUMMARY

A model of competence in communicating, if it is to be comprehensive, needs to encompass more than just behavior or just cognitions. In this chapter, we have proposed a model of relational competence in an attempt to provide a framework for a comprehensive approach to competence in communicating. The model is composed of five major components for each individual of interest in an interaction: motivation, knowledge, skills, context, and outcomes. It is suggested that to be perceived as a competent communicator, one is likely to need to be motivated to communicate, knowledgeable about how to communicate, skilled in communicating, and sensitive to the expectations of the context in which the communication occurs. This model is grounded in several assumptions regarding the most heuristic way of conceptualizing competence.

5

IMPLICATIONS AND FUTURE DIRECTIONS

THEORETICAL IMPLICATIONS

WHAT HAS BEEN PRESENTED thus far is an extensive review of the theories and constructs relevant to the issue of competence in communicating and a conceptual model to integrate these constructs. The model is not intended as "a theory" of competence so much as a way of organizing extant concepts and analyzing their possible interrelationships. In the process of constructing the model of relational competence, several assumptions and propositions were made, the most important of which are summarized here.

(1) Competence is an interpersonal inference rather than a set of skills or behaviors.
(2) Competence inferences are continuous rather than dichotomous.
(3) Competence inferences are based upon an interdependent and complex process of interaction.
(4) Competence inferences are anchored by the dimensions of appropriateness and effectiveness.

(5) Although competence is an inference, this inference is made more probable by the individual attributes of motivation, knowledge, and skill in interaction.

(6) Competence inferences are a function not only of individual attributes but also of the perceived congruence of valenced expectancies of an individual's performance and the context for that performance.

A long list of potential constructs exist that can serve to operationalize the major components outlined in the model of relational competence. Most of these constructs were considered in prior chapters. Instead of examining these variables in greater detail, the purpose of this section is to suggest productive avenues of theoretical development in the area of competence.

The typical approach to theory in competence has been to posit a set of skills or traits as important to human interaction (self-disclosure, empathy, adaptability, listening, assertiveness, conversation initiation, and so on). Relatively little effort has been expended either to explain the cognitive and affective processes underlying such skills and traits or to organize this eclectic set of characteristics into a higher-order theoretical framework.

There is an obvious risk in reducing competence to a small set of cognitive and affective intrapersonal constructs: Many of the common sense pragmatic implications tend to become obscured. A theoretical purist may find comfort in reducing everyday interactional behavior to phenomena such as schemas, information bits, memory traces, and expected utility schedules. It is less clear that such phenomena comport with laypersons' understanding of why and how they act as they do. Just as important, if a theory of competence in communicating is to have pragmatic utility, it needs to be cast at a level at which it could be used in training and education, as well as theoretical explanation and prediction. There can be a substantial difference between explaining how competence impressions are formed and instructing a person how to interact in a way that is likely to be perceived as competent. The implication is that an optimal theory of competence in communicating should be cast at a level that provides predictive precision and intuitive theoretical explanation as well as therapeutic utility. These criteria are not always as compatible as they might seem. The discussion that follows attempts to balance these concerns in presenting a possible theoretical approach to competence in communicating.

One of the more parsimonious approaches to competence is the self-efficacy/social learning theory. Social learning, of which self-efficacy is a part, is actually an integration of cognitive and behaviorist notions. Two theories that are useful in elaborating social learning theory are motor skills analogues for social skills and attribution theory.

Welford (1980) traces the concept of social skills directly to research in motor skills (that is, physical performance skills) in the early 1960s. In developing and refining a motor skills model of social interaction, Argyle (1969) considers six basic components: motivation or goal, perception, translation, motor responses, changes in the outside world, and feedback loop to perception. A person is motivated to accomplish some task or goal, selectively perceives information relevant to the task to be performed, translates this information into appropriate plans of action, and implements the selected plans through nerve impulses to the appropriate muscles. The progress of these actions in accomplishing the desired effects in the environment are monitored, and this feedback is used to adjust the subsequent plans of action and resulting motor responses.

The motor skills model, though originally developed primarily to represent person-machine interaction, has been applied productively to social interaction in a series of studies by Argyle and colleagues (Argyle, 1969, 1979, 1980; Argyle et al., 1981; Trower, 1979, 1980; Trower et al., 1978). In a social setting, the model represents "social skills" as behavioral capacities implemented as strategies occurring as the need is indicated by feedback. Such a social skills model clearly illustrates why accurate social perception, analytical thinking, behavioral flexibility, and anxiety are such important constructs in skills approaches to competence. A person must perceive the situation and task accurately in order to implement the most efficient strategies. Accurate perception has been cast under the guise of numerous skills such as role taking, empathy, cognitive complexity, interpersonal problem-solving skills, listening, attentiveness, and analytical ability. In addition to perceiving the situation and task accurately, if the feedback is not perceived and interpreted correctly, plans of action will be maladjusted to the task. Even if an individual possesses excellent perceptual skills, such skills will be severely limited if the person does not have sufficient behavioral flexibility to adapt his or her behavior to the task at hand. As feedback indicates needed changes in motor responses, the person needs to be adaptable enough to change plans and responses. Finally, if a person is anxious about interacting in a situation, such anxiety can divert the person's attention away from an objective analysis of the feedback, suppress the person's motivation to interact, and even keep the person away from many situations in which he or she could learn to develop more competent interaction skills.

While the motor skills analogue to social skills has generated some excellent research (see Argyle, 1969; Trower et al., 1978), it is not without problem. It is linear and overly rational. Interactants may be capable of performing the various functions simultaneously (for example, formulating plans while monitoring feedback and performing) rather than in a strict linear sequence. The idea that a behavior produces effects that are then monitored as feedback is again too simplistic. Feedback in social interaction is rarely a discrete, packaged effect; instead it is a continuous, ongoing stream of behaviors on the part of the other person(s) involved. There is also some question regarding whether a person can really attend to and process social information in such an ordered way. Instead of analyzing all the relevant information in a social situation, interactants are likely to rely on prior experience and previously learned strategies that are cued to a few particular stimulus features of a given context. While modifications to the model can easily account for these faults, the model itself diverts attention away from the generative processes at work—the processes through which individuals acquire skills and motivations that can then be implemented. It is here that social learning and attribution theory can help.

Social learning theory, as elaborated by Mischel (1973), involves five interrelated constructs: construction competencies, encoding strategies and personal constructs, behavior-outcome and stimulus-outcome expectancies in particular situations, subjective stimulus values, and self-regulatory systems and plans. Construction competencies are an individual's abilities to generate cognitions and behaviors, that is, mental and social intelligence. Encoding strategies and personal constructs refer to the way a person perceives, categorizes, and interprets events and self. Behavior-outcome expectancies represent a person's perception of the relationship between the behavioral alternatives in a given situation and the probable outcomes of those alternatives. It is assumed that a person will choose the behavioral option that is perceived as most likely to produce the most positively (or least negatively) valenced outcome. The behavior-outcome expectancies are based on prior experience in similar situations and/or other information available in the context. Stimulus-outcome relations concern the implicit relationships people perceive between certain signs and correlated behaviors (for example, are "shifty eyes" indicative of untrustworthy behavior?). Subjective stimulus values simply refer to an individual's desired and undesired outcomes and the intensity of these preferences.

Self-regulatory systems and plans involve a host of related cognitions, including

> the rules that specify goals or performance standards in particular situations; the consequences of achieving or failing to achieve those criteria, self-instructions and cognitive stimulus transformations to achieve the self-control necessary for goal attainment; and organizing rules (plans) for the sequencing and termination of complex behavioral patterns in the absence of external supports and indeed, in the face of external hindrances. (Mischel, 1973, p. 275)

Self-regulation is made possible by contingency rules that specify the forms of behavior appropriate to, or expected in, a given situation, the level of performance necessary to accomplish the salient goal(s) in that situation, and the consequences of not accomplishing the goal(s).

Mischel's (1973) outline of social learning theory specifies many of the vital components of a cognitive theory of competent behavior but does little to elucidate the interrelationship of the components. In an attempt to make social learning theory more precise, Bandura (1977) and Saltzer (1982) detail some of the contingency rules and relationships that are only

implicit in Mischel's (1973) writing. Bandura's (1977) self-efficacy theory places major importance on beliefs regarding self-
competence. Whether a person undertakes a course of action
depends upon whether the person believes that he or she *can*
perform such action and can do so *successfully*. These beliefs,
in turn, depend on the person's knowledge of what needs to
be done and how it needs to be done. How does a person know
what to perform and how to perform it? The "learning" of such
behaviors can occur through several routes. A person can be
instructed in social behavior (etiquette, for example). A person
can experience several similar situations and, through trial and
error, learn the behavioral routines that are most consistently
rewarding (or least punishing). Faced with an unfamiliar situation, a person may search memories of past situations that
shared certain similar features, assess the range of appropriate
or allowable behaviors, and implement the closest "fitting"
behaviors. A person may even generate novel behavior through
the creative combination of familiar interaction episodes.
Finally, a vital source of social learning is the use of social
"models," whether imagined or real. When confronted with
problematic or novel situations, people often think intuitively
of "what X (person) would do in this situation." By constructing
what someone else was observed to have done in a similar
situation, or by conjecturing what someone else would do in
such a situation, interactants expand their repertoire to include
not only what they do but what everyone else does as well.

Whereas Bandura's (1977, 1982) theory is particularly relevant to the *acquisition* of social skills, Saltzer's (1982) personal
efficacy model is more applicable to predicting the *performance* of learned behaviors. Saltzer (1982) describes three
types of personal efficacy beliefs: self-efficacy ("Can I perform
this behavior?"), behavioral efficacy ("Will the behavior produce
the desired outcome?"), and outcome attributions ("Did I, or
did something else, produce the observed outcome?"). The beliefs fit into a cognitive model of behavior.

Behavior in Saltzer's (1982) model is a function of a person's self-efficacy beliefs, behavioral efficacy beliefs, perceived
value of anticipated outcomes and behavioral intention, all of
which are influenced by the peculiarities of the specific situation. In brief, a person who believes he or she can perform a
sequence of behaviors, believes the behavior will achieve (rela-

tively) desirable outcomes, and is disposed to perform the behaviors will enact those behaviors. The behaviors produced in turn alter the parameters of the situation and contribute to behavioral outcomes. The extent to which the behavioral outcomes are attributed to self rather than uncontrollable or contextual factors in turn reinforces the other components. The origin of the self-efficacy beliefs, behavioral efficacy beliefs, and value expectancies are based upon past experiences in such episodes and modeling.

The extent to which self-efficacy, behavioral efficacy, and outcome contingencies are believed or perceived depend significantly on the attributions made regarding the observed outcomes of behavior. If desirable interactional outcomes are attributed to external or uncontrollable causes, then self- and behavioral efficacy beliefs are diminished and effort in producing effective behavior is likely to be reduced. If, on the other hand, positive effects in the social environment are attributed to one's own intentional behavior, beliefs in self- and behavioral efficacy are enhanced, increasing the likelihood of interacting competently or effectively. Attribution theory is concerned not only with self-perception but also with interpersonal perception. To date, however, little effort has been made to apply attribution theory to the perception of competence in communicating. Most relevant to this concern would be the correspondent inference theory of Jones and colleagues (Jones & Davis, 1965; Jones & McGillis, 1976). "Correspondence" refers to the degree to which information available in an episode leads to the inference of dispositions in the person(s) perceived. That is, in viewing someone's behavior, to what extent does that behavior imply personality traits or interpretation of motives to the viewer? The greater the information gained regarding the strength of an attribute-effect linkage (attribution), the greater is the correspondence.

Several propositions arise out of the correspondent inference theory. First, an episode can be correspondent only if an actor is perceived to have choice, knowledge, and ability. An actor who is forced to produce an effect or behave in a certain way reveals little about his or her motives. Further, an actor cannot be attributed with a disposition if he or she possesses neither the knowledge nor the ability to perform consistent with the disposition. For example, in observing a salesperson make a big sale, the effect (the successful sale) could be attributed to luck, the desires of the purchaser, or the persuasiveness of the seller. But persuasiveness implies that the salesperson knows how to be persuasive and has the communicative abilities to perform persuasive strategies competently.

Second, the "logic" of correspondent inferences involves a systematic process of thinking and perception. In order to attribute a motive or disposition to an actor, a perceiver needs to be cognizant of alternative choices the actor could have made, to examine possible or plausible reasons the actor selected the observed course of action, to rule out the unlikely reasons, and then to assess the relative importance of the remaining reason(s) the actor had for performing the observed course of action. Supposedly, this logic is not necessarily sequential, and some perceivers may be more efficient and comprehensive than others in utilizing it.

Third, role-deviant action is more correspondent than role-governed action. This proposition follows from the element of choice in behavior. An actor who simply does what is common or expected in a situation (that is, fulfills a defined social role) is perceived to have done what "anyone" would have done. Since anyone would have done essentially the same thing, there is little information available to differentiate the observed person from others—hence, minimal correspondence or inference of underlying attributes. However, a person who deviates from a role or from expected behavior demonstrates that something unusual is motivating his or her behavior. A person who insults the host at a party is much more likely to be attributed a disposition (that of an ingrate, a snob, an arrogant person, or the like) than someone who compliments the host. The idea of role behavior also defines a concept of social desirability. A person who performs actions low in social acceptability or desirability provides more correspondence than someone who behaves in socially acceptable ways.

This last statement suggests a potential interface of attribution and competence theory. Since competent interaction is appropriate behavior (that is, in role, socially acceptable), it follows that the attribution of competence is not usually very strong but that the attribution of incompetence is. This implies that people may be far more able to recall and form impressions of incompetent interaction than of competent interaction.

It also suggests that behavior that is merely appropriate to the expected role behavior generally will not lead others to attribute substantial competence to the observed actors.

If simply being appropriate does not consistently lead to attributions of competence, what does? Competent interaction, as conceived in Chapter 4, entails both appropriate and effective interaction. Effectiveness is closely associated with the notions of power and interpersonal influence. The attribution of power (that is, the ability to be effective) is contingent upon several factors. The attribution that A has been effective in influencing B and obtaining some desired outcome in the transaction involves a parsing out of potential causes. Suppose a subjective probability that B's behavior after encountering A is predictable from B's state before the encounter—for example, B would have "submitted" regardless of A's efforts. The lower this subjective value is, the less likely it is that B was responsible for observed changes in behavior. A second subjective probability is associated with A's intervention, that is, the probability that B's state after the encounter is predictable from A's behavior. The higher this value is, the more likely it is that A will be attributed with power or effectiveness (Hinkle et al., 1980; Schopler & Layton, 1974). In essence, then, effectiveness will be attributed to A when outcomes are perceived to be consistent with A's desires and inconsistent with B's.

Beyond the level of the specific episode, competence can be an attribution made about a person *in general*. In an effort to elucidate the process of such personality attributions, Kelley (1967; Kelley & Michela, 1980) has identified three relevant attributional dimensions: distinctiveness, consistency, and consensus. A person will be attributed with competence the more distinctively, consistently, and consensually he or she is perceived to be appropriate and effective in interaction episodes. Distinctiveness refers to the uniqueness of a cause-effect linkage. For example, A observes persons B, C, and D interact in similar episodes over several occurrences, and only B seems to interact appropriately and effectively over all the observations. Positive outcomes are distinctive to B's presence. Over time, the more consistently B can accomplish desirable outcomes and avoid rule violation, the more competent B will be viewed to be. Finally, the more that A discovers that other people concur that B is competent, the more A will also attribute competence to B.

This foray into the attibution of competence only scratches the surface of the potential propositions attribution theory could supply (see Seibold & Spitzberg, 1981). Two interesting avenues of exploration are the concepts of role ambiguity and role restraint. Role ambiguity refers to enigmatic episodes in which it is unclear what the actors are supposed or expected to do. In such situations, observers may rely on very general social norms (one should not insult others without provocation, one should thank those who do something nice for others, and the like) to judge appropriateness and may base most of their attribution of competence on effectiveness information. Role restraint would refer to apparent impediments to interacting competently (he did as well as could be expected, she did quite well considering the situation, I don't know how anyone could have done any better given the circumstances, and so on). The extent to which a person avoids rule violation and accomplishes (relatively) desirable outcomes despite opposing forces and task demands, the more competent that person will be perceived to be.

Another approach to attributions in interaction has been investigated by Giles and Powesland (1975) and Ickes et al. (1982). Giles and Powesland present a model of accommodation, which refers to the tendency to converge one's own speech style with that of another interactant. Accommodation functions to associate or identify oneself with another. Response or style matching in accommodation is likely to lead to comprehensibility, predictability, and attraction because it is the style understood and mastered by the other interactant. The prediction is also implied that accommodation is likely to lead to impressions of competence as well.

An integral feature of the speech accommodation model concerns the attributions that interactants make regarding accommodation and nonaccommodation. Specifically, if A does not accommodate to B's speech style, B can attribute that nonaccommodation to three causes. If lack of effort is perceived to be the cause, then B will have negative impressions and will not accommodate to A. If lack of ability is the perceived cause, then an attenuated negative impression results, and there is no reason for B to attempt accommodation because it could not be reciprocated. If external pressure of constraints is seen to be the cause and attenuated negative impression again results, B may or may not accommodate because of uncertainty regarding A's motives.

In the event that A does accommodate to B, then B can attribute it to effort, in which case favorable impressions and reciprocation are likely. B can also attribute A's accommodation to external pressure (such as peer group pressure), leading B to a favorable impression and tentative reciprocity, again because of uncertainty about A's motives. The speech accommodation model, therefore, provides a framework for predicting impressions of competence based upon the convergence of speech style (dialect, pause, rate, and talk-time patterning, and the like) observed in a conversation.

Accommodation is only one type of reaction to another's speech style. Another possible reaction is compensation. If accommodation reflects a *reciprocity* of interaction styles, then compensation represents the adoption of an opposite or contrasting style of interaction (Capella, 1983). According to Ickes et al. (1982), the two interaction strategies of reciprocity and compensation result from distinct and identifiable preinteraction expectancies, and further, the implementation of these strategies evokes predictable impressions in the interactants. The authors speculate that the two key expectancies mediate the selection of strategy: "the desirability of the anticipated target behavior, as well as the perceiver's awareness of or motivation to engage in contrasting behavior" (Ickes et al., 1982, p. 163). More specifically, A is expected to reciprocate when B's anticipated behavior is not undesirable (unpleasant, incompetent, embarrassing, or the like) or when B's behavior is expected to be undesirable but A either does not believe B would reciprocate A's contrasting behavior in turn or does not perceive self as possessing the motivation or ability to implement a contrasting pattern of behavior, which, if reciprocated, would produce a more desirable pattern of interaction for A. In contrast, compensation is likely to be used

> when the perceiver (1) views the target's anticipated behavior as undesirable, but (2) believes that it is modifiable via the norm of reciprocity, and (3) is aware of and willing and able to display a contrasting pattern of behavior that, if reciprocated by the target, would render the target's behavior more desirable. (Ickes et al., 1982, p. 163)

In two independent experiments, these investigators found consistent support for these predictions. Subjects were given a friendly, an unfriendly, or no expectancy regarding another interactant with whom they were about to converse. Both friendly and unfriendly expectancy conditions were hypothesized to reveal greater interactional involvement than the no-expectancy condition. However, unfriendly expectancy subjects were expected to have less favorable postinteraction ratings of their partners than the friendly expectancy subjects. Subjects with the friendly and unfriendly expectancies did reveal greater involvement (they sat closer, initiated more conversations, talked more, directed gazes more, and expressed more positive affect) than the no-expectancy control subjects. Interestingly, although subjects in the unfriendly expectation condition effectively compensated for their partners' anticipated lack of warmth (thereby producing a reciprocation of the friendly interaction the subjects initiated), these subjects formed post interaction impressions of their partners consistent with the preinteraction expectancies. That is, despite an interaction pattern that resembled the friendly expectancy condition, unfriendly expectancy subjects rated their partners as less compassionate, sensitive, and friendly than did the friendly expectancy subjects. These results were replicated in a second study with slight variations in methodology.

The results of these studies are very illuminating. First, they indicate the importance of attributions in mediating not only interactant behavior but also the impressions formed, and maintained, of others. Second, they reveal that objective behaviors in conversations are not necessarily the stimuli that produce impressions of competence. Even though the conversations were similar in several specific behaviors, the interactants came away with very different impressions because of their preinteraction expectancies. Does this mean that we should give up looking for a domain of competent behavior? No. It means that we need to investigate the conditions under which behaviors are most likely to be perceived as competent. Nor does the explication of a model of relational competence, a context-specific model, mean that we need to disregard the search for cross-contextual consistencies. It does mean that whatever consistencies are found are likely to be a function of consistencies in the contexts themselves, and that the conditions that make these contexts similar are of considerable importance in developing a comprehensive theory of competence.

METHODOLOGICAL IMPLICATIONS

Competence in communicating is a complex concept, which implies the need for complex assessment procedures. Certainly, there are many diverse measures used to operationalize competence and related constructs. Questions remain, however, regarding the validity of these measures and the procedures in which the measures are used. This section will review some selected classes of competence measures (and competence-related constructs) with an eye toward identifying some advantages and disadvantages of each category. Then some general methodological concerns will be elaborated. These general points of critique will serve to guide a discussion of ways to enhance the utility of competence measures.

Competence measures (as distinct from experimental methods per se) can be grouped according to two very broad sets: self-report of self (or self measures) and self-report of other (or other measures). This division is a purely operational one, although it does have conceptual implications. Self-report of self measures require that person A respond to items or stimuli in which self (person A) is the reference person being rated. Self-report of other measures includes all measures in which a person A assesses person B. One obvious difference between "self" and "other" measures is that a unique type of data is available is self-assessment. Specifically, only person A knows how person A feels, thinks, perceives, and so on. Goals, emotions, strategies, and perceptions of situations are all within the private realm of intrapersonal phenomena. Person B may guess about or even be confident in attributing certain thoughts and feelings of person A. But only person A knows the feelings and thoughts of self.

Another set of conceptual implications regarding the self-other distinction were considered in Chapter 3. There may be significant differences in the way a person processes information about self and about others. To the extent that self-enhancing biases are at work, self-assessment measures are likely to reflect such impressions.

Beyond the basic self-other dichotomy, measures of competence are further divided according to their levels of abstraction. The level of abstraction in this case refers to the degree to which a measure generalizes across communicative episodes (that is, is a trait measure) or is episode-specific. Thus, many general dispositional measures have been developed as self-assessments. Some of these measures assess a person's self-perceived ability to cognitively decenter (e.g., Kelley et al., 1979) and feel others' emotions (see Mehrabian & Epstein, 1972). Other measures reference a person's "social self-esteem"; that is, the degree to which a person perceives self's collective social history positively (see Helmreich & Stapp, 1974; Lawson, Marshall, & McGrath, 1979). Still other measures reflect a person's general motivation to persist in controlling the (social) environment (see Lamont, 1983). Role taking, empathy, social self-esteem, and effectance are in turn reflected to some degree in the composite measures of competence (see Duran et al., 1981; Holland & Baird, 1968; Kelly & Chase, 1978; Phelps & Snavely, 1980). Taken together, general dispositional measures indicate a person's perceived proclivity or general tendency to interact competently.

At another level of abstraction are the multiple-episode stimuli measures, which present a subject with several possible communicative stimuli/situations. The responses of the subject to these stimuli are then summed to provide an aggregate indication of the subject's competence in dealing with a specific set of interactional situations. The format of these measures is relatively flexible, allowing Likert-type responses (see Levenson & Gottman, 1978), open-ended written responses (see Fisher, 1973), and role-play responses (see Rehm & Marston, 1968). Also, these measures permit inferences about particular episode types (see Levenson & Gottman, 1978; Williams & Ciminero, 1978). This control over the types of situations to which the subject responds makes these measures more focused than the general dispositional measures, even though both types of measure produce a sum score indicating a *tendency* to be competent.

There are few existing measures that ask a person to rate self-competence in a given specific communicative episode.

Such measures refer to an episode as "a conversation" and the subject rates his or her performance in that conversation. The conversation may be one recalled from past weeks or one that occurred immediately prior to response to the questionnaire. These measures provide a researcher considerable control over the type of situation to which the subject responds but are obviously limited to inferences about the particular stimulus episode used.

There are times when a researcher is interested in obtaining ratings of another person's competence from someone other than the person being rated. The motivation for developing such self-report of other measures originates from several possible sources. A researcher may distrust the validity of self-reports of self. A researcher may be interested in variables too complex for the average subject to comprehend, or phenomena of which the interactant is not fully aware, requiring trained or expert third-party raters. A researcher may be interested in the theoretical and empirical differences between perceptions of self and other. Whatever the reason, significant work has been done to develop measures of competence in which the point of reference is another person.

Self-report measures of other vary by their levels of abstraction in much the same way that self-report of self measures do. However, a little more detail can be assigned to the classification of other measures. Under general dispositional measures are four types: demographic/sociological, peer/sociometric, expert/parent/teacher, and general inference. These types represent distinctions based upon the rater and types of inferences used in the ratings. Thus, demographic/sociological measures use such broad-level variables as social maturity, age, and education as indicators of competence. Peer/sociometric measures require people who interact with a person to rate that person's general interaction competence. Measures that use extremely knowledgeable raters rather than those with passing acquaintances fit into the expert/parent/teacher class. This somewhat eclectic class of measures usually includes rating instruments that request information that would not be obvious to peers or strangers (for example, in preschool populations, the teacher is far more able to respond to questions of competence regarding a child than are the other children) or acquaintances (as in cases when a trained interviewer knows what types of theoretical questions to ask and pursue in depth). General inference measures are those for which a particular type of rater is not required and that use general rating items (for example, s/he is not afraid to talk to strangers, s/he is friendly).

Multiple-episode stimuli measures of other competence are those which utilize diverse communication situations to which a subject responds. Some utilize videotaped situations to evoke subject reactions (see Rubin, 1982; Stricker, 1982), others use written descriptions of situations (see Martinez-Diaz & Edelstein, 1980; Mead, 1980b), and one even uses a programmed computer presentation of situations (Remer, 1978). Several of these measures provide differing types of episodes (Curran, 1982; Rubin, 1982), while others concentrate on differing stimuli within a particular type of episode (see Remer, 1978; Stricker, 1982). These instruments provide varied stimuli to which the subject responds, and the collective responses are then rated or scored by third parties familiar with the assessment criteria. Like the self-report of self measures of this class, these other measures provide considerable control over the types of episodes used for drawing inferences.

Episode-specific other measures are assessments of another person's competence in an actual conversation. The conversational performance can be recalled from weeks before or minutes before the assessment. Some measures are flexible enough to be used by "lay" interactants or trained third-party observers (see Cupach & Spitzberg, 1981; Eadie & Paulson, 1983). Others presume more knowledge on the part of the rater than the typical interactant is likely to posses (see Barlow et al., 1977; Gillingham, Griffiths, & Care, 1977; Ruben, 1976; Shepherd, 1977; Trower et al., 1978). Still other measures require detailed coding of verbal transcripts (by trained coders; see Argyris, 1965a; Getter & Nowinski, 1981; Sieburg, 1973; Viney & Westbrook, 1979). Finally, a large and diverse set of studies use trained observers to code nonverbal behaviors of interactants, usually from videotapes. Most researchers use their own preferred operational definitions of behaviors, and the number of behaviors coded vary greatly from one study to the next.

Each of the types of measurement identified in Table 5.1 has its advantages and disadvantages, depending upon the theoretical inclinations of the researcher, the resources and sample(s) available, and the types of inferences sought. Additionally, each instrument is subject to the normal debate concerning its validity and reliability. It is not the purpose of this examination to review and critique the record of each measure and its development. Such a task not only would be cumbersome but also would divert attention from the broader measurement issues. What follows is an exploration of some of these broader issues. Our intent is to isolate several problems and choices faced by researchers in the competence arena and, in the process, develop some suggestions for improving measures of competence. It is now readily accepted that the measurement of competence involves the observation of both molar and molecular elements (Bellack, 1979, 1983; Hops, 1983; McFall, 1982): "molecular measures target specific response characteristics, such as gaze and speech duration. These variables are presumed to be the basic elements of interpersonal communication, which together comprise the social-skill construct. . . . Molar ratings consist of global, qualitative judgments" (Bellack, 1983, p. 33). This distinction is useful as a separation of social skills and competence, with skills as molecular behaviors and competence as an evaluative judgment applied to the quality of the molecular behaviors (see Chapter 4 "Assumptions").

Despite the usefulness of the distinction between molar and molecular ratings, many extant measures rely on one or the other or haphazardly combine the two. A measure that is totally molecular necessarily presumes the competence of the behaviors assessed. Without an evaluative criterion to assess the subjective quality of the behavioral responses, there is no guarantee that those responses will actually be functional in real contexts. Measures that are entirely molar are so abstract that it is often impossible to know what it is that is being assessed. There is little doubt that interactants attend to molecular cues when drawing molar inferences about self or other's competence, but it is uncertain *how* they draw these inferences and which cues are most important. Among other things, attention to particular behavioral cues varies by

(text continues on page 174)

TABLE 5.1 Selected Competence Measures and Related Contructs

I. Self-report of self measures
   A. General dispositional
      1. Bienvenu (1971): Interpersonal Communication Inventory (self-confirmation, listening, clarity of experession, dealing with angry feelings)
      2. Cegala (1978, 1981): Interaction Involvement (responsiveness, perceptiveness, attentiveness)
      3. Curran et al. (1980a): (disapproval or criticism of others, social assertiveness and visibility, confrontation and anger expression, heterosexual contact, intimacy and interpersonal warmth, conflict with or rejection by parents)
      4. Duran (1983a): Cognitive Competence (self, other, audience, setting, topic, occasion)
      5. Duran & Wheeless (1980): Social Management (social adaptability, rewarding impression, meaning-centered empathy)
      6. Duran, Zakahi, & Parrish (1981): Communicative Adaptability Scale (social composure, articulation, wit, appropriate disclosure)
      7. Hart, Carlson, & Eadie (1980): Rhetorical Sensitivity (rhetorical reflector, noble self)
      8. Helmreich & Stapp (1974): Texas Social Behavior Inventory (confidence, dominance, social competence, social withdrawal, relations with authority figures)
      9. Holland & Baird (1968): Interpersonal Competency Scale (popularity, physical energy, expressiveness, sensitivity, social participation, leadership)
      10. Hughey & Harper (1983): Conversation Self-Report Inventory (mastery responsiveness, flexibility responsiveness, neutral responsiveness)
      11. Kelly & Chase (1978): California Interpersonal Competence Questionnaire (empathy, task completion, need for achievement, activity, physical attractiveness)
      12. Lamont (1983): Effectance Task (effect on self, effect on people, effect on objects)
      13. Lanyon (1967): Biographical Survey III
      14. Lawson, Marshall & McGrath (1979): Social Self-Esteem Inventory
      15. Macklin & Rossiter (1976): Interpersonal Communication Report (expressiveness, self-disclosure, understanding)
      16. Norton & Pettegrew (1979): Attentiveness (inactivity, attentiveness signals, attentiveness sensitivities, attentiveness evaluation)
      17. Phelps & Snavely (1980): Composite Interpersonal Communication Competence Inventory (empathy, anxiety, listening, self-disclosure)
      18. Sherer et al. (1982): Self-Efficacy Scale (general, social)
      19. Tyler (1978): Behavioral Attributes of Psychosocial Competence Scale (self-attitudes, world attitudes, behavioral attitudes)

   B. Multiple-episode stimuli
      1. Fisher (1973): Social Competence (cognitive accessibility, social accessibility)
      2. Kieren & Tallman (1972): Spousal Adaptability Scale (flexibility, empathy, motivation)
      3. Levenson & Gottman (1978): Dating and Assertion Questionnaire
      4. Rehm & Marston (1968), Lavin & Kupke (1980): Situation Test (self-rated anxiety, rated anxiety, rated adequacy, rated likability, average number of words per response, average latency, anxiety signs)
      5. Williams & Ciminero (1978): Survey of Heterosexual Interactions for Females

TABLE 5.1 Continued

C. Episode-specific

1. Cupach & Spitzberg (1981): Self-Rated Competence (interaction management, expressiveness, anxiety)
2. Hecht (1978a): Communication Satisfaction
3. Spitzberg & Phelps (1982), Spitzberg & Canary (1983): Perceived Appropriateness and Effectiveness

II. Self-report of other measures

A. General dispositional

1. Demographic/Sociological
   Lanyon (1967): Biographical Inventory (social activity, social extroversion, independence from parents, social conformity)
2. Peer/Sociometric
   Wright, Bond, & Denison (1968); Wright & Dunn (1970): Expanded Sociometric Device (task and perceptual effectiveness, autonomy and self-actualization, commitment, openness, self-perception)
3. Expert/parent/teacher
   a. Aumack (1962): Social Adjustment Behavior Rating Scale (work level, socialization level)
   b. Elder, Wallace, & Harris (1980): Camarillo Interpersonal Behavior Scale
   c. Havighurst (1957): Scales for Rating Role Performance (worker, parent, spouse, homemaker, leisure, friend, citizen, association, church)
   d. Lowe & Cautela (1978): Social Performance Survey Schedule (positive behaviors, negative behaviors)
4. General inference
   a. Barrett-Lennard (1962), Schumm, Jurich, & Bollman (1980): Relationship Inventory (level of regard, empathic understanding, unconditionality of regard, willingness to be known)
   b. Farber (1962): (empathy, autonomy, resourcefulness, cooperativeness, tested empathy)
   c. Monge, Bachman, Dillard, & Eisenberg (1982): Communicator Competence Questionnaire (encoding, decoding)
   d. Ruesch, Block, & Bennett (1953), Block & Bennett (1955): Interpersonal Test (actions, feelings, attitudes/expectations, traits)
   e. Walters & Snavely (1981): Other-Perceived Competency Scale (self-disclosure, social anxiety, listening, empathy)
   f. Wiemann (1977): Communicative Competence (empathy, interaction management, affiliation/support, social relaxation, behavioral flexibility)

B. Multiple-episode stimuli

1. Curran (1982): Simulated Social Interaction Test (skill, anxiety)
2. Martinez-Diaz & Edelstein (1980): Social Activity Questionnaire
3. Mead (1980b): Massachusetts Basic Skills Assessment of Listening and Speaking
4. Perri & Richards (1978): Heterosocial Adequacy Test
5. Remer (1978): Potential Interpersonal Competence Scale (understanding, prejudgment, responsibility, post hoc judgment, confidentiality, accurate empathy, personal communication)
6. Rose, Cayner, & Edelson (1977): Social Competence (assertiveness)

(continued)

TABLE 5.1 Continued

7. Rubin (1982): Communication Competency Assessment Instrument (communication codes, oral message evaluation, basic speech communication skills, human relations)
8. Stanton & Litwak (1955): Short Form Test of Interpersonal Competence
9. Stricker (1980, 1982): Interpersonal Competence Instrument

C. Episode-specific

1. Interactant or third party
   a. Brandt (1979): (Communication effectiveness, social attractiveness, task attractiveness)
   b. Cupach & Spitzberg (1981): Rating of Alter Competence (other orientation, expressiveness)
   c. Eadie & Paulson (1983): (empathy, creativity, enmeshment)
2. Trained third party
   a. Barlow, Able, Blanchard, Bristow, & Young (1977): Heterosocial Skills Behavior Checklist (voice, form of conversation, affect, motor behavior)
   b. Gillingham, Griffiths, & Care (1977): Social Behavior Assessment
   c. Ruben (1976): (respect, interaction posture, orientation to knowledge, empathy, role behavior, interaction management, ambiguity tolerance)
   d. Shepherd (1977): Social Behavior Rating Scales (eye contact, facial expression, tension, response latency, tone, attentiveness, feeling content, interruptions, spontaneity, aggressiveness)
   e. Trower, Bryant, & Argyle (1978): Social Interaction Test (voice quality, nonverbal, conversation)
   f. West, Goethe, & Kallman (1980): Nonverbal (eye contact, gestures, head nods, facial expressions, voice tone, voice volume, interpersonal distance, posture, body orientation); Verbal (initiation of conversation, minimal encouragement, open-ended questions, parallel experiences, reflective statements)
3. Verbal content ratings
   a. Argyris (1965a): Interpersonal Competence Scoring System (owning—self/other, openness—self/other, experimenting—self/other)
   b. Bavelas & Smith (1982): Disqualification (content, sender, receiver, context)
   c. Getter & Nowinski (1981): (effective responses, avoidant responses, inappropriate responses, dependent responses)
   d. Sieburg (1973), Cissna (1976): Interpersonal Confirmation (dialogue, indifference, disqualification, imperviousness)
   e. Viney & Westbrook (1979): Sociality Scale (solidarity, intimacy, influence, shared experience)

III. Special population/context measures

A. Children and adolescents (see Doucette & Freedman, 1980: Green & Forehand, 1980; Gresham, 1981)

1. Flint, Hick, Horan, Irvine, & Kukuk (1980): California Preschool Social Competency Scale (considerateness, extraversion, task orientation, verbal facility, response to the unfamiliar)
2. Freedman, Rosenthal, Donahoe, Schlundt, & McFall (1978): Adolescent Problems Inventory

TABLE 5.1 Continued

3. Harter (1982): Perceived Competence Scale (cognitive, social, physical, general)
4. Jones (1977): Rochester Adaptive Behavior Inventory (angry-oppositional-defiant, social isolation, easily upset-complaining, quiet-sad, fearful of strangers and other caretakers, dependent-demanding, anxious, strange or extreme behavior, fantasy play and feminine preference, immature-unhappy)
5. Jennings, Suwalsky, & Fivel (1981): Children's Social Competence Coding System (conflict, nonconflict)
6. Kohn & Rosman (1972): Social Competence Scale and Symptom Checklist (use of opportunities, living within the norms and roles)
7. Matson, Rotatori, & Helsel (1983): Matson Evaluation of Social Skills with Youngsters (appropriate social skill, inappropriate assertiveness, impulsive-recalcitrant, overconfident, jealousy-withdrawal)
8. Ollendick (1981): Children's Assertiveness Inventory (positive, negative)
9. Reardon, Herson, Bellack, & Foley (1979): Self-Report Assertiveness Test for Boys (positive, negative)
10. Rothenberg (1970): (leadership, gregariousness, cruelty, sensitivity, mood, friendly-apprehensive, sense of humor)
11. Sanson-Fisher (1977): (appropriate behavior, inappropriate behavior)
12. Wheeler & Ladd (1982): Children's Self-Efficacy for Peer Interaction Scale (conflict, nonconflict)
13. Wright (1980): (seeking attention, using others as a resource, leading, expressing affection/hostility, competing, following/failing to follow)

B. Mentally impaired

1. Aumack (1962): Social Adjustment Behavior Rating Scale (work level, socialization level)
2. Doll (1935): Vineland Social Maturity Scale (self-help locomotion, occupation, communication, self-direction, socialization)
3. Farina, Arenberg, & Guskin (1957): Minimal Social Behavior Scale
4. McConkey & Walsh (1982): Index of Social Competence (additional handicaps, communication skills, self-care skills, community skills)
5. Reynolds (1981): Personal Competency Scale (adaptive, cognitive, affective)
6. Zigler & Levine (1981): Premorbid Social Competence Scale (age, education, marital status, occupation, employment history)

C. Assertiveness

1. Alberti & Emmons (1974): Assertiveness Inventory
2. Del Greco (1983): Del Greco Assertive Behavior Inventory (noncoercive-coercive, overt-covert)
3. Fensterheim & Baer (1975): Assertiveness Inventory
4. Galassi, Delo, Galassi, & Bastein, (1974): College Self-Expression Scale (positive assertiveness, negative assertiveness, self-denial)
5. Gambrill & Richey (1975): Assertion Inventory
6. Lazarus (1971): Assertive Questionnaire
7. Leah, Law & Synder (1979): Difficulty in Assertiveness Inventory (distant-close, positive-negative, difficulty in assertiveness—general, difficulty in assertiveness in risky situations, difficulty in assertiveness in new relationships and in business situations, difficulty in assertiveness in confiding and expressing positive feelings to parents)

(continued)

TABLE 5.1   Continued

8. Levenson & Gottman (1978): Dating and Assertion Questionnaire
9. Lorr & More (1980): (directiveness, social assertiveness, defense of rights and interests, interdependence)
10. McFall & Lillesand (1971): Conflict Resolution Inventory
11. Rathus (1973): Rathus Assertiveness Schedule
12. Schwartz & Gottman (1976): Assertiveness Self-Statement Test
13. Sundel & Sundel (1980): Sundel Assertiveness Scale I (relationships with clients, coworkers, subordinates, superiors, professionals from other disciplines)
14. Weeks & Lefebvre (1982): Assertive Interaction Coding System
15. Wolpe & Lazarus (1967): Assertion Questionnaire

D. Empathy and role taking

1. Carkhuff, in Hefele & Hurst (1972): (empathy, respect, genuineness, concreteness, self-disclosure)
2. Cochrane (1974): Measure of Empathic Communication (internal-external, separation-fusion, accuracy-nonaccuracy, concrete-abstract, high energy-low energy, caring-noncaring)
3. Elliot et al. (1983): Response Empathy Rating Scale (frame, inference, accuracy, here and now, centrality, words, voice, manner, impact)
4. Hogan (1969): Empathy Scale
5. Kelley et al., in Chmelewski & Wolf (1979): Role-Taking Ability (role conceptualizaton, communication adaptation)
6. Mehrabian & Epstein (1972): Emotional Empathy Scale (humanistic orientation, considerateness, fictional involvement, emotional contagion)
7. Truax (1967a, 1967b), Kiesler (1967): (accurate empathy, unconditional positive regard, congruence)

respondent, behavior, situation, sequence, and discordance among cues (Bellack, 1983). Measures that mix molar and molecular items often have no systematic rationale for combining the items. Such measures make interpretation of their summative scores difficult, because the cues that are used in responding to its molar components are not known.

A second measurement issue is the generalizability of various inductions. An immense amount of research utilizes a specific context or episode type (interview, conversation initiation, requesting a date, assertion, and so forth). Such inductions have certain clear advantages. A researcher is able to control the stimuli to reach inferences about the particular domain (that is, context) of interest. Further, such inductions typically elicit actual communication behavior (usually role-play or written) from the respondent. Despite the extensive use of such measurement approaches, two important questions re-

main relatively unaddressed. First, is the measure of competence used relevant to the stimulus context? Different contexts
generate different goal structures, and rule systems (Argyle et
al., 1981). If the specific goals and rules of the context are not
elaborated or referred to, the competence of the respondent
may be assessed improperly. For example, instructing a respondent to react "as he or she normally would" may stimulate
responses very different from the instructions "behave as effectively as possible" or "as you think most people would." These
instructions generate goal structures that real-world contexts
might not. This problem is accentuated by brief or ambiguous
instructions regarding specific items or context descriptions. A
logical but often unanswered question in a conversation-initia-
tion induction is "Why am I initiating this conversation?" Similarly, a subject instructed to "ask the other person for a date"
faces an externally generated goal. Finally, it is still largely unknown what the goals and rules are in the various situations
used in the study of competence. In a highly formal context
such as an interview, such goals and rules may be fairly obvious, but heterosocial interactions and assertion situations offer
complex rule systems and often ambiguous goals for the subject. Thus, many context-based inductions are too incomplete
or ill-formed to generalize to the real world they were intended
to reflect.

A further problem with measures based on a given type of
context is that the context itself may not generalize to different
kinds of contexts. That is, using a dating-request instruction
seems unlikely to generalize to an assertion situation or interview situation: "Clearly, heterosocial interactions require different responses than assertion situations. There are also substantial differences within these broad categories. Structural
characteristics, such as sex of partner, status, race, familiarity
and age all play a role in shaping behavior" (Bellack, 1983, p.
36). As obvious as this argument sounds, it is often missing
or obscured in the discussion sections of competence studies.
Studies utilizing an interview situation still refer to their construct as communicative and social competence. Studies assessing assertiveness and dating requests also refer to their
constructs as social competence. An instrument that assesses
listening and speaking skills in a public speaking situation is
only tapping a partial domain of possible communicative behavior and contexts, even though such a measure may be in-

terpreted as a measure of communicative competence. It is entirely likely that there are some skills that do generalize across contexts, but this is an empirical question in search of stronger support.

A closely related issue in the assessment of competence is the assessment of contexts and context perception. While virtually all current competence theorists presume the importance of contexts, only a fraction of the measures used are event-focused. By "event-focused" is meant that the measures (via items, inferences, or outcomes) refer to the specific episode of interaction being studied. For example, the items in the measures developed by Bienvenu (1971), Wiemann (1977), Duran, Zakahi, and Mumper (1981), and many others rely on trait items requiring cross-situational inferences (X interacts well with strangers, Y is not afraid to talk to others, and so on). If contexts are important in influencing communicative behavior, then such measures simply obscure these influences.

Assuming that contexts are important, then it is a fault of many competence measures that no effort is made to assess the subject's perceptions of the context. The role that context perception plays in competent interaction is highlighted in a study by Forgas (1983a). Subjects evaluated a number of contexts and responded to several social skill measures. A clear four-dimensional representation of the contexts emerged consistent with prior research (self-confidence, evaluation, seriousness, involvement), and a clear difference was found between high-skilled and low-skilled subjects in the way they perceived (that is, differentiated) situations. "Low-skilled subjects are captivated by the social difficulty of episodes, with very little sensitivity for other episode characteristics, while high-skilled subjects have a much better differentiated, and more evaluative critical representation of interaction routines" (Forgas, 1983a, p.46). This indicates that part of what commonly is referred to as competence is not just behavioral skills, but the *way* perception guides behavioral skills. "Subjects must . . . know when and where to emit the various responses in their repertoires" (Bellack, 1979, p. 171). Until systematic efforts are made to assess how the perception of episodes affects the competence of interactants' performances, comprehensive competence measures will not be developed.

Researchers in the area of social behavior continually face a dilemma in attempting to assess "natural" behavior. In studying social skills, role-playing techniques are the method of choice. Role-playing techniques are popular because they evoke interactional responses to a particular social situation under the control of the researcher. In the broader realm of competence research, however, self-report questionnaires are very common. Self-report questionnaires are convenient, inexpensive, and can elicit a rich source of psychological data. In order to collect such data, self-report questionnaires often require or are used in conjunction with a recall procedure, where the respondent is asked to recall a recent conversation in rating self or other. There is little research regarding the types of biases involved in such procedures. Conversational memory research reveals a substantial loss of specific verbal content after only a few minutes, although general themes are remembered well (Stafford & Daly, 1983). Other research indicates that recall accuracy is facilitated by such factors as intellectual skills, prior knowledge of the content, positive attitudes toward the experimental setting, and attitudes consistent with the positions espoused (Weldon & Malpass, 1981). Research in conversational attributions reveals a "dispositional shift." Interactants rating their interaction immediately after the conversation attribute more responsibility to the situation, whereas after three weeks, they attribute more responsibility for the conversational interaction to self (Funder & Van Ness, 1983; Moore, Sherrod, Liu, & Underwood, 1979). One study found that third-party observer behavior ratings of interactants agreed more with the interactants' behavior ratings made immediately after their interaction than three weeks later (Funder & Van Ness, 1983). This finding was interpreted as a deterioration of interactant recall over time. Such perceptual biases indicate that, generally, the closer in time the assessment is to the conversation being rated, the more accurate the perceptions will be. It is important to note, of course, that accuracy is not synonymous with theoretical importance. People's long-term impressions of their conversational successes and failures are just as important to understand as are their short-term impressions. Researchers simply need to be sensitive to the possible effects of elapsed time between the conversation and the assessment.

A final methodological issue to be explored is the broad area of media and demand effects. Little is known of the effects of different types of measurement and experimental induction. One of the most obvious questions is whether self-report Likert-type items, interactive interviews, videotape stimulus presentation, open-ended written response, and role-play inductions can or do measure similar competence constructs. To what extent are possible anxieties, task demands, and expectations generated in a role-play setting that do not exist in simple self-report settings? Is writing out one's possible strategies in a situation a more conscious and strategic activity than spontaneously enacting them upon prompting? These different measurement formats and inductions not only represent different task and skill requirements on the part of respondents, but also may actually affect the motivations and ways of thinking of the subjects. Research has found only small to moderate relationships between self-report and role-play performance, even when the constructs being measured are similar (anxiety, social skill, competence, and so on). Some research has revealed powerful demand effects of confederate prompt style (Steinberg et al., 1982) and method variations (Martinez-Diaz & Edelstein, 1980). Other research has found ratings of social skill to generalize across audio, video, and live rating conditions and across observers (Monroe, Conger, Conger, & Moisan-Thomas, 1982). Until more is understood about the various method and demand effects associated with the assessment of competence, researchers would do well to avoid overconfidence in their procedures. Obviously, the study of these effects is a high priority in future research.

No single research method in the area of competence is clearly superior to its alternatives. Each method has its advantages and disadvantages, only some of which have been elucidated above. Instead, the selection of a method depends on the researcher's theoretical orientation and the types of inferences on intends to draw from the results. Given our assumptions and model of relational competence, and the issues raised here, a useful research strategy is outlined below.

If competence is an interpersonal impression, then measurement efforts should be aimed primarily at the interactant's level of meaning and perception. This calls for the use of self-reports at least. If competence is contextually mediated, the measurement should be event-focused (that is, episode-specific). This means that the items should reference a specific conversation. If competence is relationally mediated, then measurement should include both self and other reports. This requires relatively equivalent item content for both (or all) participants involved in the interaction. If competence involves both molar and molecular features, then measurement should include the domain of specific behavioral cues and selected general evaluative items. If competence is functional, then measurement should involve a situation with functional relevance and outcome assessment. This requires that the outcomes assessed be related to the functional objectives of the stimulus encounter. Finally, if competence does depend upon motivation and knowledge, as well as skill, then these constructs need to be measured also.

One approach that appears to meet these criteria reasonably well involves several stages. First, a target population (such as mental patients, students, married couples, or disturbed children) is chosen for reasons of theoretical interest. Second, from this population an initial small representative sample of respondents is administered an open-ended questionnaire requesting information on the types of conversations they have, with whom they have these conversations, how long and where the conversations occur, which ones were easy and which were difficult, which were enjoyable and which were not, in which the subjects would most like to perform better, and what behaviors are recalled as important, inappropriate, and competent. Some researchers have subjects keep a conversation diary for a few days which could be focused along these lines. Third, these reports are reviewed (a) to call in some of the respondents for in-depth interviewing, in turn facilitating (b) the abstraction of an item pool of conversational behaviors, settings, outcomes, and possible relevant inductions. Fourth, the literature is reviewed for the inclusion of possible relevant behaviors not found in the initial sampling process. Fifth, a questionnaire packet is compiled. From the perspective of the relational competence model, such a questionnaire would assess motivation to interact in a given conversation, knowledge of how to interact in that conversation, skills (of self and other) in interacting in that conversation, outcomes functionally related to the context, and context perceptions (such as expectation discrepancies). Such measures have been developed and partially validated in several studies (for competence measures, see Cupach & Spitzberg, 1981, 1983; Spitzberg, 1982c, Spitzberg & Canary, 1983; Spitzberg & Hecht, 1984; for context measures, see Forgas, 1979; Argyle et al., 1981; Smith-Lovin, 1979; Wish, D'Andrade, & Goodnow, 1981). More work is needed in developing such measures, however, especially given the context-specific nature of such projects. Sixth, initial psychometric analysis would be performed from another (non-redundant) sample of the target population. Reliability, factor structure, and simple intercorrelation and regressions would be examined for all constructs at this point. Requisite changes in item content and format could be made in order to refine the psychometric properties of the measures. The induction used could be a recall instruction focused on a particular type of recent conversation, or a stimulated conversational episode. Obviously, the former would more easily provide the sample size needed for psychometric analysis, but the latter would provide far greater control over the type of behavior being evaluated.

The instrument that results from the foregoing procedures is intended to be representative of the conversations of interest and relevant to the respondents involved. Even though the items reference a specific conversational context, over repeated studies of similar and distinct contextual forms certain cross-contextual consistencies may emerge. In addition, the development of a domain of conversational behaviors allows the researcher to regress the items onto evaluative items and outcome measures. This type of analysis permits the assessment of the relative importance of molecular behaviors to valued conversational outcomes. Finally the instrument easily can be combined with interactional data (by means of videotape or audiotape, for example) to explore the interrelationships among interactant self and other perceptions and third-party ratings or codings of the encounter.

PEDAGOGICAL IMPLICATIONS

In assessing the pedagogical implications of competence in communicating, three questions are salient: (a) What should be taught? (b) How should it be taught? (c) How should competence be assessed? These three questions constitute the central issues that teachers, researchers, and theorists must grapple with in order to engender competence on the part of actual communicators. Answers to these questions are not yet definitive or universally accepted. Indeed, in many instances, answers are not even available at this time. The purpose of this section is to highlight some directions suggested by the relational competence model. The first two questions will be addressed here; the latter question concerning assessment has already been dealt with in this chapter under the heading "Methodological Implications."

In considering what to teach, it is worth noting that the development of theoretical explanations of competence is (or at least should be) integrally related to the teaching of competence. In the absence of theoretical frameworks, instructors must rely on common sense, intuition, arm-chair reasoning, time-honored principles, and the like to guide the content of instruction. Many unfounded generalizations are taught because of inadequate conceptualization and empirical research. Where possible, teachers should utilize knowledge that is theory-based to guide what they teach. Propositions based upon clear concepts and empirical research are generally superior in terms of efficiency and validity. Thus, the adequacy of communication competence instruction ultimately depends, in part, on the use of theoretical frameworks. By the same token, the academic community has a responsibility to provide such frameworks. Theory and research on communication competence should be applicable to instruction, training, and skill development. In short, theoretical frameworks must be usable by educators, and they must be used.

An advantage of the relational competence model is that it is parsimonious. Its components are fundamental and comprehensible. Relational competence suggests that there are four macro components that are essential to understanding interpersonal communication competence. The elements of person (knowledge, motivation, and skill) are seen as interacting with elements of the situation (such as goals, roles, and physical environment) to produce messages, which, in turn, lead to functional outcomes. What follow are relevant questions about competence indicated by these components. These questions represent the essence of what competent interpersonal communicators should know and, consequently, what should ultimately concern communication instructors and researchers.

(1) What knowledge is important to have in order to communicate competently?
(2) How is such knowledge acquired by communicators?
(3) How is such knowledge appropriately matched to particular communication situations?

Knowledge required for successful communication comes in many forms. One such type of knowledge is in regard to the co-communicators. It is desirable for individuals to be familiar with strategies for attaining information about fellow interactants (or potential interactants; see Berger, 1979). Likewise, communicators must learn a repertoire of message options relevant to the fulfillment of various communication functions. That is, successful communicators must know how to achieve particular goals—such as compliance gaining, compliance resisting, conflict management, relationship disengagement, and information dissemination—through the use of messages. Competence additionally requires knowledge about what communication behaviors are consistent with social and interpersonal rules. Thus, information about communication situations and their respective rules allows an individual to select an appropriate communication strategy, as well as an efficacious one.

(4) What factors motivate individuals to communicate competently? What motivational factors stifle competence?
(5) Under what conditions (in what situations) should we attempt to enhance the awareness, involvement, and motivation of communicators?
(6) How can the awareness, involvement, and motivation of communicators be enhanced?

An important step in education will be to help communicators recognize the consequences of self-awareness and to control the effects when they are adverse. One goal is to help communicators understand that they can largely control their involvement in communication. It is important that when communicators are deemed incompetent due to a lack of attentiveness or involvement, it is because they have chosen not to be involved. This may help prevent negative self-fulfilling prophecies.

Self-awareness can be analogized to anxiety. It is desirable to attempt a balance between too much and not enough. Just as a modicum of anxiety, properly channeled, is desirable, so too is a moderate degree of self-awareness. We must try to teach communicators properly to monitor their self-presentations without being overly distracted. We must also seek to indicate under what conditions it is more important to monitor closely and under what conditions spontaneity is in order. Teaching someone how to strike the proper balance between strategic orientation and spontaneity is extremely difficult— akin to teaching creativity.

(7) What skills are relevant to behaving competently in which situations?

(8) How are relevant skills best developed?

Skills reflect the transition from knowing to doing. Consequently, it is significant to note that in part, communicators must learn by doing. Skill development necessitates the use of communication knowledge. Whereas knowledge represents the substantive content indicating what communicators can and should do, skill reflects the procedural implementation of knowledge.

It should be reiterated here that most skills are probably related to general competence in a curvilinear fashion. That is, too much of a good thing can be a bad thing. For example, most educators would teach the desirability of exhibiting confidence during communication. But in certain situations, a certain amount of anxiety or timidity would be expected and a high level of confidence would be perceived as clearly inappropriate to the context. Likewise, although assertiveness is generally deemed preferable to aggressiveness or nonassertiveness, there are circumstances under which nonassertion may indeed be superior. Although communicators' skills can often be easily identified, their proper implementation is not defined so simply.

(9) How are message differences related to the degree and kind of knowledge, motivation, and skill?

(10) How are message differences related to differences in the communication situation?

(11) How are message differences related to differential attributions of communication competence?

Message behaviors are the principal stuff with which attributions of competence are made. Skills are reflected in actual message behaviors. Such message behaviors result in functional outcomes and serve as stimuli for competence evaluations. Competence judgments are derived from a range of both molar impressions and molecular behaviors. The concept of message is broad, referring to any interpersonal behaviors that are generative of meaning to the interactants. Thus, messages can range from single utterances or gestures, to patterns, sequences, and cycles of behavior, to an entire conversation. Each of these units may be useful in explaining and predicting attributions of competence. In the rush to embrace nonverbal, affective displays of behavior, the significance of verbal content to appropriate and effective interaction is often overlooked.

The foregoing list of questions is only partial, but it suggests essential foci for the teaching, research, and development of communication competence. While we have attempted to deal with some of these issues throughout the last several chapters, there are not unequivocal answers to many of these questions. We hope, however, that the questions can serve as springboards for developing the knowledge base necessary for competence theory and instruction.

Related to the issue of what should be taught is the question of *how* competence should be taught. As vital as this question is, it remains sorely neglected. Unfortunately, specific answers regarding how to teach competence are beyond the scope of the relational competence model. One implication is nevertheless clear: Pedagogical tools need to be devised that will facilitate the development of relevant skills by communicators. It is the responsibility of instructors, clinicians, and researchers to create feasible techniques for translating scholarly knowledge into a usable form for those who need it in everyday life. Simply lecturing about communication principles is clearly inadequate. We must develop, test, and refine methods that will assist communicators in becoming behaviorally skilled as well as knowledgeable. Communicators must be "exposed" to diverse, real-life communication situations, and they must be given direct experience in coping with those contexts. It is unclear to what extent such firsthand experience can be provided in the traditional classroom, but experiential learning techniques are being developed for just such purposes (see Breen et al., 1977; Cox & Gunn, 1980; Rotheram, 1980). A useful outline for organizing many of the issues raised in this section has been elaborated by Ladd and Mize (1983). These authors present a cognitive-social learning model of social skill training and instruction. The instruction consists of three main components: enhancing skill concepts, promoting skill performance, and fostering skill maintenance and generalization. To enhance skill concepts, an instructor would attempt the following activities:

A. Establishing an intent to learn the skill concept
    Providing an advanced organizer
    Stressing the functional relevance of the concept
B. Defining the skill concept in terms of its attributes
    Conveying concepts meaning
    Identifying relevant and irrelevant attributes
C. Generating examplars
    Identifying positive and negative examples
D. Promoting rehearsal and recall of the skill concept
    Encouraging verbal rehearsal
    Establishing a memory code
E. Refining and generalizing the concept
    Correcting misconceptions
    Identifying alternative applications. (Ladd & Mize, 1983, p. 131)

The model assumes that performance of socially skilled behavior presupposes knowledge of the appropriate skills to perform. Once this knowledge is attained, skill performance is then developed by:

A. Providing opportunities for guided rehearsal
    Requesting overt skill rehearsal
    Conducting rehearsals in a sheltered context
B. Evaluation of performance by the instructor
    Communicating performance standards
    Providing feedback about the match between standards
        and performance
C. Fostering skill refinement and elaboration
    Recommending corrective action including concept
        reformulation and skill modification.
    (Ladd & Mize, 1983, p. 131)

Even though a student may know what skills to perform and can demonstrate that knowledge, there is a need to instruct the student in how to replicate and guide the use of this knowledge. This maintenance and generalization task is accomplished by:

A. Providing opportunities for self-directed rehearsal
    Skill rehearsal in a series of contexts that
        approximate real-life situations
B. Promoting self-initiation of performance
    Encouraging skill usage while withdrawing performance
        cues or aids
C. Fostering self-evaluation and skill adjustment
    Self-appraisals of skill performance
    Self-monitoring of skill outcomes
    Adoption of nondefeating self-attributions
        and affective states
    Use of information from self-monitoring to modify
        performance. (Ladd & Mize, 1983, p. 131)

Clearly, strides are being made in integrating both the content and procedures of instruction in competence. Much more needs to be done. It may be some time before solid outcome-based evidence points unequivocally to the best methods of skills instruction. Therefore, it is all the more important that efforts get under way to attempt such pedagogical strategies on a small-scale basis, to assess their efficacy, and to establish a base of data upon which to guage the optimal directions to take. This section has attempted to offer some directions to explore.

EPILOGUE

In the course of exploring approaches and issues relevant to competence in communicating, some significant features have become salient. In Chapter 1, we attempted to highlight the historical development of competence as a concept. The importance of competent communication is fundamental—deriving from the scholarly interests of both scientists and humanists. The conceptual and empirical paths of the development of competence have been diverse and diffuse. Nevertheless, its roots in ancient rhetorical theory are still apparent. After more than two centuries, there is strong adherence to classical ideas, such as the importance of adapting one's messages to the "audience," the significance of creating a desirable image, and the relevance of both pragmatic and ethical dimensions to "good communication." Although often not explicitly recognized, current thinking about competence owes much to the ancients.

It is also obvious, though, that there has been a tremendous expansion in scholarly work since Aristotle and Quintilian. For one thing, the scope of human activity germane to communication competence has broadened. The relevant domain has extended from the traditional conception of persuasion to such divergent areas as mental disorder, problem solving, relationship maintenance, and identity management. It seems that as communication studies have expanded and become more interdisciplinary, the range of applicability for competence has grown concomitantly.

The number and diversity of theoretical perspectives applied to the concept of competence have also multiplied—ranging from psychiatric to dramaturgic to systemic. This, in conjunction with the proliferation of measurement devices, has produced an ever-accumulating pool of research findings.

Despite these developments, it is safe to say that advances in the study of communication competency are quite minimal in comparison to the advances that should and will be made in the not-so-distant future. We have only scratched the surface. The study of competence has raised many more questions than it has answered. Each discovery serves as the impetus for further investigation.

In Chapters 2 and 3, we presented a review and critique of modern perspectives on communication competence. Different approaches to competence provide different answers—in part because they ask different questions. As the perspective on competence varies, so does the definition of competence, the "location" of competence, and the focus of inquiry. Some approaches are more behavioral; others are more mentalistic. Some focus on consequences and effects while others attend to processes of development, acquisition, and deterioration. Although the underlying assumptions of various approaches to competence are sometimes at odds, in many cases the approaches are compatible and complementary. More attempts need to be made to understand different aspects of the general phenomenon of competence vis-à-vis the testing of competing or mutually exclusive models.

Above all, there is a growing recognition of the complexity and richness of competence as a construct. Competence is not dichotomous, it is not objectively determined, it is not inherently pleasant. In an effort to capture the complexity of communication competence in an elegant fashion, the model of relational competence was presented in Chapter 4. Our purpose was to construct a useful framework for understanding competence in everyday interaction. This framework is intended to serve as a stimulus for academic argument, theory construction, and research.

Although the relational competence model is not a formal theory, it can be evaluated as a theoretical framework. In short, what is the utility of the relational competence model? One benefit of the model is its parsimony. Relational competence recognizes the complexity of communication processes in several ways: (a) by including both cognitions and behaviors, (b) by realizing the "interactive" nature of communication, and (c) by incorporating the dyad rather than the individual as the appropriate unit of analysis. This complexity, moreover, is accounted for with a minimum of constructs; in comparison to other approaches (and given its sophistication), the relational competence model characterizes communication efficiently. Furthermore, the model is flexible. It is based upon the integration of diverse literature, and it is compatible with other theories, as indicated earlier in this chapter.

Perhaps the most significant criterion is that of explanatory power. Relational competence is a powerful model to the extent that it provides a sense of understanding of competence in communicating. The model seems to provide an intuitively satisfying framework for describing what leads to behaving optimally and what leads to the attribution of competence. Moreover, the model is heuristic. It stimulates a host of ideas for scholarly inquiry. It is a fecund source of theoretical and empirical questions.

On the other side of the ledger, it is appropriate to note the weaknesses of the relational competence model. The most obvious question mark is that of predictiveness. Although predictive relationships deriving from the relational competence model have been investigated and supported, the model is more descriptive than predictive at this stage. The model clearly requires some sophistication and additional precision to enhance its predictive value.

Another question concerns the generality of the model. The model has been applied most directly to dyadic encounters. It is not yet clear to what extent this model is applicable or adaptable to other forms of communication. Such forms would include groups, organizations, electronically mediated communications, and public communication. The model does apply to the diverse contexts that may be considered "interpersonal" in nature. However, its utility for clinical and pedagogical applications remains to be demonstrated.

It is important to realize that the relational competence model is not offered as a theory. It is hoped that it can serve as a catalyst in the generation of theory. What is required is the development and refinement of the constructs identified and the specification and testing of meaningful empirical relationships.

This final Chapter has offered some recommendations for future efforts to study competence. To the extent that the relational competence model is heuristic, it suggests avenues for research in the future. Other recommendations may be specified as well. One fruitful endeavor is the combination of compatible theories and models. We briefly demonstrated such an effort at the beginning of this chapter by exploring the relevance of social learning theories. The combination of models can provide a richer explanation of phenomena and can help to integrate existing knowledge by providing a more systematic picture. In this chapter we have also identified methodological and pedagogical implications that suggest some logical areas of scholarly effort. Additionally, there are numerous directions for theory and research that we have specifically neglected.

One such crucial topic concerns the developmental aspects of competence (see Allen & Brown, 1976; Johnson, 1983; Stohl, 1982). It is important to discover how individuals acquire, refine, update, and increase the sophistication of their communication repertoires. In particular, it is useful to study communication skill development among chilfren. Given that communication skill deficits may result from a particular developmental history, and given that children learn more easily than adults, intervention during childhood may be most efficacious.

A related question is how competence varies across the life span. Standards for competence seem to vary as a function of age. Being "youthful" or "elderly" seems to be taken into account when attributions of competence are made. This suggests a line of research into the connection between attributions of competence and perceived "ability." That is, to what extent is perceived competence a function of what a person is perceived as being capable of doing? Competence judgments are partially related to expectations we have of people. We tend to expect more of some individuals in certain contexts, and less of others.

In all, we seem to have raised more questions than we have answered. This is not inconsistent with our primary goal. We intend this work to be a beginning—a point of departure—rather than a destination.

REFERENCES

Abelson, R. P. (1981). Psychological status of the script concept. *American Psychologist, 36,* 715-729.

Adcock, D., & Segal, M. (1979). *Two-years-olds' social competence.* Rolling Hills Estates, CA: B. L. Winch.

Ainsworth, M. D. S., & Bell, S. M. (1974). Mother-infant interaction and the development of competence. In K. Connolly & J. Bruner (Eds.), *The growth of competence* (pp. 97-118). New York: Academic Press.

Alberti, R. E., & Emmons, M. L. (1974). *Your perfect right: A guide to assertive behavior* (2nd Ed.). San Luis Obispo, CA: Impact.

Alden, L., & Cappe, R. (1981). Nonassertiveness: Skill deficit or selective self-evaluation? *Behavior Therapy, 12,* 107-114.

Allen, A., & Thompson, T. (1983). *Agreement, understanding, realization and feeling understood as predictors of communicative satisfaction.* Paper presented at the meeting of the International Communication Association, Dallas.

Allen, B. P., & Potkay, C. R. (1981). On the arbitrary distinction between states and traits. *Journal of Personality and Social Psychology, 41,* 916-928.

Allen, R. R., & Brown, K. L. (Eds.). (1976). *Developing communication competence in children.* Skokie, IL: National Textbook.

Allen, R. R., & Wood, B. S. (1978). Beyond reading and writing to communication competence. *Communication Education, 27,* 286-292.

Altman, I., Vinsel, A. & Brown, B. B. (1981). Dialectic conceptions in social psychology: An application to social penetration and privacy regulation. In L. Berkowitz (Ed.), *Advances in experimental social psychology* (Vol. 14, pp. 107-160). New York: Academic Press.

Altman, I., & Taylor, D. A. (1973). *Social penetration.* New York: Holt, Rinehart & Winston.

Ames, R., Ames, C., & Garrison, W. (1977). Children's causal ascriptions for positive and negative interpersonal outcomes. *Psychological Reports, 41,* 595-602.

Andersen, P. A. (1983). *Nonverbal immediacy in interpersonal communication.* Paper presented at the meeting of the International Communication Association, Dallas.

Appleton, T., Clifton, R., & Goldberg, S. (1975). The development of behavioral competence in infancy. In F. D. Horowitz (Ed.), *Review of child development research* (Vol. 4). Chicago: University of Chicago Press.

Archer, J., Jr., & Kagan, N. (1973). Teaching interpersonal relationship skills on campus: A pyramid approach. *Journal of Counseling Psychology, 20,* 535-540.

Argyle, M. (1969). *Social interaction*. London: Tavistock.

Argyle, M. (1979). New developments in the analysis of social skills. In A. Wolfgang (Ed.), *Nonverbal behavior: Applications and cultural implications* (pp. 139-158). New York: Academic Press.

Argyle, M. (1980). Interaction skills and social competence. In P. Feldman & J. Orford (Eds.), *Psychological problems: The social context* (pp. 123-150). New York: John Wiley.

Argyle, M. (1981). The contribution of social interaction research to social skills training. In J. D. Wine & M. D. Smye (Eds.), *Social competence* (pp. 261-189). New York: Guilford Press.

Argyle, M., Furnham, A., & Graham, J. A. (1981). *Social situations.* London: Cambridge University Press.

Argyle, M., & Little, B. R. (1972). Do personality traits apply to social behavior? *Journal for the Theory of Social Behavior, 2,* 1-33.

Argyris, C. (1962). *Interpersonal competence and organizational effectiveness.* Homewood, IL: Irwin.

Argyris, C. (1965a). Explorations in interpersonal competence—I. *Journal of Applied Behavioral Science, 1,* 58-83.

Argyris, C. (1965b). Explorations in interpersonal competence—II. *Journal of Applied Behavioral Science, 1,* 255-269.

Argyris, C. (1968). The nature of competence-acquisition activities and their relationship to therapy. In W. G. Bennis, E. H. Schein, F. I. Steele, & D. E. Berlew (Eds.), *Interpersonal dynamics: Essays and readings on human interaction* (pp. 749-766). Homewood, IL: Irwin.

Aristotle (1926). *The "art" of rhetoric* (J. H. Freese, Trans.). New York: Putnam's.

Arkes, H. R. (1979). Competence and the overjustification effect. *Motivation and Emotion, 3*(20), 143-150.

Arkowitz, H. (1977). Measurement and modification of minimal dating behavior. In M. Hersen, R. M. Eisler, & P. M. Miller (Eds.), *Progress in behavior modification* (Vol. 5, pp. 1-61). New York: Academic Press.

Arkowitz, H., Lichtenstein, E., McGovern, K., & Hines, P. (1975). The behavioral assessment of social competence in males. *Behavior Therapy, 6,* 3-13.

Athay, M., & Darley, J. M. (1981). Toward an interaction-centered theory of personality. In N. Cantor & J. F. Kihlstrom (Eds.), *Personality, cognition, and social interaction* (pp. 281-308). Hillsdale, NJ: Erlbaum.

Aumack, L. (1962) A social adjustment behavior rating scale. *Journal of Clinical Psychology, 18,* 436-441.

Austin, J. L. (1971). Performative-constative. In J. R. Searle (Ed.), *The philosophy of language* (pp. 13-22). Oxford: Oxford University Press.

Bach, G. R., & Deutsch, R. M. (1970). *Pairing.* New York: Peter H. Wyden.

Backlund, P. M. (1977). *Issues in communication competence theory.* Paper presented at the meeting of the Speech Communication Association, Washington, DC.

Backlund, P. M. (1978). *Speech communication correlates of perceived communication competence. Dissertation Abstracts International, 38,* 3800A.

Backlund, P. M. (1982). A response to "Communication competence and performance: A research and pedagogical perspective." *Communication Education, 31,* 365-366.

Backlund, P. M., Booth, J., Moore, M., Parks, A. M., & VanRheenen, D. (1982). A national survey of state practices in speaking and listening skill assessment. *Communication Education, 31,*125-129.

Backlund, P. M., Brown, K. L., Gurry, J., & Jandt, F. (1982). Recommendations for assessing speaking and listening skills. *Communication Education, 31,* 10-17.

Backlund, P. M., VanRheenen, D., Moore, M., Parks, A. M., & Both, J. (1981). A national survey of state practices in speaking and listening assessment. *Perspectives on the assessment of speaking and listening skills for the 1980s* (pp. 3-24). Symposium presented by Clearinghouse for Applied Performance Testing, Northwest Regional Educational Laboratory, Portland, OR.

Baird, J. E., & Bradley, P. H. (1978). Communiction correlates of employee morale. *Journal of Business Communication, 15*(3), 47-56.

Baldwin, A. L. (1958). The role of an "ability" construct in a theory of behavior. In D. C. McClelland, A. L. Baldwin, U. Bronfenbrenner, & F. L. Stronbeck (Eds.), *Talent and society* (pp. 195-233). Princeton, NJ: D. Van Nostrand.

Bandura, A. (1977). Self-efficacy: Toward a unifying theory of behavioral change. *Psychological Review, 84,* 191-215.

Bandura, A. (1982). Self-efficacy mechanism in human agency. *American Psychologist, 37,* 122-147.

Bannai, H. (1980). *Teachers' perceptions of comparisons between the spoken communication competencies of Asian American and Caucasion students.* Unpublished doctoral dissertation, University of Southern California, Los Angeles.

Barbatsis, G. S. (1980). *Critical consumers and creative producers: A model for integrative language arts instruction.* Paper presented at the Speech Communication Association Convention, New York.

Barlow, D. H., Able, G. G., Blanchard, B. B., Bristow, A. R., & Young, L. D. (1977). A heterosocial skills behavior checklist for males. *Behavior Therapy, 8,* 229-239.

Barrett-Lennard, G. T. (1962). Dimensions of therapist response as causal factors in therapeutic change. *Psychological Monographs, 76,* 1-36.

Barrios, F. X. (1980). Social skills training and psychosomatic disorders. In D. P. Rathjen & J. P. Forst (Eds.), *Social competence: Interventions for children and adults* (pp. 271-303). Elmsford, NY: Pergamon.

Bassett, D. M., Longwell, S. G., & Bulow, H. V. (1939). Social and occupational competence of idiots. *American Association of Mental Deficiency, 44,* 97-102.

Bassett, R. E., Whittington, N., & Staton-Spicer, A. (1978). The basics in speaking and listening for high school graduates: What should be assessed? *Communication Education, 27,* 293-303.

Baumrind, D., & Black, A. E. (1967). Socialization practices associated with dimensions of competence in preschool boys and girls. *Child Development, 38,* 291-327.

Bavelas, J. B. (1983). Situations that lead to disqualification. *Human Communication Research, 9,* 130-145.

Bavelas, J. B., & Smith, B. J. (1982). A method for scaling verbal disqualification. *Human Communication Research, 8,* 214-227.

Baxter, L. A. (1980). The fundamental attribution error in interpersonal communication research. *The Communicator, 10,* 25-42.

Baxter, L. A., & Philpott, J. (1981). *The effects of relational goal, communicator age, and communicator sex role orientation on communication competence.* Paper presented at the meeting of the Western Speech Communication Association, San Jose, CA.

Baxter, L. A., & Wilmot, W. W. (1983). Communication characteristics of relationships with differential growth rates. *Communication Monographs, 50,* 264-272.

Bayes, M. A. (1972). Behavioral cues of interpersonal warmth. *Journal of Consulting and Clinical Psychology, 39,* 333-339.

Beattie, G. W. (1980). The skilled art of conversational interaction: Verbal and nonverbal signals in its regulation and management. In W. T. Singleton, P. Spurgeon, & R. B. Stammers (Eds.), *The analysis of social skill* (pp. 193-211). New York: Plenum.

Becker, S. P. (1977). Competency analysis: Looking at attitudes and interests as well as technical job skills. *Training HRD, 14*(12), 21-22.

Begin, G. (1983). A reassessment of the Kohn Social Competence Scale and the Walker Problem Behavior Identification Checklist. *Journal of Psychology, 114,* 223-226.

Bellack, A. S. (1979). A critical appraisal of strategies for assessing social skill. *Behavioral Assessment, 1,* 157-176.

Bellack, A. S. (1983). Recurrent problems in the behavioral assessment of social skill. *Behaviour Research and Therapy, 21,* 29-41.

Bellack, A. S., & Hersen, M. (1978). Chronic psychiatric patients: Social skills training. In M. Hersen & A. S. Bellack (Eds.), *Behavior therapy in the psychiatric setting* (pp. 169-195). Baltimore: Williams & Wilkins.

Bellack, A. S., Hersen, M., & Lamparski, D. (1979). Role-play tests for assessing social skills: Are they valid? Are they useful? *Journal of Consulting and Clinical Psychology, 47,* 335-342.

Bellack, A. S., Hersen, M., & Turner, S. M. (1978). Role-play tests for assessing social skills: Are they valid? *Behavior Therapy, 9,* 448-461.

Bellack, A. S., Hersen, M., & Turner, S. M. (1979). Relationship of role playing and knowledge of appropriate behavior to assertion in the natural environment. *Journal of Consulting and Clinical Psychology, 47,* 670-678.

Bennis, W. G., Berlew, D. E., Schein, E. H., & Steele, F. I. (1968). Toward better interpersonal relationships. In W. G. Bennis, E. H. Schein, F. I. Steele, & D. E. Berlew (Eds.), *Interpersonal dynamics: Essays and readings on human interaction* (pp. 495-518). Homewood, IL: Irwin.

Berger, C. R. (1975). Proactive and retroactive attribution processes in interpersonal communications. *Human Communication Research, 2,* 33-50.

Berger, C. R. (1979). Beyond initial interaction: Uncertainty, understanding, and the development of interpersonal relationships. In H. Giles & R. St. Clair (Eds.), *Language and social psychology* (pp. 122-144). Oxford: Blackwell.

Berger, C. R. (1980). Self-consciousness and the adequacy of theory and research into relationship development. *Western Journal of Speech Communication, 44,* 93-96.

Berger, C. R., & Bradac, J. J. (1982). *Language and social knowledge: Uncertainty in interpersonal relations.* London: Edward Arnold.

Berger, C. R., & Calabrese, R. J. (1975). Some explorations in initial interaction and beyond: Toward a developmental theory of interpersonal communication. *Human Communication Research, 1,* 99-112.

Berger, C. R., & Douglas, W. (1982). Thought and talk: "Excuse me, but have I been talking to myself?" In F.E.X. Dance (Ed.), *Human communication theory: Comparative essays* (pp. 42-60). New York: Harper & Row.

Berger, C. R., Gardner, R. R., Parks, M. R., Schulman, L., & Miller, G. R. (1976). Interpersonal epistemology and interpersonal communications. In G. R. Miller (Ed.),*Explorations in interpersonal communication* (pp. 149-171). Beverly Hills: Sage.

Berryman-Fink, C., & Pederson, L. (1981). Testing the effects of a competency-based interpersonal communication course. *Southern Speech Communication Journal, 465,* 251-262.

Bienvenu, M. J.,Sr. (1970). Measurement of marital communication. *Family Coordinator, 19,* 26-31.

Bienvenu, M. J., Sr. (1971). An interpersonal communication inventory. *Journal of Communication, 21,* 381-388.

Bieri, J., Atkins, A., Briar, S., Leaman, R., Miller, H., & Tripodi, T. (1966). *Clinical and social judgment: The discrimination of behavioral information.* New York: John Wiley.

Billings, A. (1979). Conflict resolution in distressed and nondistressed married couples. *Journal of Consulting and Clinical Psychology, 47,* 376-386.

Black, J. (1979). Formal and informal means of assessing the communicative competence of kindergarten children. *Research in the Teaching of English, 13,* 49-68.

Blau, J. S. (1980). Changes in assertiveness and marital satisfaction after participation in an assertiveness training group. In D. Upper & S. M. Ross (Eds.), *Behavior therapy, 1980: An annual review* (pp. 63-83). Champaign, IL: Research Press.

Blechman, E. A. (1981). Competence, depression, and behavior modification with women. In M. Hersen, R. M. Eisler, & P. M. Miller (Eds.), *Progress in behavior modification* (Vol. 12, pp. 227-264). New York: Academic Press.

Block, J., & Bennett, L. (1955). The assessment of communication: Perception and transmission as a function of the social situation. *Human Relations, 8,* 317-325.

Bochner, A. P. (1978). On taking ourselves seriously: An analysis of some persistent problems and promising directions interpersonal research. *Human Communication Research, 4,* 179-191.

Bochner, A. P., & Kelly, C. W. (1974). Interpersonal competence: Rationale, philosophy, and implementation of a conceptual framework. *Speech Teacher, 23,* 270-301.

Bochner, A. P., & Yerby, J. (1977). Factors affecting instruction in interpersonal competence. *Communication Education, 26,* 91-103, 120.

Bohart, A. C., Landeros, D. D., Hewitt, B. N., & Heilman, A. (1979). Two methods of interpersonal skills training: Conceptual versus response-oriented approaches. *Small Group Behavior, 10,* 299-312.

Borden, A. W. (1981). *Interpersonal values, Machiavellianism, and social cognition as indicators of communicative competence in persuasive contexts.* Paper presented at the meeting of the Speech Communication Association, Anaheim, CA.

Bordewick, M. C., & Bornstein, P. H. (1980). Examination of multiple cognitive response dimensions among differentially assertive individuals. *Behavior Therapy, 11*, 440-448.

Bornstein, M. R., Bellack, A. S., & Hersen, M. (1977). Social skills training for unassertive children: A multiple-baseline analysis. *Journal of Applied Behavior Analysis, 10*, 183-195.

Bourque, P., & Ladduceur, R. (1979). Self-report and behavioral measures in the assessment of assertive behavior. *Journal of Behavior Therapy and Experimental Psychiatry, 10*, 287-292.

Bowers, J. W., & Bradac, J. J. (1982). Issues in communication theory: A metatheoretical analysis. In M. Burgoon (Ed.), *Communication yearbook 5.* New Brunswick, NJ: Transaction.

Boyd, L. A., & Roach, A. J. (1977). Interpersonal communication skills differentiating more satisfying from less satisfying marital relationships. *Journal of Counseling Psychology, 24*, 540-542.

Bradway, K. P. (1937). Social competence of exceptional children: II. The mentally subnormal. *Journal of Exceptional Children, 4*, 38-42.

Bradway, K. P. (1938). Social competence of grade school children. *Journal of Experimental Education, 6*, 326-331.

Braen, B. B. (1960). Development of a theoretically-based manifest rigidity inventory. *Psychological Reports, 6*, 75-88.

Brandt, D. R. (1979). On linking social performance with social competence: Some relations between communicative style and attributions of interpersonal effectiveness. *Human Communication Research, 5*, 223-237.

Brandt, D. R., Miller, G. R., & Hocking, J. E. (1980). Effects of self-monitoring and familiarity on deception. *Communication Quarterly, 28*, 3-10.

Branham, R. J. (1980). Ineffability, creativity, and communication competence. *Communication Quarterly, 28*, 11-21.

Breen, P., Donlon, T. F., & Whitaker, U. (1977). *Teaching and assessing interpersonal competence—A CAEL handbook.* Columbia, NJ: CAEL.

Brenner, S. O., & Hjelmquist, E. (1978). The production and understanding of utterances in dyadic communication. *Scandinavian Journal of Psychology, 19*, 121-131.

Breskin, S. (1968). Measurement of rigidity, a nonverbal test. *Perceptual and Motor Skills, 27*, 1203-1206.

Briedis, I. (1978). The facilitation of social competence through the implementation of an interpersonal coping skills program. *Dissertation Abstracts International, 39*, 1430A.

Briere, E. J. (1979). Testing communication-language proficiency. In R. Silverstein (Ed.), *Proceedings of the Third International Conference on Frontiers in Language Proficiency and Dominance Testing.* (pp. 254-275). Carbondale: Southern Illinois University.

Briggs, S. R., Cheek, J. M., & Buss, A. H. (1980). An analysis of the self-monitoring scale. *Journal of Personality and Social Psychology, 38*, 679-686.

Brim, J., Witcoff, C., & Wetzel, R. D. (1982). Social network characteristics of hospitalized depressed patients. *Psychological Reports, 50,* 423-433.

Brockner, J., & Eckenrode, J. (1979). Self-monitoring and the actor-observer bias. *Representative Research in Social Psychology, 9,* 81-88.

Bronfenbrenner, U., Harding, J., & Gallwey, M. (1958). The measurement of skill in social perception. In D. C. McClelland, A. L. Baldwin, U. Bronfenbrenner, & F. L. Stronbeck (Eds.), *Talent and society,* (pp. 29-111). Princeton, NJ: D. Van Nostrand.

Bronson, W. C. (1974). Competence and the growth of personality. In K. Connolly & J. Bruner (Eds.), *The growth of competence* (pp. 241-264). New York: Academic Press.

Broucek, F. (1979). Efficacy in infancy: A review of some experimental studies and their possible implication for clinical theory. *International Journal of Psychoanalysis, 60,* 311-316.

Brown, I., Jr., & Inouye, D. K. (1978). Learned helplessness through modeling: The role of perceived similarity in competence. *Journal of Personality and Social Psychology, 36,* 900-908.

Brown, K., Ecroyd, K., Hopper, R., McCambridge, M., Nance, T., & Wood, B. S. (Eds.). (1977). *Development of functional communication competencies: Grades 7-12.* Falls Church, VA: Speech Communication Association.

Brown, P., & Fraser, C. (1979). Speech as a marker of situation. In K. R. Scherer & H. Giles (Eds.), *Social markers in speech* (pp. 33-62). London: Cambridge University Press.

Brown, S. D. (1980). Videotape feedback: Effects on assertive performance and subjects' perceived competence and satisfaction. *Psychological Reports, 47,* 455-461.

Bruch, M. A., Heisler, B. D., & Conroy, C. G. (1981). Effects of conceptual complexity on assertive behavior. *Journal of Counseling Psychology, 28,* 377-385.

Brunner, C. C., & Phelps, L. A. (1979, May). *An examination of the relationship between interpersonal competence and androgyny.* Paper presented at the Communication Language and Gender Conference, Madison, WI.

Brunner, C. C., & Phelps, L. A. (1980). *Interpersonal competence and androgyny.* Paper presented at the meeting of the International Communication Association, Acapulco, Mexico.

Bucci, W., & Freedman, N. (1978). Language and hand: The dimension of referential competence. *Journal of Personality, 46,* 594-622.

Buckingham, T., & Rosenfeld, L. B. (1978) The conversant program and the development of communicative competence. *Communication Education, 27,* 349-354.

Buley, J. L. (1977). *Relationships and communication.* Dubuque, IA: Kendall/Hunt.

Buley, J. L. (1979). *Communication competence for ongoing relationships.* Paper presented at the meeting of the Western Speech Communication Association, Los Angeles.

Burgess, R. L., & Huston, T. L. (Eds.). (1979). *Social exchange in developing relationships.* New York: Academic Press.

Burgoon, J. K. (1976). The unwillingness-to-communicate scale: Development and validation. *Communication Monographs, 43,* 60-69.

Burgoon, J. K., & Hale, J. L. (1981). *Dimensions of relational messages.* Paper presented at the meeting of the Speech Communication Association, Anaheim, CA.

Burke, J. A., & Clark, R. A. (1980). *The development of persuasive skills: A research summary with a discussion of pedagogical implications.* Paper presented at the meeting of the Speech Communication Association, New York.

Burke, K. (1945). *A grammar of motives.* Englewood Cliffs, NJ: Prentice-Hall.

Burke, K. (1950). *A rhetoric of motives.* Englewood Cliffs, NJ: Prentice-Hall.

Burke, K. (1966). *Language as symbolic action.* Berkeley: University of California Press.

Burleson, B. R., & Kline, S. L. (1979). Habermas' theory of communication: A critical explication. *Quarterly Journal of Speech, 65,* 379-392.

Buss, D. M., & Craik, K. H. (1980). The frequency concept of disposition: Dominance and prototypically dominant acts. *Journal of Personality, 48,* 379-392.

Buss, D. M. & Craik, K. H. (1981). The act frequency analysis of interpersonal dispositions: Aloofness, gregariousness, dominance and submissiveness. *Journal of Personality, 49,* 175-192.

Caldwell, A. T., Calhoun, K. S., Humphreys, L., & Cheney, T. H. (1978). Treatment of socially anxious women by a skills training program. *Journal of Behavior Therapy and Experimental Psychiatry, 9,* 315-320.

Campbell, G. (1963). *The philosophy of rhetoric* (L. F. Bitzer). Carbondale, IL: Southern Illinois University Press.

Campbell, J. D., & Yarrow, M. R. (1961). Perceptual and behavioral correlates of social effectiveness. *Sociometry, 24,* 1-20.

Campbell, R. J., Kagan, N., Krathwohl, D. R. (1971). The development and validation of a scale to measure affective sensitivity (empathy). *Journal of Counseling Psychology, 18,* 407-412.

Capella, J. N. (1983). Conversational involvement: Approaching and avoiding others. In J. M. Wiemann& R. P. Harrison (Eds.), *Nonverbal interaction.* (pp. 113-148). Beverly Hills, CA: Sage.

Carkhuff, R. R., & Truax, C. B. (1966). Toward explaining success or failure in interpersonal experience. *Personnel and Guidance Journal, 44,* 723-728.

Cartledge, G., & Milburn, J. F. (1978). The case for teaching social skills in the classroom: A review. *Review of Educational Research, 48,* 133-156.

Cazden, C. B. (1970). The situation: A neglected source of social class differences in language use. *Journal of Social Issues, 26,* 35-60.

Cedergen, H. J., & Sankoff, D. (1974). Variable rules: Performance as a statistical reflection of competence. *Language, 50,* 333-355.

Cegala, J. J. (1978). *Interaction involvement: A fundamental dimension of interpersonal communication competence.* Paper presented at the meeting of the Speech Commuication Association, Minneapolis.

Cegala, D. J. (1981). Interaction involvement: A cognitive dimension of communicative competence. *Communication Education, 30,* 109-121.

Cegala, D. J., & Brunner, C. C. (1983). *A study of interaction involvement and mood state during unstructured and competitive interactions.* Unpublished manuscript. Ohio State University, Columbus.

Cegala, J. J., Savage, G. T., Brunner, C.C., & Conrad, A. B. (1982). An elaboration of the meaning of interaction involvement: Toward the development of a theoretical concept. *Communication Monographs, 49,* 229-248.

Cervin, V. (1957). Personality dimensions of emotional responsiveness and rigidity, and scales for measuring them. *Journal of Personality, 25*, 626-642.

Cherulnik, P. D., Neely, W. T., Flanagan, M., & Zachau, M. (1978). Social skill and visual interaction. *Journal of Social Psychology, 104*, 263-270.

Chiauzzi, E., Heimburgg, R. G., & Doty, D. (1982). Task analysis of assertive behavior revisited: The role of situational variables with female college students. *Behavioral Counseling Quarterly, 2*, 42-50.

Chmielewski, T. L., & Wolf, L. (1979). *Assessing the reliability of a scale to measure role-taking ability.* Paper presented at the meeting of the Speech Communication Association, San Antonio.

Chomsky, N. (1965). *Aspects of the theory of syntax.* Cambridge, MA: MIT Press.

Chomsky, N. (1970). Topics in the theory of generative grammar. In J. R. Searle (Ed.), *The philosophy of language* (pp. 71-100). Oxford: Oxford University Press.

Christensen, D., Farina, A., & Boudreau, L. (1980). Sensitivity to nonverbal cues as a function of social competence. *Journal of Nonverbal Behavior, 4*, 146-156.

Christie, R., & Geis, F. L. (1970). *Studies in Machiavellianism.* New York: Academic Press.

Cicero. (1959). *De Oratore I, II* (E. W. Sutton, Trans.). Cambridge, MA: Harvard University Press. (original work published 1942)

Cissna, K. N. (1976). *Interpersonal confirmation: A review of current theory, measurement and research.* Paper presented at the meeting of the Central States Speech Association, Chicago.

Cissna, K. N., & Keating, S., Sr. (1979). Speech communication antecedents of perceived confirmation. *Western Journal of Speech Communication, 43*, 48-60.

Clark, J. V., & Arkowitz, H. (1975). Social anxiety and self-evaluation of interpersonal performance. *Psychological Reports, 36*, 211-221.

Clark, R. A., & Delia, J. G. (1979). *Topoi* and rhetorical competence. *Quarterly Journal of Speech, 65*, 187-206.

Clatterbuck, G. W. (1979). Attributional confidence and uncertainty in initial interaction. *Human Communication Research, 5*, 147-157.

Clinard, H. (1979). Interpersonal communication skills training. *Training and Development Journal, 33*, 34-38.

Cochrane, C. T. (1974). Development of a measure of empathic communication. *Psychotherapy: Theory, Research and Practice, 11*, 41-47.

Cody, M. J., & McLaughlin, M. L. (1980). Perceptions of compliance-gaining situations. A dimensional analysis. *Communication Monographs, 47*, 132-148.

Cody, M. J., Woelfel, M. L., & Jordan, W. J. (1983). Dimensions of compliance-gaining situations. *Human Communication Research, 9*, 99-113.

Collie, S. J. (1981). *Relationship initiation.* Paper presented at the meeting of the Illinois Speech and Theatre Association, St. Louis.

Colson, E. (1967). Competence and incompetence in the context of independence. *Current Anthropology, 8*, 92-111.

Colten, S. I., & Langlois, J. (1976). The test of behavioral rigidity: A measure of change. *Psychology, 13*, 61-63.

Conger, A. J., Wallander, J. L., Mariotto, M. J., & Ward, D. (1980). Peer judgments of heterosexual-social anxiety and skills: What do they pay attention to anyhow? *Behavioral Assessment, 2,* 243-295

Conger, A. J., Wallander, J. L., Ward, D. G., & Farrell, A. D. (1980). *Ratings of heterosocial anxiety and skill: 1 + 1 = 1.* Unpublished manuscript. Purdue University, Lafayette, IN.

Conger, J. C., & Conger, A. J. (1982). Components of heterosocial competence. In J. P. Curran & P. M. Monti (Eds.), *Social skills training* (pp. 313-347). New York: Guilford Press.

Conger, J. C., & Farrell, A. D. (1981). Behavioral components of heterosocial skills. *Behavior Therapy, 12,* 41-55.

Connolly, K. J., & Bruner, J. S. (1974). Competence: Its nature and nurture. In K. J. Connolly & J. S. Bruner (Eds.), *The growth of competence* (pp. 3-7). New York: Academic Press.

Corriveau, D. P., Vespucci, R., Curran, J. P., Monti, P. M., Wessberg, H. W., & Coyne, N. A. (1981). The effects of various rater training procedures on the perception of social skills and social anxiety. *Journal of Behavioral Assessment, 3*(2), 93-97.

Cottrell, L. S., & Dymond, R. F. (1949). The empathic response: A neglected field for research. *Psychiatry, 12,* 355-359.

Coulter, W. A., & Morrow, H. W. (1978). A collection of adaptive behavior measures. In W. A. Coulter & H. W. Morrow (Eds.), *Adaptive behavior: Concepts and measurements* (pp. 141-152). New York: Grune & Stratton.

Cox, R. D., & Gunn, W. B. (1980). Interpersonal skills in the schools: Assessment and curriculum development. In D. P. Rathjen & J. P. Foreyt (Eds.), *Social competence: Interventions for children and adults* (pp. 113-132). New York: Plenum.

Crino, M. D., & White, M. C. (1981). Satisfaction in communication: An examination of the Downs-Hazen measure. *Psychological Reports, 49,* 831-838.

Crites, J. O., & Fitzgerald, L. F. (1978). The competent male. *Counseling Psychologist, 7*(4), 10-14.

Crowley, T. J., & Ivey, A. E. (1976). Dimensions of effective interpersonal communications: Specifying behavioral components. *Journal of Counseling Psychology, 23,* 267-271.

Cunningham, M. R. (1977). Personality and the structure of the nonverbal communication of emotion. *Journal of Personality, 45,* 564-584.

Cupach, W. R. (1981). *The relationship between perceived communication competence and choice of interpersonal conflict message strategies.* Unpublished doctoral dissertation, University of Southern California, Los Angeles.

Cupach, W. R. (1982a). *Communication satisfaction and interpersonal solidarity as outcomes of conflict message strategy use.* Paper presented at the meeting of the International Communication Association, Boston.

Cupach, W. R. (1982b). *Perceived communication competence and choice of interpersonal conflict message strategies.* Paper presented at the meeting of the Western Speech Communication Association, Denver.

Cupach, W. R., & Hazleton, V. (1982). *A language-action approach to situation*. Paper presented at the meeting of the Speech Communication Association, Louisville.

Cupach, W. R., & Spitzberg, B. H. (1981). *Relational competence: Measurement and validation*. Paper presented at the meeting of the Western Speech Communication Association, San Jose, CA.

Cupach, W. R., & Spitzberg, B. H. (1983). Trait versus state: A comparison of dispositional and situational measures of interpersonal communication competence. *Western Journal of Speech Communication, 47*, 364-379.

Curran, J. P. (1977). Skills training as an approach to the treatment of heterosexual-social anxiety: A review. *Psychological Bulletin, 84*, 140-157.

Curran, J. P. (1979a). Pandora's box reopened? The assessment of social skills. *Journal of Behavioral Assessment, 1*(1), 55-71.

Curran, J. P. (1979b). Social skills: Methodological issues and future directions. In A. S. Bellack & M. Hersen (Eds.), *Research and practice in social skills training* (pp. 319-354). New York: Plenum.

Curran, J. P. (1982). A procedure for the assessment of social skills: The Simulated Social Interaction Test. In J. P. Curran & P. M. Monti (Eds.), *Social skills training* (pp. 348-398). New York: Guilford Press.

Curran, J. P., Corriveau, D. P., Monti, P. M., & Haberman, S. B. (1980). Social skill and social anxiety: Self-report measurement in a psychiatric population. *Behavior Modification, 4*, 493-512.

Curran, J. P., & Mariotto, M. J. (1980). A conceptual structure for the assessment of social skills. In M. Hersen, R. M. Eisler, & P. M. Miller (Eds.), *Progress in behavioral modification* (Vol. 10). New York: Academic.

Curran, J. P., Monti, P. M., Corriveau, D. P., Hay, L. R., Hagerman, S., Zwick, W. R., & Farrell, A. D. (1980). The generalizability of a procedure for assessing social skills and social anxiety in a psychiatric population. *Behavioral Assessment, 2*, 389-401.

Curran, J. P., Wallander, J. L., & Fischetti, M. (1980). The importance of behavioral and cognitive factors in heterosexual-social anxiety. *Journal of Personality, 48*, 285-292.

Cushman, D. P., & Craig, R. T. (1976). Communication systems: Interpersonal implications. In G. R. Miller (Ed.), *Explorations in interpersonal communication* (pp. 37-58). Beveral Hills: Sage.

Dabbs, J.M., Jr., Evans, M. S., Hopper, C. H., & Purvis, J. A. (1980). Self-monitors in conversations: What do they monitor? *Journal of Personality and Social Psychology, 39*, 278-284.

Duncan, S., Jr. (1983). Speaking turns: Studies of structure and individual differences. In J. M. Wiemann & R. P. Harrison (Eds.), *Nonverbal interaction* (pp. 149-178). Beverly Hills, CA: Sage.

Dance, F. E. X., & Larson, C. E. (1972). *Speech communication: Concepts and behaviors*. New York: Holt, Rinehart & Winston.

Daly, J. A. (1977). Communication apprehension in the classroom. *Florida Speech Communication Journal, 5*, 9-26.

D'Augelli, A. R. (1973). Group composition using interpersonal skills on peer ratings and group cohesiveness. *Journal of Counseling Psychology, 30*, 531-534.

Davis, J. D. (1978). When boy meets girl: Sex roles and the negotiation of intimacy in an acquaintance exercise. *Journal of Personality and Social Psychology, 36*, 684-692.

Davis, M. H. (1980). A multidimensional approach to individual differences in empathy. *JSAS Catalog of Selected Documents in Psychology, 10*(4, Ms. 2124).

Dawley, H.H., Jr., & Wenrich, W. W. (1976). *Achieving assertive behavior: A guide to assertive training.* Monterey, CA: Brooks/Cole.

Day, C. L. (1981). *Relationship termination.* Paper presented at the meeting of the Illinois Speech and Theatre Association, St. Louis.

Del Greco, L. (1983). The Del Greco Assertive Behavior Inventory. *Journal of Behavioral Assessment, 5*(1), 49-63.

Delia, J. (1980). Some tentative thoughts concerning the study of interpersonal relationships and their development. *Western Journal of Speech Communication, 44*, 97-103.

Derber, C. (1979). *The pursuit of attention.* Cambridge, MA: Schenkman.

DeVito, J. A. (1980). *The interpersonal communication book* (2nd ed). New York: Harper & Row.

Doll, E. A. (1935). The measurement of social competence. *American Association of Mental Deficiency, 40*, 103-126.

Doll, E. A. (1939). Growth studies in social competence. *American Association of Mental Deficiency, 44*, 90-96.

Doll, E. A. (1948). The relation of social competence to social adjustment. *Educational Record* (Suppl. 12), 77-85.

Doll, E. A. (1953). *The measurement of social competence.* Circle Pines, MN: Educational Publishers.

Donahoe, C.P., Jr. (1978). *Definitions of competence and the assessment of social skills of adolescent boys.* Unpublished master's thesis, University of Wisconsin, Madison.

Dosser, D. A., Jr., Balswick, J. O., & Halverson, C.F., Jr. (1983). Situational context of emotional expressiveness. *Journal of Counseling Psychology, 30*, 375-387.

Doucette, J., & Freedman, R. (1980). *Progress tests for the developmentally disabled: An evaluation.* Cambridge, MA: Abt Books.

Dow, M. G., Glaser, S. R., & Biglan, A. (1981). The relevance of specific conversational behaviors to ratings of social skill: A review and experimental analysis. *Journal of Behavioral Assessment, 3*, 233-242.

Duck, S. (1980). The personal context: Intimate relationships. In P. Feldman & J. Orford (Eds.), *Psychological problems: The social context* (pp. 73-96). New York: John Wiley.

Duhamel, P. A. (1949). The function of rhetoric as effective expression. *Journal of the History of Ideas, 10*, 344-356.

Duncan, S., Jr. (1983). Speaking turns: Studies of structure and individual differences. In J. M. Wiemann & R. P. Harrison (Eds.), *Nonverbal interaction.* Beverly Hills, CA: Sage.

Duran, R. L. (1983a). *Cognitive competence: Conceptualization and measurement.* Unpublished manuscript. University of Hartford, West Hartford, CT.

Duran, R. L. (1983b). Communicative adaptability: A measure of social communicative competence. *Communication Quarterly, 31*, 320-326.

Duran, R. L., & Wheeless, V. E. (1980). *Social management: Toward a theory based operationalization of communication competence.* Paper presented at the meeting of the Speech Communication Association, New York.

Duran, R. L., Zakahi, W. R., & Mumper, M. A. (1982). *Competence vs style: A dyadic assessment of the relationship among communication performance variables and communication satisfaction.* Paper presented at the meeting of the International Communication Association, Boston.

Duran, R. L., Zakahi, W. R., & Parrish, S. C. (1981). *Communicative adaptability: An extension of content and construct validity.* Paper presented at the meeting of the Speech Communication Association, Anaheim, CA.

Durham, R. C. (1979). Lewinsohn's behavioral measures of social skill: Their stability and relationship to mood level and depression among college students. *Journal of Clinical Psychology, 35*, 599-604.

Duval, S., & Wicklund, R. A. (1972). *A theory of objective self-awareness.* New York: Academic Press.

Dymond, R. F. (1948). A preliminary investigation of the relation of insight and empathy. *Journal of Consulting Psychology, 12*, 228-233.

Dymond, R. F. (1949). A scale for the measurement of empathic ability. *Journal of Consulting Psychology, 13*, 127-133.

Dymond, R. F., Hughes, A. S., & Raabe, V. L. (1952). Measurable changes in empathy with age. *Journal of Consulting Psychology, 16*, 202-206.

Eadie, W. F. (1983). *Influences of attitudes toward communication and relational factors on rhetorical force.* Paper presented at the meeting of the Western Speech Communication Association, Albuquerque.

Eadie, W. F., & Paulson, J. W. (1983). *Relationships among attitudes toward communication, communicator style, and communication competence.* Paper presented at the meeting of the International Communication Association, Dallas.

Edgerton, R. B. (1967). *The cloak of competence: Stigma in the lives of the mentally retarded.* Berkley: University of California Press.

Edwards, C. N. (1973). Interactive styles and social adaptation. *Genetic Psychology Monographs, 87*, 123-174.

Ehninger, D. (1968). On systems of rhetoric. *Philosophy and Rhetoric, 1*, 131-144.

Ehninger, D. (1975). A synoptic view of systems of Western rhetoric. *Quarterly Journal of Speech, 61*, 448-453.

Eidelson, R. J. (1980). Interpersonal satisfaction and level of involvement: A curvilinear relationship. *Journal of Personality and Social Psychology, 39*, 460-470.

Eisler, R. M. (1978). Behavioral assessment of social skills. In M. Hersen & A. S. Bellack (Eds.), *Behavioral assessment: A practical handbook* (pp. 369-395). Elmsford, NY: Pergamon.

Eisler, R. M., & Fredericksen, L. W. (1980). *Perfecting social skills.* New York: Plenum.

Eisler, R. M., Fredericksen, L. W., & Peterson, G. L. (1978). The relationship of cognitive variables to the expression of assertiveness. *Behavior Therapy, 9*, 419-427.

Elder, J. P., Wallace, C. J., & Harris, F. C. (1980). Assessment of social skills using a Thurstone equal-appearing interval scale. *Journal of Behavioral Assessment, 2*(3), 161-165.

Elliot, J., & Connolly, K. J. (1974). Hierarchical structure in skill development. In K. J. Connolly & J. S. Bruner (Eds.), *The growth of competence* (pp. 135-168). New York: Academic Press.

Elliot, R., Filipovich, H., Harrigan, L., Gaynor, J., Reimschuessel, C., & Zapadka, J. K. (1982). Measuring response empathy: The development of a multicomponent rating scale. *Journal of Counseling Psychology, 29,* 379-387.

Ellis, R., & Whittington, D. (1981). *A guide to social skill training.* London: Croom Helm.

Ervin-Tripp, S. M. (1973). *Language acquisition and communicative choice.* Stanford, CA: Stanford University Press.

Ezekiel, R. S. (1968). The personal future and Peace Corps competence. *Journal of Personality and Social Psychology Monographs, 8*(2, Pt. 2), 1-26.

Farber, B. (1962). Elements of competence in interpersonal relations: A factor analysis. *Sociometry, 25,* 30-47.

Farina, A., Arenberg, D., & Guskin, S. (1957). A scale for measuring minimal social behavior. *Journal of Consulting Psychology, 21,* 265-268.

Farrell, A. D., Mariotto, M. J., Cooper, A. J., Curran, J. P., & Wallander, J. L. (1979). Self-ratings and judges' ratings of heterosexual social anxiety and skill: A generalizability study. *Journal of Consulting and Clinical Psychology, 47,* 164-175.

Fasold, R. W. (1978). Language variation and linguistic competence. In D. Sankoff (Ed.), *Linguistic variation: Models and methods* (pp. 85-95). New York: Academic Press.

Feingold, P. C. (1977). Toward a paradigm of effective communication: An empirical study of perceived communication effectiveness. *Dissertation Abstracts International, 37,* 4697A-4698A.

Fenigstein, A. (1979). Self-consciousness, self-attention, and social interaction. *Journal of Personality and Social Psychology, 37,* 75-86.

Fenigstein, A., Scheier, M. F., & Buss, A. H. (1975). Public and private self-consciousness: Assessment and theory. *Journal of Consulting and Clinical Psychology, 43,* 522-527.

Fensterheim, H., & Baer, J. (1975). *Don't say yes when you want to say no.* New York: Dell.

Fillmore, C. J. (1979). On Fluency. In C. J. Fillmore, D. Kemper, & W.S.Y. Wang (Eds.), *Individual differences in language ability and language behavior* (pp. 85-101). New York: Academic Press.

Filsinger, E. E., & Lamke, L. K. (1983). The lineage transmission of interpersonal competence. *Journal of Marriage and the Family, 45,* 75-80.

Finch, B. E., & Wallace, C. J. (1977). Successful interpersonal skills training with schizophrenic inpatients. *Journal of Consulting and Clinical Psychology, 45,* 885-890.

Fischetti, M., Curran, J. P., & Wessberg, H. W. (1977). Sense of timing: A skill deficit in heterosexual-socially anxious males. *Behavior Modification, 1,* 179-194.

Fisher, B. A. (1978). *Perspectives on human communication.* New York: Macmillan.

Fisher, B. A. (1981). *On relationship and competence: Contemporary issues in interpersonal communication research.* Critique presented at the meeting of the Western Speech Communication Association, San Jose, CA.

Fisher, J. (1973). Competence, effectiveness, intellectual functioning, and aging. *The Gerontologist, 13*, 62-68.

Fisher, W. R. (1978). Toward a logic of good reasons. *Quarterly Journal of Speech, 64*, 376-384.

Fisher, W. R. (1980). Rationality and the logic of good reasons. *Philosophy and Rhetoric, 13*, 121-130.

Fisher-Beckfield, D. E. (1979). *The relationship of competence to both depression and depression-proneness in male college students.* Unpublished master's thesis. University of Wisconsin, Madison.

Fisher—Beckfield, D. E., & McFall, R. M. (1982) Development of a competence inventory for college men and evaluation of relationships between competence and depression. *Journal of Consulting and Clinical Psychology, 50*, 699-705.

Fitts, W. H. (1970). *Interpersonal competence: The wheel model* (Studies on the self-concept and rehabilitation: Research monograph no. 2). Nashville, TN: Dede Wallace Center.

Fitzpatrick, M. A., & Indvik, J. (1982). The instrumental and expressive domains of marital interaction. *Human Communication Research, 8*, 195-213.

Flavell, J. H., Botkin, P. B., Fry, C.L., Jr., Jarvis, P. E., & Wright, J. W. (1968). *The development of role-taking and communication skills in children.* New York: John Wiley.

Flint, D. L., Hick, T. L., Horan, M. D., Irvine, D. J., & Kukuk, S. E. (1980). Dimensionality of the California preschool social competency scale. *Applied Psychological Measurement, 4*, 203-212.

Foa, U. G. (1961). Convergences in the analysis of the structure of interpersonal behavior. *Psychological Review, 68*, 341-353.

Fodor, J., & Garrett, M. (1966). Some reflections on competence and performance. In J. Lyons & R. J. Wales (Eds.), *Psycholinguistic papers* (Proceedings of the 1966 Edinburgh Conference, pp. 135-154). Edinburgh: Edinburgh University Press.

Foote, N. N., & Cottrell, L. S., Jr. (1955). *Identity and interpersonal competence.* Chicago: University of Chicago Press.

Forgas, J. P. (1979). *Social episodes: The study of interaction routines.* New York: Academic Press.

Forgas, J. P. (1982). Episode cognition: Internal representations of interaction routines. In L. Berkowitz (Ed.), *Advances in experimental social psychology* (Vol. 15). New York: Academic.

Forgas, J. P. (1983). The effects of prototypicality and cultural salience on perceptions of people. *Journal of Research in Personality, 17*, 153-173.

Forgas, J. P. (1983b). Episode cognition and personality: A multidimensional analysis. *Journal of Personality, 51*, 34-48.

Forgas, J. P., & Dobosz, B. (1980). Dimensions of romantic involvement: Towards a taxonomy of heterosexual relationships. *Social Psychological Quarterly, 43*, 290-300.

Foster, S. L., & Ritchey, W. L. (1979). Issues in the assessment of social competence in children. *Journal of Applied Behavior Analysis, 12*, 625-638.

Foy, D. W., Massey, F. H., Duer, J. D., Ross, J. M., & Wooten, L. S. (1979). Social skills training to improve alcoholics: Vocational interpersonal competency. *Journal of Counseling Psychology, 26*, 128-132.

Franks, D. D., & Morolla, J. (1976). Efficacious action and social approval as interacting dimensions of self-esteem: A tentative formulation through construct validation. *Sociometry, 29,* 324-341.

Freedman, B. J., Rosenthal, L., Donahoe, C.P., Jr., Schlundt, D. G., & McFall, R. M. (1978). A social-behavioral analysis of skill deficits in delinquent and nondelinquent adolescent boys. *Journal of Consulting and Clinical Psychology, 46,* 1448-1462.

French, J.R.P., Jr., Rodgers, W., & Cobb, S. (1974). Adjustment as person-environment fit. In G. V. Coelho, D. A. Hamburg, & J. E. Adams (Eds.), *Coping and adaptation* (pp. 316-333). New York: Basic Books.

French, P. L. (1976). Disintegrating theoretical distinctions and some future directions in psycholinguistics. In E. C. Carterette & M. P. Friedman (Eds.), *Handbook of perception: Vol 7: Language and speech* (pp. 445-465). New York: Academic Press.

Friedman, H. S., DiMatteo, M. R., & Taranta, A. (1980). A study of the relationship between individual differences in nonverbal expressiveness and factors of personality and social interaction. *Journal of Research in Personality, 14,* 351-364.

Friedman, H. S., Prince, L. M., Riggio, R. E., & DiMatteo, M. R. (1980). Understanding and assessing nonverbal expressiveness: The affective communication test. *Journal of Personality and Social Psychology, 39,* 333-351.

Friedrich, G. W. (1981). *Atomistic versus holistic approaches to teaching communication skills.* Paper presented at the meeting of the Speech Communication Association, Anaheim, CA.

Funder, D. C., & Van Ness, M. J. (1983). On the nature and accuracy of attributions that change over time. *Journal of Personality, 51,* 17-33.

Furnham, A., & Argyle, M. (Eds.). (1981). *The psychology of social situations: Selected readings.* Elmsford, NY: Pergamon.

Gabrenya, W.K., Jr., & Arkin, R. M. (1980). Self-monitoring scale: Factor structure and correlates. *Personality and Social Psychology Bulletin, 6,* 13-22.

Galassi, J. P., DeLo, J. S., Galassi, M. D., & Bastien, S. (1974). The college self-expression scale: A measure of assertiveness. *Behavior Therapy, 5,* 165-171.

Galassi, J. P., Galassi, M. D., & Vedder, M. J. (1981). Perspectives on assertion as a social skills model. In J. D. Wine & M. D. Smye (Eds.), *Social competence* (pp. 287-345). New York: Guilford Press.

Galassi, J. P., Hollandsworth, J.G., Jr., Radeki, J. C., Gay, M. L., Howe, M. R., & Evans, C. L. (1976). Behavioral performance in the validation of an assertiveness scale. *Behavior Therapy, 7,* 447-452.

Galassi, M. D., & Galassi, J. P. (1976). The effects of role playing variations on the assessment of assertive behavior. *Behavior Therapy, 7,* 343-347.

Gambrill, E. D. (1977). *Behavior modification: Handbook of assessment, intervention, and evaluation.* San Francisco: Jossey-Bass.

Gambrill, E. D., & Richey, C. A. (1975). An assertion inventory for use in assessment and research. *Behavior Therapy, 6,* 550-561.

Garland, D. R. (1981). Training married couples in listening skills: Effects on behavior, perceptual accuracy and marital adjustment. *Family Relations, 30,* 297-306.

Garmezy, N., Masten, A., Nordstrom, L., & Ferrarese, M. (1979). The nature of competence in normal and deviant children. In M. W. Kent & J. E. Rolf (Eds.), *Primary prevention of psychopathology: Volume 3—Social competence in children* (pp. 23-43). Hanover, NH: University Press of New England.

Garner, A. (1980). *Conversationally speaking*. New York: McGraw-Hill.

Garrison, J. P., & Powell, R. G. (1977). *Interpersonal solidarity and communication contexts: The study of relational communication in a multi-causal paradigm*. Paper presented at the meeting of the Western Speech Communication Association, Phoenix.

Garrison, J. P., Sullivan, D. L., & Pate, L. E. (1976). *Interpersonal valence dimensions as discriminators of communication contexts: An empirical assessment of dyadic linkages*. Paper presented at the meeting of the Speech Communication Association, San Francisco.

Geest, T.V.D., Gerstel, R., Appel, R., & Tervoort, B. T. (1973). *The child's communicative competence*. The Hague: Mouton.

Getter, H., & Nowinski, J. K. (1981). A free response test of interpersonal effectiveness. *Journal of Personality Assessment, 45*, 301-308.

Gibb, J. R. (1961). Defensive communication. *Journal of Communication, 11*, 141-148.

Giffin, K. (1970). Social alienation by communication denial. *Quarterly Journal of Speech, 56*, 347-356.

Giffin, K., & Gilham, S. M. (1971). Relationships between speech anxiety and motivation. *Speech Monographs, 38*, 70-73.

Giles, H., & Powesland, P. F. (1975). *Speech style and social evaluation*. New York: Academic Press.

Gillingham, P. R., Griffiths, R.D.P., & Care, D. (1977). Direct assessment of social behaviour from videotape recordings. *British Journal of Social and Clinical Psychology, 16*, 181-187.

Ginsburg, G. P. (1980). Situated action: An emerging paradigm. In L. Wheeler (Ed.), *Review of personality and social psychology* (Vol. 1, pp. 295-325). Beverly Hills: Sage.

Girodo, M. (1978). *Shy? You don't have to be*. New York: Pocket Books.

Gladwin, T. (1967). Social competence and clinical practice. *Psychiatry, 30*, 30-38.

Glaser, S. R. (1980). *Toward communication competency: Developing interpersonal skills*. New York: Holt, Rinehart & Winston.

Glaser, S. R. (1983). Interpersonal communication instruction: A behavioral competency approach. *Communication Education, 32*, 221-225.

Glasgow, R. E., & Arkowitz, H. (1975). The behavioral assessment of male and female social competence in dyadic heterosexual interactions. *Behavior Therapy, 6*, 488-498.

Goffman, E. (1967). *Interaction ritual: Essays on face-to-face behavior*. New York: Pantheon.

Goffman, E. (1969). *Strategic interaction*. Philadelphia: University of Pennsylvania Press.

Goldberg. L. R. (1981). Language and individual differences: The search for universals in personality lexicons. In L. Wheeler (Ed.), *Review of personality and social psychology* (Vol. 2, pp. 141-165). Beverly Hills: Sage.

Goldberg, S. (1977). Social competence in infancy: A model of parent-infant interaction. *Merrill-Palmer Quarterly, 23,* 163-177.

Goldfried, M. R., & D'Zurilla, T. J. (1969). A behavioral-analytic model for assessing competence. In D. D. Spielberger (Ed.), *Current topics in clinical and community psychology* (Vol. 1, pp. 151-196). New York: Academic Press.

Goldsmith, J. B., & McFall, R. M. (1975). Development and evaluation of an interpersonal skill-training program for psychiatric inpatients. *Journal of Abnormal Psychology, 84,* 51-58.

Gompertz, K. (1960). The relation of empathy to effective communication. *Journalism Quarterly, 37,* 533-546.

Gorecki, P. R., Dickson, A. L., & Ritzler, B. (1981). Convergent and concurrent validation of four measures of assertion. *Journal of Behavioral Assessment, 3,* 85-91.

Gormally, J. (1982). Evaluation of assertiveness: Effects of gender, rater, involvement, and level of assertiveness. *Behavior Therapy, 13,* 219-225.

Gotlib, I. H., & Asarnow, R. F. (1980). Independence of interpersonal and impersonal problem-solving skills: Reply to Rohsenow. *Journal of Consulting and Clinical Psychology, 48,* 286-288.

Gottman, J. M. (1979). *Marital interaction: Experimental investigations.* New York: Academic Press.

Gottman, J. M., Gonso, J., & Rasmussen, B. (1975). Social interaction, social competence, and friendship in children. *Child Development, 46,* 709-718.

Gottman, J. M., & Porterfield, A. L. (1981). Communicative competence in the nonverbal behavior of married couples. *Journal of Marriage and the Family, 43,* 817-824.

Gouran, D. S. (1973). Correlates of member satisfaction in group decision-making discussions. *Central States Speech Journal, 24,* 91-96.

Grayson, M., Nugent, C., & Oken, S. L. (1977). A systematic and comprehensive approach to teaching and evaluating interpersonal skills. *Journal of Medical Education, 52,* 906-913.

Green, K. D., & Forehand, R. (1980). Assessment of children's social skills: A review of methods. *Journal of Behavioral Assessment, 2*(3), 143-159.

Greene, J. (1977). Psycholinguistics: Competence and performance. In G. Vesey (Ed.), *Communication and understanding* (pp. 79-90). Atlantic Highlands, NJ: Humanities Press.

Greenwald, D. P. (1977). The behavioral assessment of differences in social skill and social anxiety in female college students. *Behavior Therapy, 8,* 925-937.

Greif, E. B., & Hogan, R. (1973). The theory and measurement of empathy. *Journal of Counseling Psychology, 20,* 280-284.

Gresham, F. M. (1981). Assessment of children's social skills. *Journal of School Psychology, 19,* 120-129.

Griffiths, R.D.P. (1980). Social skills and psychological disorder. In W. T. Singleton, P. Spurgeon, & R. B. Stammers (Eds.), *The analysis of social skill* (pp. 39-78). New York: Plenum.

Grimshaw, A. D. (1971). Sociolinguistics. In J. A. Fishman (Ed.), *Contributions to the sociology of language* (Vol. 1, pp. 92-151). The Hague: Mouton.

Groot, P.J.M. (1975). Testing communicative competence in listening comprehension. In R. L. Jones & B. Spolsky (Eds.), *Testing language proficiency* (pp. 45-58). Arlington, VA: Center for Applied Linguistics.

Guerney, B.G., Jr. (1977). *Relationship enhancement.* San Francisco: Jossey-Bass.

Gunzberg, H. C. (1973). *Social competence and mental handicap: An introduction to social education.* Baltimore: Williams & Wilkins.

Gutkin, T. B. (1981). Relative frequency of consultee lack of knowledge, skills, confidence, and objectivity in school settings. *Journal of School Psychology, 19,* 57-61.

Haase, R. S., & Tepper, D. T., Jr. (1972). Nonverbal components of empathic communication. *Journal of Counseling Psychology, 19,* 417-424.

Habermas, J. (1970). Toward a theory of communicative competence. In H. P. Dreitzel (Ed.), *Recent sociology* (No. 2, pp. 115-148). New York: Macmillan.

Haight, L., & Pavitt, C. (1982). *Implicit theories of communication competence: I. Traits, behaviors, and situational differences.* Paper presented at the meeting of the Speech Communication Association, Louisville.

Hale, C. L. (1980). Cognitive complexity-simplicity as a determinant of communication effectiveness. *Communication Monographs, 47,* 304-311.

Hale, C. L., & Delia, J. G. (1976). Cognitive complexity and social perspective-taking. *Communication Monographs, 43,* 195-203.

Hamburg, D. A., Coelho, G. V., & Adams, J. E. (1974). Coping and adaptation: Steps towards a synthesis of biological and social perspectives. In G. V. Coelho, D. A. Hamburg, & J. E. Adams (Eds.), *Coping and adaptation* (pp. 403-440). New York: Basic Books.

Hargie, O., Saunders, C., & Dickson, D. (1981). *Social skills in interpersonal communication.* London: Croom Helm.

Harris, L. (1979). *Communication competence: An argument for a systemic view.* Paper presented at the meeting of the International Communication Association Convention, Philadelphia.

Hart, R. P., & Burks, D. M. (1972). Rhetorical sensitivity and social interaction. *Speech Monographs, 39*(2), 75-91.

Hart, R. P., Carlson, R. E., & Eadie, W. F. (1980). Attitudes toward communication and the assessment of rhetorical sensitivity. *Communication Monographs, 47,* 1-22.

Harter, S. (1978). Effectance motivation reconsidered: Toward a developmental model. *Human Development, 21,* 34-64.

Harter, S. (1982). The perceived competence scale for children. *Child Development, 53,* 87-97.

Harvey, P. D. (1983). Speech competence in manic and schizophrenic psychoses: The association between clinically rated thought disorder and cohesion and reference performance. *Journal of Abnormal Psychology, 92,* 368-377.

Haspel, E. C. (1976). *Marriage in Trouble.* Chicago: Nelson-Hall.

Havighurst, R. J. (1957). The social competence of middle-aged people. *Genetic Psychology Monographs, 56,* 297-375.

Hayano, D. M. (1980). Communicative competency among poker players. *Journal of Communication, 30,* 113-120.

Haynes, S. N., & Wilson, C. C. (1979). *Behavioral assessment: Recent advances in methods, concepts, and applications*. San Francisco: Jossey-Bass.

Hecht, M. L. (1978a). The conceptualization and measurement of interpersonal communication satisfaction. *Human Communication Research, 4*, 253-264.

Hecht, M. L. (1978b). *Contextual correlates of communication satisfaction.* Paper presented at the meeting of the International Communication Association, Minneapolis.

Hecht, M. L. (1978c). Measures of communication satisfaction. *Human Communication Research, 4*, 350-368.

Hecht, M. L. (1978d). Toward a conceptualization of communication satisfaction. *Quarterly Journal of Speech, 64*, 47-62.

Hecht, M. L. (1981). *A developmental study of satisfying communication*. Unpublished manuscript. University of Southern California, Los Angeles.

Hecht, M. L. (1982). *Persuasive efficacy: An integrative study of the relationships among type of change, strategy, and communication satisfaction.* Unpublished manuscript. University of Southern California, Los Angeles.

Hecht, M. L., & Sereno, K. K. (1982). *Interpersonal communication satisfaction: Relationship to satisfaction with self and other.* Paper presented at the meeting of the Western Speech Communication Association, Denver.

Hefele, T. J., & Hurst, M. W. (1972). Interpersonal skill measurement: Precision, validity, and utility. *The Consulting Psychologist, 3*(3), 62-70.

Heise, D. R. (1977). Social action as the control of affect. *Behavioral Science, 22*, 163-177.

Heise, D. R. (1979). *Understanding events: Affect and the construction of social action*. London: Cambridge University Press.

Helmreich, R., & Stapp, J. (1974). Short forms of the Texas Social Behavior Inventory, an objective measure of self-esteem. *Bulletin of the Psychonomic Society, 4*, 473-475.

Helper, M. M. (1970). Message preferences: An approach to the assessment of interpersonal standards. *Journal of Projective Techniques and Personality Assessment, 34*, 64-70.

Henderson, M., & Furnham, A. (1982). Self-reported and self-attributed scores on personality, social skills, and attitudinal measures as compared between high and low nominated friends and acquaintances. *Psychological Reports, 50*, 88-90.

Henzl, S., Mabry, E. A., & Powell, R. G. (1983). *The effects of cognitive complexity and gender on assessments of communication competence.* Paper presented at the meeting of the International Communication Association, Dallas.

Hersen, M., & Bellack, A. S. (1976). Social skills training for chronic psychiatric patients: Rationale, research findings, and future directions. *Comprehensive Psychiatry, 17*, 559-580.

Hersen, M., & Bellack, A. S. (1977). Assessment of social skills. In A. R. Ciminero, K. S. Calhoun, & H. S. Adams (Eds.), *Handbook of behavioral assessment* (pp. 509-544). New York: John Wiley.

Hersen, M., Bellack, A. S., & Turner, S. M. (1978). Assessment of assertiveness in female psychiatric patients: Motor and autonomic measures. *Journal of Behavior Therapy and Experimental Psychiatry, 9*, 11-16.

Hess, R. D. (1974). Social competence and the educational process. In K. J. Connolly & J. S. Bruner (Eds.), *The growth of competence* (pp. 283-299). New York: Academic Press.

Hewes, D. E. (1978). Interpersonal communication theory and research: A metamethodological overview. In B. D. Ruben (Ed.), *Communication year-book 2* (pp. 155-169). New Brunswick, NJ: Transaction.

Hinkle, S., Corcoran, C. J., & Greene, A. E. (1980). Self-attributions of having exerted influence: The effect of target admission of denial of influence. *Personality and Social Psychology Bulletin, 6,* 447-453.

Hocker-Wilmot, J. L. (1981). *Couple communication training: A model for prac-titioners.* Paper presented at the meeting of the Western Speech Communi-cation Association, San Jose, CA.

Hoffman, M. L. (1977). Empathy: Its development and prosocial implications. In H. E. Howe, Jr. (Ed.), *Nebraska symposium on motivation* (Vol. 25, pp. 169-217). Lincoln: University of Nebraska Press.

Hogan, R. (1969). Development of an empathy scale. *Journal of Consulting and Clinical Psychology, 33,* 307-316.

Holland, J. L., & Baird, L. L. (1968). An interpersonal competency scale. *Educa-tional and Psychological Measurement, 28,* 503-510.

Hollandsworth, J.G., Jr. (1977). Differentiating assertion and aggression: Some behavioral guidelines. *Behavior Therapy, 8,* 347-352.

Honeycutt, J. M., Knapp, M. L., & Powers, W. G. (1983). On knowing others and predicting what they say. *Western Journal of Speech Communication, 47,* 157-174.

Hops, H. (1983). Children's social competence and skill: Current research prac-tices and future directions. *Behavior Therapy, 14,* 3-18.

Horowitz, L. M., French, R.D.S., Gani, M., & Lapid, J. S. (1980). The co-occur-rence of semantically similar interpersonal problems. *Journal of Consulting and Clinical Psychology, 48,* 413-415.

Hosman, L. A., & Tardy, C. H. (1980). Self-disclosure and reciprocity in short- and long-term relationships: An experimental study of evaluational and at-tributional consequences. *Communication Quarterly, 28*(1), 20-30.

Howard, G. S., Maxwell, S. E., Wiener, R. L., Boynton, K. S., & Rooney, W. M. (1980). Is a behavioral measure the best estimate of behavioral parame-ters? Perhaps not. *Applied Psychological Measurement, 4,* 293-311.

Howell, W. S. (1982). *The empathic communicator.* Belmont, CA: Wadsworth.

Hughey, J. D., & Harper, B. (1983). *Instructor responsiveness and outcomes of the basic course.* Paper presented at the meeting of the International Communication Association, Dallas.

Hull, J. G., & Levy, A. S. (1979). The organizational functions of the self: An alternative to the Duval and Wicklund model of self-awareness. *Journal of Personality and Social Psychology, 37,* 756-768.

Hymes, D. (1971). Competence and performance in linguistic theory. In R. Hux-ley & E. Ingram (Eds.), *Language acquisition: Models & Methods* (pp. 3-26). New York: Academic Press.

Hymes, D. (1972a). Introduction. In C. B. Cazden, V. P. John, & D. Hymes (Eds.), *Functions of language in the classroom* (pp. xi-lvii). New York: Teachers College Press.

Hymes, D. (1972b). On communicative competence. In J. B. Pride & J. Holmes
    (Eds.), *Sociolinguistics* (pp. 269-293). New York: Penguin.
Hymes, D. (1979). Sapir, competence, voices. In C. J. Fillmore, D. Kempler,
    & W.S.Y. Wang (Eds.), *Individual differences in language ability and lan-
    guage behavior* (pp. 33-45). New York: Academic Press.
Ickes, D. W., & Barnes, R. D. (1977). The role of sex and self-monitoring in
    unstructured dyadic interactions. *Journal of Personality and Social Psychol-
    ogy, 35*, 315-330.
Ickes, D. W., Patterson, M. L., Rajecki, D. W., & Tanford, S. (1982). Behavioral
    and cognitive consequences of reciprocal versus compensatory responses
    to pre-interaction expectancies. *Social Cognition, 1*, 160-190.
Inkeles, A. (1966). Social structure and the socialization of competence. *Har-
    vard Educational Review, 36*, 265-283.
Ivey, A. E., & Hurst, J. C. (1971). Communication as adaptation. *Journal of
    Communication, 21*, 199-207.
Jackson, H. J., King, N. J., & Heller, V. R. (1981). Social skills assessment and
    training for mentally retarded persons: A review of research. *Australian
    Journal of Developmental Disabilities, 7*, 113-123.
Jacob, T., Kornblith, S., Anderson, C., & Hartz, M. (1978). Role expectation
    and role performance in distressed and normal couples. *Journal of Abnor-
    mal Psychology, 87*, 286-290.
Jacobson, N. S., Waldron, H., & Moore, D. (1980). Toward a behavioral profile
    of marital distress. *Journal of Consulting and Clinical Psychology, 48*, 696-
    703.
Jahoda, M. (1953). The meaning of psychological health. *Social Casework,
    34*(8), 349-354.
Jain, H. C. (1973). Supervisory communication and performance in urban hos-
    pitals. *Journal of Communication, 23*, 103-117.
Jakobovitz, L. A. (1969). A functional approach to the assessment of language
    skills. *Journal of English as a Second Language, 4*(2), 63-76.
Jakobovitz, L. A. (1970). Prolegomena to a theory of communicative compe-
    tence. In R. C. Lugton (Ed.), *Language and the teacher: A series in applied
    linguistics* (Vol. 6 of English as a Second Language: Current Issues).
    Philadelphia: Center for Curriculum Development.
Jandt, F. E., & Armstrong, R. N. (1978). [Review of CAEL project on interper-
    sonal competence]. *Communication Education, 27*, 175-177.
Jansen, D. G., Robb, G. P., & Bonk, E. G. (1973). Peer ratings and self-ratings
    on twelve bipolar items and practicum counselors ranked high and low in
    competence by their peers. *Journal of Counseling Psychology, 20*, 419-424.
Jennings, K. D., Suwalsky, T. D., & Fivel, M. W. (1981). Measuring childrens'
    social competence by coding discrete social acts. *JSAS Catalog of Selected
    Documents in Psychology, 11*(3, Ms. 2291).
Johnson, F. L. (1979). Communicative competence and the Bernstein perspec-
    tive. *Communication Quarterly, 27*(4), 12-19.
Johnson, J. R. (1983). A developmental-biological perspective of human com-
    munication competency. *Western Journal of Speech Communication, 47*,
    193-204.
Johnson, J. R., & Powell, R. G. (1981a). *Theoretical issues and concerns for
    human communication competence.* Paper presented at the meeting of the
    Central States Speech Association, Chicago.

Johnson, J. R., & Powell, R. G. (1981b). *What do we know to teach? Taking theory into the classroom*. Paper presented at the meeting of the Speech Communication Association, Anaheim, CA.

Johnson-George, C., & Swap, W. C. (1982). Measurement of specific interpersonal trust: Construction and validation of a scale to assess trust in a specific other. *Journal of Personality and Social Psychology, 43*, 1306-1317.

Jones, E. E., & Davis, K. (1965). From acts to dispositions: The attribution process in person perception. *Advances in Experimental Social Psychology, 2*, 219-266.

Jones, E. E., & McGillis, D. (1976). Correspondent inferences and the attribution cube: A comparative reappraisal. In J. H. Harvey, W. J. Ickes, & R. F. Kidd (Eds.), *New directions in attribution research* (Vol. 1). Hillsdale, NJ: Lawrence Erlbaum.

Jones, F. H. (1977). The Rochester adaptive behavior inventory: A parallel series of instruments for assessing social competence during early and middle childhood and adolescence. In J. S. Strauss, H. M. Babigian, & M. Roff (Eds.), *The origins and course of psychopathology*. New York: Plenum.

Jones, T. S., & Brunner, C. C. (1981). *Communicator style and its relationship to interpersonal communication competence: An exploratory investigation*. Paper presented at the meeting of the Speech Communication Association, Anaheim, CA.

Kagan, J. (1979). The form of early development: Continuity and discontinuity in emergent competencies. *Archives of General Psychiatry, 36*, 1047-1054.

Kaufer, D. S. (1979). The competence/performance distinction in linguistic theory. *Philosophy of the Social Sciences, 9*, 257-275.

Keefe, T. (1976). Empathy: The critical skill. *Social Work, 21*, 10-14.

Keenan, E. O. (1974). Conversational competence in children. *Journal of Child Language, 1*, 163-183.

Kelley, H. H. (1950). The warm-cold variable in first impressions of persons. *Journal of Personality, 18*, 431-439.

Kelley, H. H. (1967). Attribution theory in social psychology. *Nebraska Symposium on Motivation, 15*, 192-238.

Kelley, H. H., & Michela, J. L. (1980). Attribution theory and research. *Annual Review of Psychology, 31*, 457-501.

Kelly, C. W., & Chase, L. J. (1978). *The California Interpersonal Competence Questionnaire: I. An exploratory search for factor structure*. Paper presented at the meeting of the International Communication Association, Chicago.

Kelly, C. W., Chase, L. J., & Wiemann, J. M. (1979). *Interpersonal competence: Conceptualization, measurement, and future considerations*. Paper presented at the meeting of the Speech Communication Association, San Antonio.

Kelly, E. M. (1939). Social competence of public school children. *Binet Review, 6*, 9-26.

Kelly, J. A. (1982). *Social skills training: A practical guide for interventions*. New York: Springer.

Kelly, J. A., Urey, J. R., & Patterson, J. T. (1980). Improving heterosocial conversational skills of male psychiatric patients through a small group training procedure. *Behavior Therapy, 11*, 179-188.

Kelly, R. L., Osborne, W. J., & Hendrick, C. (1974). Role-taking and role-playing in human communication. *Human Communication Research, 1*, 62-74.

Kent, G. G., Davis, J. D., & Shapiro, D. A. (1981). Effect of mutual acquaintance on the construction of conversation. *Journal of Experimental Social Psychology, 17,* 197-209.

Kern, J. M. (1982). The comparative external and concurrent validity of three role-plays for assessing heterosocial performance. *Behavior Therapy, 13,* 666-680.

Kern, J. M., Miller, C., & Eggers, J. (1983). Enhancing the validity of role-play tests: A comparison of three role-play methodologies. *Behavior Therapy, 14,* 482-492.

Kieren, D., & Tallman, I. (1972). Spousal adaptability: An assessment of marital competence. *Journal of Marriage and the Family, 34,* 247-255.

Kiesler, D. J. (1967). A scale for the rating of congruence. In C. R. Rogers (Ed.), *The therapeutic relationship and its impact* (pp. 581-584). Madison: University of Wisconsin Press.

King, L. W., Liberman, R. P., Roberts, J., & Bryan, E. (1977). Personal effectiveness: A structured therapy for improving social and emotional skills. *Behavioral Analysis and Modification, 2,* 82-91.

Kirkpatrick, T. G. (1977). *Conceptualizing and measuring relationship satisfaction.* Paper presented at the meeting of the Western Speech Communication Association, Phoenix.

Knapp, M. L. (1978). *Social intercourse: From greeting to goodbye.* Boston, MA: Allyn & Bacon.

Knapp, M. L., Ellis, D. G., & Williams, B. A. (1980). Perceptions of communication behavior associated with relationship terms. *Communication Monographs, 47,* 262-278.

Koch, D. A., Chandler, M. J., Harder, D. W., & Paget, K. F. (1982). Parental defense style and child competence: A match-mismatch hypothesis. *Journal of Applied Developmental Psychology, 3,* 11-21.

Koffman, A., Getter, H., & Chinsky, J. M. (1978). Social skills and the effect of a group psychotherapy analogue. *Small Group Behavior, 9,* 92-101.

Kohn, M. (1977). *Social competence, symptoms and underachievement in childhood: A longitudinal perspective.* Silver Spring, MD: V. H. Winston.

Kohn, M., & Rosman, B. L. (1972). A social competence scale and symptom checklist for the preschool child: Factor dimensions, their cross-instrument generality, and longitudinal persistence. *Developmental Psychology, 6,* 430-444.

Konsky, C. W., & Murdock, J. I. (1980). Interpersonal communication. In J. F. Cragan & D. W. Wright (Eds.), *Introduction to speech communication* (pp. 83-113). Prospect Heights, IL: Waveland Press.

Koren, P., Carlton, K., & Shaw, D. (1980). Marital conflict: Relations among behaviors, outcomes, and distress. *Journal of Consulting and Clinical Psychology, 48,* 460-468.

Krauss, R. M., & Glucksberg, S. (1969). The development of communication competence as a function of age. *Child Development, 40,* 255-266.

Krembs, P. (1980). *Diagnosing and determining communication competencies: A theoretical model.* Paper presented at the meeting of the Speech Communication Association, New York.

Kupke, T. E., Calhoun, K. S., & Hobbs, S. A. (1979). Selection of heterosocial skills: II. Experimental validity. *Behavior Therapy, 10,* 336-346.

Kupke, T. E., Hobbs, S. A., & Cheney, T. H. (1979). Selection of heterosocial skills: I. Criterion-related validity. *Behavior Therapy, 10,* 327-335.

Ladd, G. W., & Mize, J. (1983). A cognitive-social learning model of social-skill training. *Psychological Review, 90,* 127-157.

LaFrance, M. (1974). Nonverbal cues to conversational turn taking between black speakers. *Proceedings of the Division of Personality and Social Psychology—1974.* Washington, DC: American Psychological Association.

LaFromboise, T. D., & Rowe, W. (1983). Skills training for bicultural competence: Rationale and application. *Journal of Counseling Psychology, 30,* 589-595.

Lamont, D. J. (1983). A three dimensional test for White's effectance motive. *Journal of Personality Assessment, 47,* 91-99.

Lane, S. D. (1981). *Empathy and assertive communication.* Paper presented at the meeting of the Western Speech Communication Association, San Jose, CA.

Lane, S. D. (1983). Compliance, satisfaction, and physician-patient communication. In R. N. Bostrom (Ed.), *Communication yearbook 7* (pp. 772-799). Beverly Hills: Sage.

Lange, J. I. (1980). *Rhetorical sensitivity and understanding.* Paper presented at the meeting of the Western Speech Communication Association, Portland, OR.

Langer, E. J. (1978). Rethinking the role of thought in social interaction. In J. H. Harvey, W. J. Ickes, and R. F. Kidd (Eds.), *New directions in attribution research* (Vol. 2, pp. 35-58). Hillsdale, NJ: Erlbaum.

Langer, E. J. (1979). The illusion of incompetence. In L. C. Perlmuter & R. A. Monty (Eds.), *Choice and perceived control* (pp. 301-313). Hillsdale, NJ: Erlbaum.

Langer, E. J., & Imber, L. G. (1979). When practice makes imperfect: Debilitating effects of overlearning. *Journal of Personality and Social Psychology, 37,* 2014-2024.

Lanyon, R. I. (1967). Measurement of social competence in college males. *Journal of Consulting Psychology, 31,* 495-498.

Larson, C. E. (1967). Interaction patterns and communication effectiveness in the marital context: A factor analytic study. *Journal of Communication, 17,* 342-353.

Larson, C. E. (1978). Problems in assessing functional communication. *Communication Education, 27,* 304-309.

Larson, C. E., Backlund, P., Redmond, M., & Barbour, A. (1978). *Assessing functional communication.* Falls Church, VA: Speech Communication Association.

Larzelere, R. E., & Huston, T. L. (1980). The dyadic trust scale: Toward understanding interpersonal trust in close relationships. *Journal of Marriage and the Family, 42,* 595-604.

Lavin, P. F., & Kupke, T. E. (1980). Psychometric evaluation of the situation test of heterosocial skill. *Journal of Behavioral Assessment, 2*(2), 111-121.

Lawson, J. S., Marshall, W. L., & McGrath, P. (1979). The social self-esteem inventory. *Educational and Psychological Measurement, 39,* 803-811.

Lazarus, A. A. (1971). *Behavior therapy and beyond.* New York: McGraw-Hill.

Leader, G. C. (1973). Interpersonally skillful bank officers view their behavior. *Journal of Applied Behavior Analysis, 9,* 484-497.

Leah, J. A., Law, H. G., & Snyder, C.W., Jr. (1979). The structure of self-reported difficulty in assertiveness: An application of three-mode common factor analysis. *Multivariate Behavioral Research, 14,* 443-462.

Leary, M. R. (1983a). A brief version of the fear of negative evaluation scale. *Personality and Social Psychology Bulletin, 9,* 371-375.

Leary, M. R. (1983b). Social anxiousness: The construct and its measurement. *Journal of Personality Assessment, 47,* 66-75.

Lerner, B. (1981). The minimum competence testing movement: Social, scientific, and legal implications. *American Psychologist, 36,* 1057-1066.

Levenson, R. W., & Gottman, J. M. (1978). Toward the assessment of social competence. *Journal of Consulting and Clinical Psychology, 46,* 453-462.

Liberman, R. P. (1982). Assessment of social skills. *Schizophrenia Bulletin, 8,* 62-83.

Libet, J. M., & Lewinsohn, P. M. (1973). Concept of social skill with special reference to the behavior of depressed persons. *Journal of Consulting and Clinical Psychology, 40,* 304-312.

Liska, J. R. (1978). Situational and topical variations in credibility criteria. *Communication Monographs, 45,* 85-92.

Loacker, S. G. (1981). *Alverno College's program in developing and assessing oral communication skills.* Paper presented at the meeting of the Speech Communication Association, Anaheim, CA.

Lofland, J. (1976). *Doing social life: The qualitative study of human interaction in natural settings.* New York: John Wiley.

Lorr, M., & More, W. W. (1980). Four dimensions of assertiveness. *Multivariate Behavioral Research, 15,* 127-138.

Lowe, M. R. (1978). *The validity of a measure of social performance in an inpatient population.* Unpublished manuscript. Washington University, St. Louis.

Lowe, M. R., & Cautela, J. R. (1978). A self-report measure of social skill. *Behavior Therapy, 9,* 535-544.

Lustig, M. W., & King, S. W. (1980). The effect of communication apprehension and situation on communication strategy choices. *Human Communication Research, 7,* 74-82.

MacDonald, M. L., & Cohen, J. (1981). Trees in the forest: Some components of social skills. *Journal of Clinical Psychology, 37,* 342-347.

Macklin, T. J., & Rossiter, C. M. (1976). Interpersonal communication and self-actualization. *Communication Quarterly, 24*(4), 45-50.

Magnusson, D. (1971). An analysis of situational dimensions. *Perceptual and Motor Skills, 32,* 851-867.

Mahaney, M. M., & Kern, J. M. (1983). Variations in role-play tests of heterosocial performance. *Journal of Consulting and Clinical Psychology, 51,* 151-152.

Malott, R., Tillema, M., & Glenn, S. (n.d.). *Behavior analysis and behavior modification: An introduction.* Bridgewater, NJ: F. Fournes & Associates.

Margolin, G., & Wampold, B. E. (1981). Sequential analysis of conflict and accord in distressed and nondistressed marital partners. *Journal of Consulting and Clinical Psychology, 49,* 554-567.

Marsh, D. T. (1982). The development of interpersonal problem-solving among elementary school children. *Journal of Genetic Psychology, 140,* 107-118.

Marsh, D. T., Serafica, F. C., & Barenboim, C. (1981). Interrelationships among perspective taking, interpersonal problem solving, and interpersonal functioning. *Journal of Genetic Psychology, 138,* 37-48.

Martinez-Diaz, J. A., & Edelstein, B. A. (1979). Multivariate effects of demand characteristics on the analogue assessment of heterosocial competence. *Journal of Applied Behavior Analysis, 12*, 679-689.

Martinez-Diaz, J. A., & Edelstein, B. A. (1980). Heterosocial competence: Predictive and construct validity. *Behavior Modification, 4*, 115-129.

Matarazzo, J. D., & Wiens, A. N. (1977). Speech behavior as an objective correlate of empathy and outcome in interview and psychotherapy research: A review with implications for behavior modification. *Behavior Modification, 1*, 453-480.

Mathews, P. H. (1979). *Generative grammar and linguistic competence.* London: Allen & Unwin.

Matson, J. L., Rotatori, A. F., & Helsel, W. J. (1983). Development of a rating scale to measure social skills in children: The Matson Evaluation of Social Skills with Youngers (MESSY). *Behavior Research and Therapy, 21*, 335-340.

Mayo, C., & La France, M. (1978). On the acquisition of nonverbal communication: A review. *Merrill-Palmer Quarterly, 24*, 213-228.

McArthur, R. L. (1978). *The relationships among interpersonal attraction, relationship satisfaction and conformity: An experimental study.* Unpublished master's thesis. California State University, Fullerton.

McCarthy, T. A. (1973). A theory of communicative competence. *Philosophy of the Social Sciences, 3*, 135-156.

McConkey, R., & Walsh, J. (1982). An index of social competence for use in determining the service needs of mentally handicapped adults. *Journal of Mental Deficiency Research, 26*, 47-61.

McCroskey, J. C. (1977). Oral communication apprehension: A summary of recent theory and research. *Human Communication Research, 4*, 78-96.

McCroskey, J. C. (1980). On communication competence and communication apprehension: A response to Page. *Communication Education, 29*, 109-111.

McCroskey, J. C. (1981). *Oral communication apprehension: Reconceptualization and a new look at measurement.* Paper presented at the meeting of the Central States Speech Association, Chicago.

McCroskey, J. C. (1982a). Oral communication apprehension: A reconceptualization. In M. Burgoon (Ed.), *Communication yearbook 6* (pp. 136-170). Beverly Hills: Sage.

McCroskey, J. C. (1982b). Communication competence and performance: A research and pedagogical perspective. *Communication Education, 31*, 1-8.

McCroskey, J. C., & McCain, T. A. (1974). The measurement of interpersonal attraction. *Speech Monographs, 41*, 261-266.

McFall, R. M. (1982). A review and reformulation of the concept of social skills. *Behavioral Assessment, 4*, 1-33.

McFall, R. M., & Lillesand, D. B. (1971). Behavior rehearsal with modeling and coaching in assertion training. *Journal of Abnormal Psychology, 77*, 313-323.

McGuire, R. R. (1977). Speech acts, communicative competence and the paradox of authority. *Philosophy and Rhetoric, 10*, 30-45.

McLaughlin, M. L., & Cody, M. J. (1982). Awkward silences: Behavioral antecedents and consequences of the conversational lapse. *Human Communication Research, 8*, 299-316.

McLaughlin, M. L., Cody, M. J., & Robey, C. S. (1980). Situational influences on the selection of strategies to resist compliance-gaining attempts. *Human Communication Research, 7,* 14-36.

McNamara, J. R., & Blumer, C. A. (1982). Role-playing to assess social competence: Ecological validity considerations. *Behavior Modification, 6,* 519-549.

Mead, G. H. (1974). *Mind, self, and society.* (C. W. Morris Ed.). Chicago: University of Chicago Press. (Original work published 1934)

Mead, N. A. (1980a). *Assessing speaking skills: Issues of feasibility, reliability, validity and bias.* Paper presented at the meeting of the Speech Communication Association, New York.

Mead, N. A. (1980b). *The Massachusetts Basic Skills Assessment of Listening and Speaking.* Paper presented at the meeting of the Speech Communication Association, New York.

Mehrabian, A. (1980). *Basic dimensions for a general psychological theory.* Cambridge, MA: Oelgeschlager, Gunn & Hain.

Mehrabian, A., & Epstein, N. (1972). A measure of emotional empathy. *Journal of Personality, 40,* 525-543.

Mehrabian, A., & Ksionzky, S. (1972). Categories of social behavior. In D. C. Speer (Ed.), *Nonverbal communication* (pp. 49-60). Beverly Hills: Sage.

Mehrabian, A., & Reed, H. (1968). Some determinants of communication accuracy. *Psychological Bulletin, 70,* 365-381.

Mehrabian, A., & Russell, J. A. (1974). *An approach to environmental psychology.* Cambridge, MA: MIT Press.

Meichenbaum, D., Butler, L., & Gruson, L. (1981). Toward a conceptual model of social competence. In J. D. Wine & M. D. Smye (Eds.), *Social competence* (pp. 36-60). New York: Guilford Press.

Metcalfe, B. A. (1981). Model of psychological processes in social interaction. *Perceptual and Motor Skills, 53,* 254.

Mettetal, G., & Gottman, J. M. (1980). *Affective responsiveness in spouses: Investigating the relationship between communication behavior and marital satisfaction.* Paper presented at the meeting of the Speech Communication Association, New York.

Miller, G. R., Boster, F., Roloff, M., & Seibold, D. (1977). Compliance-gaining message strategies: A typology and some findings concerning effects of situational differences. *Communication Monographs, 44,* 37-57.

Miller, G. R., & Steinberg, M. (1975). *Between people: A new analysis of interpersonal communication.* Chicago: Science Research Associates.

Miller, G. R., & Sunnafrank, M. J. (1982). All is for one but one is not for all: A conceptual perspective of interpersonal communication. In F. E. X. Dance (Ed.), *Human communication theory: Comparative essays* (pp. 220-242). New York: Harper & Row.

Minkin, N., Braukman, C. J., Minkin, B. L., Timbers, G. D., Timbers, B. J., Fixen, D. L., Phillips, E. L., & Wolf, M. M. (1976). The social validation and training of conversational skills. *Journal of Applied Behavior Analysis, 9,* 127-139.

Mischel, W. (1973). Toward a cognitive social learning reconceptualization of personality. *Psychological Review, 80,* 252-283.

Misgeld, D. (1977). Discourse and conversation: The theory of communicative competence and hermeneutics in the light of the debate between Habermas and Gademer. *Cultural Hermeneutics, 4,* 321-344.

Mohrmann, G. P. (1972). The civile conversation: Communication in the Renaissance. *Speech Monographs, 39,* 193-204.

Moment, D., & Zaleznik, A. (1963). *Role development and interpersonal competence.* Cambridge, MA: Harvard University Press.

Monge, P. R., Bachman, S. G., Dillard, J. P., & Eisenberg, E. M. (1982). Communicator competence in the workplace: Model testing and scale development. In M. Burgoon (Ed.), *Communication yearbook 5* (pp. 505-528). New Brunswick, NJ: Transaction.

Monroe, M. D., Conger, J. C., Conger, A. J., & Moison-Thomas, P. C. (1982). Comparability of methods of observation for global ratings of heterosexual social skill and anxiety: A generalizability study. *Journal of Behavioral Assessment, 4(1),* 87-102.

Montgomery, B., & Norton, R. (1980). *Grounding for a research program investigating marital communication.* Paper presented at the meeting of the Speech Communication Association, New York.

Monti, P. N., Corriveau, D. P., & Curran, J. P. (1982). Social skills training for psychiatric patients: Treatment and outcome. In J. P. Curran & P. M. Monti (Eds.), *Social skills training.* (pp. 185-223). New York: Guilford Press.

Moore, B. S., Sherrod, D. R., Liu, T. J., & Underwood, B. (1979). The dispositional shift in attribution over time. *Journal of Experimental Social Psychology, 15,* 553-569.

Moore, M. R., & Levison, G. K. (1977). *Communication competencies: Reality or fantasy?* Paper presented at the Eastern Communication Association Conference, New York.

Moos, R. H., & Tsu, V. D. (1976). Human competence and coping: An overview. In R. H. Moos (Ed.), *Human adaptation: Coping with life crises* (pp. 3-16). Lexington, MA: D. C. Heath.

Morganstern, B. F., & Wheeless, L. R. (1980). *The relationship of nonverbal anxiety, status/self-control and affective behaviors to relational anxiety.* Paper presented at the meeting of the Speech Communication Association, New York.

Morley, S., Shepherd, G., & Spence, S. (1983). Cognitive approaches to social skills training. In S. Spence & G. Shepherd (Eds.), *Developments in social skills training* (pp. 305-334). New York: Academic Press.

Morrison, R. L., & Bellack, A. S. (1981). The role of social perception in social skill. *Behavior Therapy, 12,* 69-79.

Morse, B. W., & Phelps, L. A. (Eds.), (1980). *Interpersonal communication: A relational perspective.* Minneapolis: Burgess.

Muhar, I. S. (1974). Intercorrelations amongst six measures of rigidity. *Indian Journal of Psychology, 49,* 59-64.

Mungas, D. M., & Walters, H. A. (1979). Pretesting effects in the evaluation of social skills training. *Journal of Consulting and Clinical Psychology, 47,* 216-218,

Myers, H. F. (1982). Coping styles and competence as mediators of self-reported responses to stress. *Psychological Reports, 50,* 303-313.

Naisbitt, J. (1982). *Megatrends: Ten new directions transforming our lives.* New York: Warner Books.

Navran, L. (1967). Communication and adjustment in marriage. *Family Process, 6,* 173-184.

Neal, W. P., & Hughey, J. D. (1979). *Personality correlates of communication sensitivity.* Paper presented at the meeting of the Speech Communication Association Convention, San Antonio.

Neer, M. R., & Hudson, D. D. (1981). *Role behavior of the apprehensive communicator: A preliminary scale development.* Paper presented at the meeting of the Speech Communication Association Convention, Anaheim, CA.

Nesbett, E. B. (1979). Rathus Assertiveness Schedule and College Self-Expression Scale scores as predictors of assertive behavior. *Psychological Reports, 45,* 855-861.

Nietzel, M. T., & Bernstein, D. A. (1976). Effects of instructionally mediated demand on the behavioral assessment of assertiveness. *Journal of Consulting and Clinical Psychology, 44,* 500.

Norton, R. W., Murray, P., & Arnston, P. (1982). *Communicative links to health: Dramatic style covariates of health perceptions.* Paper presented at the meeting of the International Communication Association, Boston.

Norton, R. W., & Pettegrew, L. S. (1979). Attentiveness as a style of communication: A structural analysis. *Communication Monographs, 46,* 13-26.

Novotny, H. R. Acquisition of social competency skills. (1977). In G. G. Harris (Ed.), *The group treatment of human problems: A social learning approach* (pp. 209-220). New York: Grune & Stratton.

Numbers, J. S., & Chapman, L. J. (1982). Social deficits in hypothetically psychosis-prone college women. *Journal of Abnormal Psychology, 91,* 255-260.

Ogbu, J. U. (1981). Origins of human competence: A cultural-ecological perspective. *Child Development, 52,* 413-429.

O'Keefe, B. J., & Delia, J. G. (1979). Construct comprehensiveness and cognitive complexity as predictors of the number and strategic adaptation of arguments and appeals in a persuasive message. *Communication Monographs, 46,* 231-240.

O'Keefe, D. J., & Sypher, H. E. (1981). Cognitive complexity measures and the relationship of cognitive complexity to communication. *Human Communication Research, 8,* 72-92.

Ollendick, T. H. (1981). Assessment of social interaction skills in school children. *Behavioral Counseling Quarterly, 1,* 227-243.

Olson, J. M., & Partington, J. T. (1977). An integrative analysis of two cognitive models of interpersonal effectiveness. *British Journal of Social and Clinical Psychology, 16,* 13-14.

O'Malley, J. M. (1977). Research perspective on social competence. *Merrill-Palmer Quarterly, 23,* 29-44.

O'Malley, S. S., Suh, C. H., & Strupp, H. H. (1983). The Vanderbilt psychotherapy process scale: A report on the scale development and a process-outcome study. *Journal of Consulting and Clinical Psychology, 51,* 581-586.

Orlofsky, J. L. (1976). Intimacy status: Relationship to interpersonal perception. *Journal of Youth and Adolescence, 5,* 73-88.

Osgood, C. E. (1970). Speculation on the structure of interpersonal intentions. *Behavioral Science, 15,* 237-254.

Osgood, C. E., May, W. H., & Miron, S. (1975). *Cross-cultural universals of affective meaning.* Champaign: University of Illinois Press.

Osgood, C. E., Suci, G. C., & Tannenbaum, P. H. (1975). *The measurement of meaning.* Champaign: University of Illinois Press.

Otness, H. R. (1941). Educating for social competence. *Training School Bulletin, 38(2),* 21-32.

Pargament, K. I., Sullivan, M. S., Tyler, F. B., & Steele, R. E. (1982). Patterns of attribution of control and individual psychological competence. *Psychological Reports, 51,* 1243-1252.

Parks, M. R. (1977a). Anomia and close friendship communication networks. *Human Communication Research, 4,* 48-57.

Parks, M. R. (1977b). *Issues in the explication of communication competence.* Paper presented at the meeting of the Western Speech Communication Association, Phoenix.

Patterson, G. R., Hops, H., & Weiss, R. L. (1975). Interpersonal skills training for couples in early stages of conflict. *Journal of Marriage and the Family, 37,* 295-302.

Paul, G. L. (1969). Chronic mental patients: Current status—future directions. *Psychological Bulletin, 71,* 81-94.

Paul, G. L. (1981). Social competence and the institutionalized mental patient. In J. D. Wine & M. D. Smye (Eds.), *Social competence* (pp. 232-260). New York: Guilford Press.

Paulston, C. B. (1974). Linguistic and communicative competence. *TESOL Quarterly, 8,* 347-362.

Pavitt, C. (1982). Preliminaries to a theory of communication: A system for the cognitive representation of person and object based information. In M. Burgoon (Ed.), *Communication yearbook 5* (pp. 211-232). New Brunswick, NJ: Transaction.

Pavitt, C. (1983). *Implicit theories of communicative competence: 3.* Paper presented at the meeting of the International Communication Association, Dallas.

Pavitt, C., & Haight, L. (1982). *Implicit theories of communicative competence: 2. The semantics of social behavior.* Paper presented at the meeting of the Speech Communication Association, Louisville.

Pearce, W. B. (1976). An overview of communication and interpersonal relationships. In R. L. Applbaum & R. P. Hart (Eds.), *Modcom: Modules in speech communication.* Chicago: Science Research Associates.

Pearce, W. B., & Cronen, V. E. (1979). *Toward a logic of interactional rules.* Paper presented at the Conference on Human Communication from an Interactional View, Asilomar, CA.

Pearce, W. B., & Cronen, V. E. (1980). *Communication, action, and meaning.* New York: Praeger.

Pearlman, C. (1982). The measurement of effectance motivation. *Educational and Psychological Measurement, 42,* 49-56.

Pearson, J. C. (1981). *The relationship between rhetorical sensitivity and self-disclosure.* Paper presented at the meeting of the Western Speech Communication Association, San Jose, CA.

Perri, M. G., Kerzner, A. B., & Tayler, A. H. (1981). The assessment of heterosocial adequacy: A cross-validation and replication. *Behavioral Counseling Quarterly, 1,* 317-319.

Perri, M. G., & Richards, C. S. (1979). Assessment of heterosocial skills in male college students. *Behavior Modification, 3,* 337-354.

Perri, M. G., Richards, C. S., & Goodrich, J. D. (1978). Heterosocial adequacy test (HAT): A behavioral role-playing test for the assessment of heterosocial skills in male college students. *JSAS Catalog of Selected Documents in Psychology, 8*(15, Ms. 1650).

Peterson, J., Fischetti, M., Curran, J. P., & Arland, S. (1981). Sense of timing: A skill deficit in heterosocially anxious women. *Behavior Therapy, 12,* 195-201.

Phelps, L. A., & Snavely, W. B. (1979). *Development of conceptual and operational definitions of interpersonal communication competencies.* Paper presented at the Midwest Basic Course Director's Conference, Ames, IA.

Phelps, L. A., & Snavely, W. B. (1980). *Toward the measurement of interpersonal communication competence.* Paper presented at the meeting of the Western Speech Communication Association, Portland, OR.

Phillips, D. C. (1949). Factors of effective and ineffective conversation. *Speech Monographs, 16,* 203-213.

Phillips, L., & Zigler, E. (1961). Social competence: The action-thought parameter and vicariousness in normal and pathological behaviors. *Journal of Abnormal and Social Psychology, 63,* 137-146.

Piaget, J. (1955). *The language and thought of the child.* (M. Gabain, Trans.). New York: New American Library.

Pierce, R. M., & Zarle, T. H. (1972). Differential referral to significant others as a function of interpersonal effectiveness. *Journal of Clinical Psychology, 28,* 230-232.

Pitcher, S. W., & Meikle, S. (1980). The topography of assertive behavior in positive and negative situations. *Behavior Therapy, 11,* 532-547.

Planalp, S. (1983). *A test of the impact of three levels of relational knowledge on memory for relational implications of messages.* Paper presented at the meeting of the International Communication Association, Dallas.

Platt, J. J., & Spivack, G. (1972). Social competence and effective problem-solving thinking in psychiatric patients. *Journal of Clinical Psychology, 28,* 3-5.

Pope, B. Nudler, S., Vonkorff, M. R., & McGhee, J. P. (1974). The experienced professional interviewer versus the complete novice. *Journal of Consulting and Clinical Psychology, 42,* 680-690.

Powell, R. G. (1979). *Differentiating among social situations: An investigation of the role of the situational element in communication competency.* Unpublished doctoral dissertation. University of Nebraska, Lincoln.

Powers, W. G., & Lowry, D. N. (1983). Basic communication fidelity: an initial investigation. Unpublished manuscript. North Texas State University, Denton.

Preston, M. G., Peltz, W. L., Hartshorne, E., & Froscher, H. B. (1952). Impressions of personality as a function of marital conflict. *Journal of Abnormal and Social Psychology, 47,* 326-336.

Price, R. H. (1974). The taxonomic classification of behaviors and situations and the problem of behavior-environment congruence. *Human Relations, 27,* 567-585.

Price, R. H., & Blashfield, R. K. (1975). Explorations in the taxonomy of behavior settings: Analysis of dimensions and classifications of settings. *American Journal of Community Psychology, 3,* 335-351.

Price, R. H., & Bouffard, D. L. (1974). Behavioral appropriateness and situational constraint as dimensions of social behavior. *Journal of Personality and Social Psychology, 30,* 579-586.

Priestly, P., McGuire, J., Flegg, D., Hemsley, V., & Welham, D. (1978). *Social skills and personal problem-solving.* London: Tavistock.

Prisbell, M. (1979). *Feeling good: Conceptualization and measurement.* Paper presented at the meeting of the Western Speech Communication Association, Los Angeles.

Prisbell, M. (1980). *Criterial attributes of interpersonal solidarity.* Paper presented at the meeting of the Western Speech Communication Association, Portland, OR.

Prisbell, M. (1981). *The relationships among uncertainty level, safety, self-disclosure, and interpersonal solidarity.* Paper presented at the meeting of the Western Speech Communication Association, San Jose, CA.

Prisbell, M. (1982). Heterosocial communicative behavior and communication apprehension. *Communication Quarterly, 30*(3) 251-257.

Prutting, C. A. (1982). Pragmatics as social competence. *Journal of Speech and Hearing Disorders, 47,* 123-134.

Pylyshyn, A. W. (1973). The role of competence theories in cognitive psychology. *Journal of Psycholinguistic Research, 2,* 21-50.

Quintilian. (1903). *Quintilian's institutes of oratory; or education of an orator.* (J. S. Bell, trans.). London: George Bell and Sons.

Rae-Grant, Q.A.F., Gladwin, T., & Bower, E. M. (1966). Mental health, social competence and the war on poverty. *American Journal of Orthopsychiatry, 36,* 652-664.

Rarick, D. L., Soldow, G. F., & Geizer, R. S. (1976). Self-monitoring as a mediator of conformity. *Central States Speech Journal, 27,* 267-271.

Rasmussen, C., Day, C. L., & Collie, S. J. (1981). *Towards interpersonal competence in relationships: A workshop on instruction and evaluation of skills through oral interpretation of literature.* Paper presented at the meeting of the Illinois Speech and Theatre Association, St. Louis.

Rathjen, D. P. (1980). An overview of social competence. In D. P. Rathjen & J. P. Foreyt (Eds.), *Social competence: Interventions for children and adults* (pp. 1-23). Elmsford, NY: Pergamon.

Rathjen, D. P., Rathjen, E. D., & Hiniker, A. (1978). A cognitive analysis of social performance: Implications for assessment and treatment. In J. P. Foreyt, & D. P. Rathjen (Eds.), *Cognitive behavior therapy: Research and application* (pp. 33-76). New York: Plenum.

Rathus, S. A. (1973). A 30-item schedule for assessing assertive behavior. *Behavior Therapy, 4,* 398-406.

Reardon, K. K. (1982). Conversational deviance: A structural model. *Human Communication Research, 9,* 59-74.

Reardon, R. C., Hersen, M., Bellack, A. S., & Foley, J. M. (1979). Measuring social skill in grade school boys. *Journal of Behavioral Assessment, 1*(1), 87-105.

Redmond, M. (1983). Communication competence and varying communication experiences. *Iowa Journal of Speech Communication, 15,* 1-9.

Rehm, L. P., & Marston, A. R. (1968). Reduction of social anxiety through modification of self-reinforcement: An instigation therapy technique. *Journal of Consulting and Clinical Psychology, 32,* 565-574.

Remer, R. (1978). Three modes of stimulus presentation in a simulation test of interpersonal communication competence. *Journal of Educational Measurement, 15,* 125-130.

Reynolds, W. M. (1981). Measurement of personal competence of mentally retarded individuals. *American Journal of Mental Deficiency, 85,* 368-376.

Reynolds, W. M., & Reynolds, S. (1979). Prevalence of speech and hearing impairment of noninstitutionalized mentally retarded adults. *American Journal of Mental Deficiency, 84,* 62-66.

Ribeau, S. A., & Hecht, M. L. (1979). *Intracultural differences in the communication satisfaction of domestic cultural groups.* Paper presented at the meeting of the Speech Communication Association, San Antonio.

Riccillo, S. C. (1983). Modes of speech as a developmental hierarchy: A descriptive study. *Western Journal of Speech Communication, 47,* 1-11.

Richards, I. A. (1965). *The philosophy of rhetoric.* Oxford: Oxford University Press.

Richardson, F. C., & Tasto, D. L. (1976). Development and factor analysis of a social anxiety inventory. *Behavior Therapy, 7,* 453-462.

Richmond, V. P. (1978). The relationship between trait and state communication apprehension and interpersonal perceptions during acquaintance stages. *Human Communication Research, 4,* 338-349.

Ridley, C. A., & Vaughn, S. R. (1982). Interpersonal problem solving: An intervention program for preschool children. *Journal of Applied Developmental Psychology, 3,* 177-190.

Ring, K., Braginksy, D., & Braginsky, B. (1966). Performance styles in interpersonal relations: A typology. *Psychological Reports, 18,* 203-220.

Ring, K., Braginsky, D., Levine, L., & Braginsky, B. (1967). Performance styles in interpersonal behavior: An experimental validation of a typology. *Journal of Experimental Social Psychology, 3,* 140-159.

Ring, K., & Wallston, K. (1968). A test to measure performance styles in interpersonal relations. *Psychological Reports, 22,* 147-154.

Ritter, E. M. (1979). Social perspective-taking ability, cognitive complexity and listener-adapted communication in early and late adolescence. *Communication Monographs, 46,* 40-51.

Rivers, W. (1973). From linguistic competence to communicative competence. *TESOL Quarterly, 7,* 25-34.

Robinson, E. A., & Price, M. G. (1980). Pleasurable behavior in marital interaction: An observational study. *Journal of Consulting and Clinical Psychology, 48,* 117-118.

Rodnick, R., & Wood, B. (1972). The communication strategies of children. *Speech Teacher, 22,* 114-124.

Rogers, C. R. (Ed.). (1967). *The therapeutic relationship and its impact.* Madison: University of Wisconsin Press.

Roloff, M. E. (1980). Self-awareness and the persuasion process: Do we really *know* what we're doing? In M. E. Roloff and G. R. Miller (Eds.), *Persuasion: New directions in theory and research* (pp. 29-66). Beverly Hills: Sage.

Roloff, M. E., & Barnicott, E. F. (1978). The situational use of pro- and anti-social compliance-gaining strategies by high and low Machiavellians. In B. D. Ruben (Ed.), *Communication yearbook 2* (pp. 193-205). New Brunswick, NJ: Transaction.

Romano, J. M., & Bellack, A. S. (1980). Social validation of a component model of assertive behavior. *Journal of Consulting and Clinical Psychology, 48,* 478-490.

Rose, J., & Tyron, W. W. (1979). Judgments of assertive behavior as a function of speech loudness, latency, content, gestures, inflection, and sex. *Behavior Modification, 3,* 112-123.

Rose, S. D. (1975). In pursuit of social competence. *Social Work, 20,* 33-39.

Rose, S. D., Cayner, J. J., & Edelson, J. L. (1977). Measuring interpersonal competence. *Social Work, 22,* 125-129.

Rosen, B., Klein, D. F., Levenstein, S., & Shahinian, S. P. (1969). Social competence and the posthospital outcome among schizophrenic and nonschizophrenic psychiatric patients. *Journal of Abnormal Psychology, 74,* 401-404.

Rosen, J. (1967). Multiple-regression analysis of counselor characteristics and competencies. *Psychological Reports, 20,* 1003-1008.

Ross, R. S., & Ross, M. G. (1982). *Relating and interacting.* Englewood Cliffs, NJ: Prentice-Hall.

Rothenberg, B. B. (1970). Children's social sensitivity and the relationship to interpersonal competence, intrapersonal comfort, and intellectual level. *Developmental Psychology, 2,* 335-350.

Rotheram, M. J. (1980). Social skills training programs in elementary and high school classrooms. In D. P. Rathjen & J. P. Foreyt (Eds.), *Social competence: Interventions for children and adults* (pp. 69-112). New York: Plenum.

Royce, W. S. (1982). Behavioral referents for molar ratings of heterosocial skill. *Psychological Reports, 59,* 139-146.

Royce, W. S., & Weiss, R. L. (1975). Behavioral cues in the judgment of marital satisfaction: A linear regression analysis. *Journal of Consulting and Clinical Psychology, 43,* 816-824.

Ruben, B. D. (1976). Assessing communication competency for intercultural adaptation. *Group and Organization Studies, 1,* 334-354.

Rubin, D. L. (1981). Using performance rating scales in large-scale assessments of oral communication proficiency. *Perspectives on the assessment of speaking and listening skills for the 1980's* (pp. 51-67). Proceedings of a symposium presented by Clearing House for Applied Performance Testing, Northwest Regional Educational Laboratory, Portland, OR.

Rubin, R.B. (1981a). Assessment of college-level speaking and listening assessment. *Perspectives on the assessment of speaking and listening skills for the 1980s* (pp. 25-42). Symposium presented by Clearing House for Applied Performance Testing, Northwest Regional Educational Laboratory, Portland, OR.

Rubin, R. B. (1981b). *The development and refinement of a communication competency assessment instrument.* Paper presented at the meeting of the Speech Communication Association, Anaheim, CA.

Rubin, R. B. (1982). Assessing speaking and listening competence at the college level: The communication competency assessment instrument. *Communication Education, 31,* 19-32.

Rubin, R. B., & Henzl, S. A. (1982). *Cognitive complexity, communication competence, and verbal ability.* Paper presented at the meeting of the International Communication Association, Boston.

Ruesch, J. (1951). Communication and mental illness: A psychiatric approach. In J. Ruesch & G. Bateson (Eds.), *Communication: The social matrix of psychiatry* (pp. 50-93). New York: W. W. Norton.

Ruesch, J. (1972). *Disturbed communication.* New York: W. W. Norton. (Originally published in 1957)

Ruesch, J. (1973). *Therapeutic communication.* New York: W. W. Norton. (Originally published in 1961)

Ruesch, J., Block, J., & Bennett, L. (1953). The assessment of communication: I. A method for the analysis of social interaction. *Journal of Psychology, 35,* 59-80.

Ruesch, J., & Prestwood, A. R. (1950). Interaction processes and personal codification. *Journal of Personality, 18,* 391-430.

Rumsey, M., & Justice, B. (1982). Social correlates of psychological dysfunction. *Psychological Reports, 59,* 1335-1345.

Sacks, H., Schegloff, E. A., & Jefferson, G. (1978). A simplest systematics for the organization of turn taking for conversation. In J. Schenkein (Ed.), *Studies in the organization of conversational interaction.* New York: Academic.

Saltzer, E. B. (1982). The relationship of personal efficacy beliefs to behavior. *British Journal of Social Psychology, 21,* 213-221.

Sankoff, G. (1974). A quantitative paradigm for the study of communicative competence. In R. Bauman & J. Sherzer (Eds.), *Explorations in the ethnography of speaking* (pp. 18-49). London: Cambridge University Press.

Sanson-Fisher, R. W., & Mulligan, B. (1977). The validity of a behavioral ratings scale: Application of a psychophysical technique. *Multivariate Behavioral Research, 12,* 357-372.

Sarason, B. R. (1981). The dimensions of social competence: Contributions from a variety of research areas. In J. D. Wine & M. D. Smye (Eds.), *Social competence.* New York: Guilford Press.

Schaefer, M. T., & Olson, D. H. (1981). Assessing intimacy: The pair inventory. *Journal of Marital and Family Therapy, 7,* 47-59.

Schaie, K. W. (1955). A test of behavioral rigidity. *Journal of Abnormal and Social Psychology, 51,* 604-610.

Schank, R. C., & Abelson, R. P. (1977). *Scripts, plans, goals and understanding.* Hillsdale, NJ: Erlbaum.

Scheier, M. F., & Carver, C. S. (1977). Self-focused attention and experience of emotion: Attraction, repulsion, elation, and depression. *Journal of Personality and Social Psychology, 35,* 625-636.

Scherer, J., & Scherer, K. R. (1980). Psychological factors in bureaucratic encounters: Determinants and effects of interactions between officials and clients. In W. T. Singleton, P. Spurgeon, & R. B. Stammers (Eds.), *The analysis of social skill* (pp. 315-328). New York: Plenum.

Schlenker, B. R. (1980). *Impression management: The self-concept, social identity, and interpersonal relations.* Monterey, CA: Brooks/Cole.

Schopler, J., & Layton, B. D. (1974). Attributions of interpersonal power. In J. T. Tedeschi (Ed.), *Perspectives on social power* (pp. 34-60). Chicago, IL: Aldine.

Schuetz, J. (1978a). Argumentative competence and the negotiation of Henry Kissinger. *Journal of the American Forensic Association, 15,* 1-16.

Schuetz, J. (1978b). Communicative competence and the bargaining of Watergate. *Western Journal of Speech Communication, 41,* 105-115.

Schumm, W. R., Jurich, A. P., & Bollman, S. R. (1980). The dimensionality of an abbreviated relationship inventory for couples. *Journal of Psychology, 105,* 225-230.

Schutz, W. C. (1966). *The interpersonal underworld.* Palo Alto, CA: Science & Behavior Books.

Schwartz, R. M., & Gottman, J. M. (1976). Toward a task analysis of assertive behavior. *Journal of Consulting and Clinical Psychology, 44,* 910-920.

Scofield, M. E., & Yoxtheimer, L. L. (1983). Psychometric issues in the assessment of clinical competencies. *Journal of Counseling Psychology, 30,* 413-420.

Scott, M. D., & Powers, W. G. (1978). *Interpersonal communication: A question of needs.* Boston: Houghton Mifflin.

Scott, R. L. (1975). A synoptic view of systems of Western rhetoric. *Quarterly Journal of Speech, 61,* 439-447.

Scott, W. A. (1966). Flexibility, rigidity, and adaptation: Toward clarification of concepts. In O. J. Harvey (Ed.), *Experience, structure and adaptability* (pp. 369-400). New York: Springer.

Scott, W. A., Osgood, D. W., & Peterson, C. (1969). *Cognitive structure: Theory and measurement of individual differences.* Silver Spring, MD: V. H. Winston.

Scott, W.D.N., & Edelstein, B. A. (1981). The social competence of two interaction strategies: An analog evaluation. *Behavior Therapy, 12,* 482-492.

Searle, J. R. (1971). What is a speech act? In J. R. Searle (Ed.), *The philosophy of language* (pp. 34-53). Oxford: Oxford University Press.

Sedano, M., & Ribeau, S. (1981). *Functional intercultural communication competence: An intercultural examination of communication competence.* Paper presented at the meeting of the Western Speech Communication Association, San Jose, CA.

Seibold, D. R., & Spitzberg, B. H. (1981). Attribution theory and research: Formalization, critique, and implications for communication. In B. Dervin & M. Voight (Eds.), *Progress in communication sciences* (Vol. 3, pp. 85-125). Norwood, NJ: Ablex.

Shanley, L. A., Walker, R. E., & Foley, J. M. (1971). Social intelligence: A concept in search of data. *Psychological Reports, 29,* 1123-1132.

Shantz, C. U. (1982). Children's understanding of social rules and the social context. In F. C. Serafica (Ed.), *Social-cognitive development in context* (pp. 167-198). New York: Guilford Press.

Sharpley, C. F., & Cross, D. G. (1982). A psychometric evaluation of the Spanier Dyadic Adjustment Scale. *Journal of Marriage and the Family, 44,* 739-741.

Shatz, M. (1977). The relationship between cognitive processes and the development of communication skills. In H. E. Howe, Jr. (Ed.), *Nebraska symposium on motivation* (Vol. 25, pp. 1-42). Lincoln: University of Nebraska Press.

Shepherd, G. (1977). Social skills training: The generalization problem. *Behavior Therapy, 8,* 1008-1009.

Shepherd, G. (1983). Introduction. In S. Spence & G. Shepherd (Eds.), *Development in social skills training* (pp. 1-19). New York: Academic Press.

Shepherd, G., & Spence, S. (1983). Concluding comments. In S. Spence & G. Shepherd (Eds.), *Developments in social skills training* (pp. 335-342). New York: Academic Press.

Sherer, M., Maddux, J. E., Mercandante, B., Prentice-Dunn, S., Jacobs, B., & Rogers, R. W. (1982). The self-efficacy scale: Construction and validation. *Psychological Reports, 51,* 663-671.

Sherer, M., & Rogers, R. W. (1980). Effects of therapist's nonverbal communication on rated skill and effectiveness. *Journal of Clinical Psychology, 36,* 696-700.

Sheridan, T. (1762). *A course of lectures on elocution: Together with two dissertations on language; and some other tracts relative to those subjects.* London: W. Strahan.

Shimanoff, S. B. (1980). *Communication rules: Theory and research.* Beverly Hills: Sage.

Shure, M. B. (1980). Real-life problem solving for parents and children: An approach to social competence. In D. P. Rathjen & J. P. Foreyt (Eds.), *Social competence: Interventions for children and adults* (pp. 54-68). Elmsford, NY: Pergamon.

Shure, M. B. (1981). Social competence as a problem-solving skill. In J. D. Wine & M. D. Smye (Eds.), *Social competence* (pp. 158-188). New York: Guilford Press.

Shure, M. B. (1982). Interpersonal problem-solving: A cog in the wheel of social cognition. In F. C. Serafica (Ed.), *Social-cognitive development in context* (pp. 133-166). New York: Guilford Press.

Sieburg, E. (1973). *Interpersonal confirmation: A paradigm for conceptualization and measurement.* Paper presented at the meeting of the International Communication Association, Montreal.

Sieburg, E., & Larson, C. (1971). *Dimensions of interpersonal response.* Paper presented at the meeting of the International Communication Association, Phoenix.

Simon, C. S. (1979). *Communicative competence: A functional-pragmatic approach to language therapy.* Tucson: Communication Skill Builders.

Singleton, W. T., Spurgeon, P., & Stammers, R. B. (Eds.). (1980). *The analysis of social skills.* New York: Plenum.

Smith, I. L., & Greenberg, S. (1979). Hierarchical assessment of social competence. *American Journal of Mental Deficiency, 83,* 551-555.

Smith, M. B. (1966). Explorations in competence: A study of Peace Corps teachers in Ghana. *American Psychologist, 21,* 555-566.

Smith, M. G. (1968). Toward a conception of the competent self. In J. A. Clausen (Ed.), *Socialization and society* (pp. 270-320). Boston: Little, Brown.

Smith, V. R. (1981). *Development and validation of a conflict and bargaining outcome scale.* Paper presented at the meeting of the International Communication Association, Acapulco.

Smith-Lovin, L. (1979). Behavior settings and impressions formed from social scenarios. *Social Psychology Quarterly, 42,* 31-43.

Snyder, D. K. (1979). Multidimensional assessment of marital satisfaction. *Journal of Marriage and the Family, 41,* 813-823.

Snyder, M. (1974). Self-monitoring of expressive behavior. *Journal of Personality and Social Psychology, 30,* 526-537.

Snyder, M. (1979a). Cognitive, behavioral, and interpersonal consequences of self-monitoring. In P. Pliner, K. R. Blakenstein, & I. M. Spigel (Eds.), *Advances in the study of communication and affect* (pp. 181-201). New York: Plenum.

Snyder, M. (1979b). Self-monitoring processes. In L. Berkowitz (Ed.), *Advances in experimental social psychology* (Vol. 12, pp. 85-128). New York: Academic Press.

Snyder, M., & Cantor, N. (1980). Thinking about ourselves and others: Self-monitoring and social knowledge. *Journal of Personality and Social Psychology, 39,* 222-234.

Snyder, M., & Swann, W. B. (1976). When actions reflect attitudes: The politics of impression management. *Journal of Personality and Social Psychology, 34,* 1034-1042.

Snyder, M., & Tanke, E. D. (1976). Behavior and attitude: Some people are more consistent than others. *Journal of Personality, 44,* 501-517.

Spady, W. G. (1977). Competency based education: A bandwagon in search of a definition. *Educational Researcher, 6(1),* 9-14.

Spady, W. G., & Mitchell, D. E. (1977). Competency based education: Organizational issues and implications. *Educational Researcher, 6(2),* 9-15.

Spanier, G. B. (1976). Measuring dyadic adjustment: New scales for assessing the quality of marriage and similar dyads. *Journal of Marriage and the Family, 38,* 15-27.

Spanier, G. B., & Thompson, L. (1982). A confirmatory analysis of the dyadic adjustment scale. *Journal of Marriage and the Family, 44,* 731-738.

Spence, S. H. (1981). Validation of social skills of adolescent males in an interview conversation with previously unknown adult. *Journal of Applied Behavior Analysis, 14,* 159-168.

Spence, S. H. (1983). The training of heterosexual skills. In S. Spence & G. Shepherd (Eds.), *Developments in social skills training* (pp. 275-303). New York: Academic Press.

Spence, S. H., & Marzillier, J. S. (1981). Social skills training with adolescent male offenders:—II. Short-term, long-term and generalized effects. *Behaviour Research and Therapy, 19,* 349-368.

Spitzberg, B. H. (1980). *Interpersonal competence and loneliness.* Paper presented at the meeting of the Western Speech Communication Association, Portland, OR.

Spitzberg, B. H. (1981a). *Competence in communicating: A taxonomy, review, critique, and predictive model.* Paper presented at the meeting of the Speech Communication Association, Anaheim, CA.

Spitzberg, B. H. (1981b). *Loneliness and communication apprehension.* Paper presented at the meeting of the Western Speech Communication Association, San Jose, CA.

Spitzberg, B. H. (1982a). *Other-orientation and relational competence.* Paper presented at the meeting of the Western Speech Communication Association, Denver.

Spitzberg, B. H. (1982b). *Performance styles, interpersonal communication competence, and communicative outcomes.* Paper presented at the meeting of the Western Speech Communication Association, Denver.

Spitzberg, B. H. (1982c). *Relational competence: An empirical test of a conceptual model.* Paper presented at the meeting of the International Communication Association, Boston.

Spitzberg, B. H., & Canary, D. J. (1983). *Attributions of loneliness and relational competence.* Paper presented at the meeting of the International Communication Association, Dallas.

Spitzberg, B. H., & Cupach, W. R. (1981). *Self-monitoring and relational competence.* Paper presented at the meeting of the Speech Communication Association, Anaheim, CA.

Spitzberg, B. H., & Dillard, J. D. (1984). *Behavioral predictors of global impressions of social skills: A meta-analysis.* Paper presented at the meeting of the International Communication Association, San Francisco.

Spitzberg, B. H., & Hecht, M. L. (1984). Component model of relational competence. *Human Communication Research, 10* (4).

Spitzberg, B. H., & Lane, S. D. (1983). *Interpersonal orientations: A review, synthesis and critique.* Paper presented at the meeting of the Western Speech Communication Association, Albuquerque.

Spitzberg, B. H., & Phelps, L. A. (1982). *Conversational appropriateness and effectiveness: Validation of a criterion measure of relational competence.* Paper presented at the meeting of the Western Speech Communication Association, Denver.

Spivack, G., Platt, J. J., & Shure, M. B. (1976). *The problem-solving approach to adjustment.* San Francisco: Jossey-Bass.

St. Lawrence, J. S. (1982). Validation of a component model of social skill with outpatient adults. *Journal of Behavioral Assessment, 4*(1), 15-26.

St. Lawrence, J. S., Kirksey, W. A., & Moore, T. (1983). External validity of role play assessment of assertive behavior. *Journal of Behavioral Assessment, 5*(1), 25-34.

Stafford, L., & Daly, J. A. (1983). *Conversational memory: The effects of recall mode and instructional set on memory for naturally occurring conversations.* Paper presented at the meeting of the International Communication Association, Dallas.

Stanton, H. R., & Litwak, E. (1955). Toward the development of a short form test of interpersonal competence. *American Sociological Review, 20,* 668-674.

Staples, F. R., & Sloane, R. B. (1976). Truax factors, speech characteristics, and therapeutic outcome. *Journal of Nervous and Mental Disease, 163,* 135-140.

Staub, E. (1978). *Positive social behavior and morality* (Vol. 1). New York: Academic.

Steele, F. (1980). Defining and developing environmental competence. In C. P. Alderfer & C. L. Cooper (Eds.), *Advances in experimental social processes* (Vol. 2, pp. 225-244). New York: John Wiley.

Steffen, J. J., Greenwald, D. P., & Langmeyer, D. (1979). A factor analytic study of social competence in women. *Social Behavior and Personality, 7,* 17-27.

Steffen, J. J., & Redden, J. (1977). Assessment of social competence in an evaluation-interaction analogue. *Human Communication Research, 4,* 30-37.

Steinberg, S. L., Curran, J. P., Bell, S., Paxson, M. A., & Munroe, S. M. (1982). The effects of confederate prompt delivery style in a standardized social simulation test. *Journal of Behavioral Assessment, 4,* 263-272.

Steiner, I. D. (1955). Interpersonal behavior as influenced by accuracy of social perception. *Psychological Review, 62,* 268-273.

Stiggins, R. J. (1981). Potential sources of bias in speaking and listening assessment. *Perspectives on the assessment of speaking and listening skills for the 1980s* (pp. 43-50). Symposium presented by Clearinghouse for Applied Performance Testing, Northwest Regional Educational Laboratory, Portland, OR.

Stohl, C. (1982). *A developmental perspective on the development of communicative competency.* Paper presented at the meeting of the Speech Communication Association, Louisville.

Stohl, C. (1983). Developing a communicative competence scale. In R. N. Bostrom (Ed.), *Communication yearbook 7* (pp. 685-716). Beverly Hills: Sage.

Stotland, E., Mathews, K.E., Jr., Sherman, S. E., Hansonn, R. O., & Richardson, B. Z. (1978). *Empathy, fantasy, and helping.* Beverly Hills: Sage.

Stricker, L. J. (1982). Interpersonal competence instrument: Development and preliminary findings. *Applied Psychological Measurement, 6* 69-81

Stricker, L. J. (1983). *Interpersonal competence, social intelligence, and general ability.* Princeton, NJ: Educational Testing Service.

Strupp, H. H., & Wallach, M. S. (1965). A further study of psychiatrists' responses in quasi-therapy situations. *Behavioral Science, 10,* 113-134.

Stryker, S. (1957). Role-taking accuracy and adjustment. *Sociometry, 20,* 286-295.

Sullivan, H. S. (1950). Tensions interpersonal and international: A psychiatrist's view. In H. Cantril (Ed.), *Tensions that cause wars.* Champaign: University of Illinois Press.

Sundberg, N. D., Snowden, L. R., & Reynolds, W. M. (1978). Toward assessment of personal competence and incompetence in life situations. *Annual Review of Psychology, 29,* 179-221.

Sundel, S. S., & Sundel, M. (1980). *Be assertive: A practical guide for human service workers.* Beverly Hills: Sage.

Sunnafrank, M. J., & Miller, G. R. (1981). The role of initial conversations in determining attraction to similar and dissimilar strangers. *Human Communication Research, 8,* 16-25.

Talley, M. A. & Richmond, V. P. (1980). The relationship between psychological gender orientation and communicator style. *Human Communication Research, 6,* 326-339.

Tanaka, J. S., & Bentler, P. M. (1983). Factor invariance of premorbid social competence across multiple populations of schizophrenics. *Multivariate Behavioral Research, 18,* 135-146.

Tepper, D.T., Jr., & Haase, R. F. (1978). Verbal and nonverbal communication of facilitative conditions. *Journal of Counseling Psychology, 25,* 35-44.

Thayer, L. (1968). *Communication and communication systems.* Homewood, IL: Irwin.

Thomas, A. P., Roger, D., & Bull, P. (1983). A sequential analysis of informal dyadic conversation using Markov chains. *British Journal of Social Psychology, 22,* 177-188.

Thomas E. J., Walter, C. L., & O'Flaherty, K. (1974). A verbal problem checklist for use in assessing family verbal behavior. *Behavior Therapy, 5,* 235-246.

Thomas, M., & Bookwalter, R. B. (1982). *Clarifying context and appropriateness in communication rules.* Paper presented at the meeting of the Western Speech Communication Association, Denver.

Thorndike, R. L. (1920). Intelligence and its uses. *Harper's Monthly, 140,* 227-235.

Thorndike, R. L. (1936). Factor analysis of social and abstract intelligence. *Journal of Educational Psychology, 27,* 231-233.

Thorngate, W. (1976). Must we always think before we act? *Personality and Social Psychology Bulletin, 2,* 31-35.

Tobey, E. L., & Tunnell, G. (1981). Predicting our impressions on others: Effects of public self-consciousness and acting, a self-monitoring subscale. *Personality and Social Psychology Bulletin, 7,* 661-669.

Tortoriello, T. R., & Phelps, L. A. (1975). Can students apply interpersonal theory? *Today's Speech, 23,* 45-48.

Toulmin, S. (1974). Rules and their relevance for understanding human behavior. In T. Mischel (Ed.), *Understanding other persons* (pp. 185-215). Totowa, NJ: Rowan & Littlefield.

Trank, D. M., & Steele, J. M. (1983). Measurable effects of a communication skills course: An initial study. *Communication Education, 32,* 227-236.

Trenholm, S., & Rose, T. (1981). The compliant communicator: Teacher perceptions of classroom behavior. *Western Journal of Speech Communication, 45,* 13-26.

Triandis H. C. (1978). Some universals of social behavior. *Personality and Social Psychology Bulletin, 4,* 1-16.

Tronick, E., Als, H., & Brazelton, T. B. (1980). The infant's communicative competencies and the achievement of intersubjectivity. In M. R. Key (Ed.), *The relationship of verbal and nonverbal communication* (pp. 261-274). The Hague: Mouton.

Trower, P. (1979). Fundamentals of interpersonal behavior: A social-psychological perspective. In A. S. Bellack & M. Hersen (Eds.), *Research and practice in social skills training* (pp. 3-40). New York: Plenum.

Trower, P. (1980). Situational analysis of the components and processes of behavior of socially skilled and unskilled patients. *Journal of Consulting and Clinical Psychology, 48,* 327-339.

Trower, P. (1981). Social skill disorder. In S. Duck & R. Gilmour (Eds.), *Personal relationships: 3. Personal relationships in disorder* (pp. 97-110). New York: Academic Press.

Trower, P. (1982). Toward a generative model of social skills: A critique and synthesis. In J. P. Curran & P. M. Monti (Eds.), *Social skills training* (pp. 399-427). New York: Guilford Press.

Trower, P., Bryant, B., & Argyle, M. (1978). *Social skills and mental health.* Philadelphia: University of Pennsylvania Press.

Truax, C. B. (1967a). A tentative scale for the rating of unconditional positive regard. In C. R. Rogers (Ed.), *The therapeutic relationship and its impact* (pp. 569-579). Madison: University of Wisconsin Press.

Truax, C. B. (1967b). A scale for the rating of accurate empathy. In C. R. Rogers (Ed.), *The therapeutic relationship and its impact* (pp. 555-568). Madison: University of Wisconsin Press.

Truax, C. B. (1970). Length of therapist response, accurate empathy and patient improvement. *Journal of Clinical Psychology, 26,* 539-541.

Tucker, C. M., & Horowitz, J. E. (1981). Assessment of factors in marital adjustment. *Journal of Behavioral Assessment, 3,* 243-252.

Tunnell, G. (1980). Intraindividual consistency in personality assessment: The effect of self-monitoring. *Journal of Personality, 48,* 220-232.

Twentyman, C., Boland, T., & McFall, R. M. (1981). Heterosocial avoidance in college males. *Behavior Modification, 5,* 523-552.

Tyler, F. B. (1978). Individual psychosocial competence: A personality configuration. *Educational and Psychological Measurement, 38,* 309-323.

Tyler, F. B. (1979). Psychosocial competence differences among adolescents on entering group counseling. *Psychological Reports, 44,* 811-822.

Tyler, F. B, & Gatz, M. (1977). Development of individual psychosocial competence in a high school setting. *Journal of Consulting and Clinical Psychology, 45,* 441-449.

Ulmer, R. A., & Timmons, E. O. (1966). An application of the minimal social behavior scale (MSBS): A short objective, empirical, reliable measure of personality functioning. *Journal of Consulting Psychology, 30,* 86.

Urbain, E. S., & Kendall, P. C. (1980). Review of social-cognitive problem-solving interventions with children. *Psychological Bulletin, 88,* 109-143.

Urey, J. R., Laughlin, C., & Kelly, J. A. (1979). Teaching heterosocial conversation skills to male psychiatric inpatients. *Journal of Behavior Therapy and Experimental Psychiatry, 10,* 323-328.

Vaillant, G. E. (1977). *Adaptation to life.* Boston: Little, Brown.

Verdeber, R. F., & Verdeber, K. S. (1980). *Inter-act* (2nd ed). Belmont, CA: Wadsworth.

Vincent, J. P., Weiss, R. L., & Birchler, G. R. (1975). A behavioral analysis of problem-solving in distressed and nondistressed married and stranger dyads. *Behavior Therapy, 6,* 475-487.

Viney, L. L., & Westbrook, M. T. (1979). Sociality: A content analysis scale for verbalizations. *Social Behavior and Personality, 7,* 129-137.

Wallander, J. L., & Albion, M. N. (1981). Modification of social interaction behavior with primary focus on social skills and assertion training: A bibliography. *JSAS Catalog of Selected Documents in Psychology, 11-12,* (Ms. 2195).

Wallander, J. L., Conger, A. J., Mariotto, M. J., Curran, J. P., & Farrell, A. D. (1980). Comparability of selection instruments in studies of heterosexual-social problem behaviors. *Behavior Therapy, 11,* 548-560.

Wallander, J. L., Curran, J. P., & Myers, P. E. (1983). Social calibration of the SSIT: Evaluating social validity. *Behavior Modification, 7,* 423-445.

Walters, E. V., & Snavely, W. B. (1981). *The relationship between social style and communication competence in an organizational setting.* Paper presented at the meeting of the Speech Communication Association, Anaheim, CA.

Walters, J. (1979). Language variation in the assessment of human communication competence. In R. Silverstein (Ed.), *Proceedings of the Third International conference on frontiers in language proficiency and dominance testing* (pp. 293-305). Carbondale: Southern Illinois University, Department of Linguistics.

Warrick, D. D. (1972). *The effect of leadership style and adaptability on employee performance and satisfaction.* Unpublished doctoral dissertation. University of Southern California, Los Angeles.

Washington, R. O. (1975). Toward a theory of social competence: Implications for measuring the effects of Head Start programs. *Urban Education, 10,* 73-85.

Waters, E., & Sroufe, L. A. (1983). Social competence as a developmental construct. *Developmental Review, 3,* 79-97.

Watson, T. R., & Petelle, J. L. (1981). *Marital adjustment: A selected review of a unique interpersonal relationship.* Paper presented at the meeting of the Speech Communication Association, Anaheim, CA.

Watzlawick, P., Beavin, J. H., & Jackson, D. D. (1967). *Pragmatics of human communication.* New York: W. W. Norton.

Weeks, R. E., & Lefebvre, R. C. (1982). The assertive interaction coding system. *Journal of Behavioral Assessment, 4, (1),* 71-85.

Wegener, C., Revenstorf, D., Hahlweg, K., & Schindler, L. (1979). Empirical analysis of communication in distressed and nondistressed couples. *Behavioural Analysis and Modification, 3,* 178-188.

Weinberg, R. B., & Marlowe, H.A., Jr. (1983). Recognizing the social in psychosocial competence: The importance of social network interventions. *Psychosocial Rehabilitation Journal, 6,* 25-34.

Weinstein, E. A. (1966). Toward a theory of interpersonal tactics. In C. W. Backman & P. F. Secord (Eds.), *Problems in social psychology* (pp. 394-398). New York: McGraw-Hill.

Weinstein, E. A. (1969). The development of interpersonal competence. In D. A. Goslin (Ed.), *Handbook of socialization theory and research* (2nd ed.). Skokie, IL: Rand McNally.

Weissman, M. M. (1975). The assessment of social adjustment: A review of techniques. *Archives of General Psychiatry, 32,* 357-365.

Weldon, D. E., & Malpass, R. S. (1981). Effects of attitudinal, cognitive, and situational variables on recall of biased communications. *Journal of Personality and Social Psychology, 40,* 39-52.

Welford, A. T. (1980). The concept of skill and its application to social performance. In W. T. Singleton, P. Spurgeon, & R. B. Stammers (Eds.), *The analysis of social skills* (pp. 11-22). New York: Plenum.

Wenegrat, A. (1974). A factor analytic study of the Truax Accurate Empathy Scale. *Psychotherapy: Theory, Research and Practice, 11,* 48-51.

Wenegrat, A. (1976). Linguistic variables of therapist speech and accurate empathy ratings. *Psychotherapy: Theory, Research and Practice, 13,* 30-33.

Wessberg, H. W., Curran, J. P., Monti, P. M., Corriveau, D. P., Coyne, N. A., & Dziadosz, T. H. (1981). Evidence for the external validity of a social simulation measure of social skills. *Journal of Behavioral Assessment, 3(3),* 209-220.

West, B. L., Goethe, K. E., & Kallman, W. M. (1980). Heterosocial skills training: A behavioral-cognitive approach. In D. Upper & S. M. Ross (Eds.), *Behavioral therapy, 1980: An annual review.* Champaign, IL: Research Press.

Wheeler, V. A., & Ladd, G. W. (1982). Assessment of children's self-efficacy for social interactions with peers. *Developmental Psychology, 18,* 795-805.

Wheeless, L. R., & Wheeless, V. E. (1981). Attribution, gender orientation, and adaptability: Reconceptualization, measurement, and research results. *Communication Quarterly, 30* (1), 56-66.

Wheeless, V. E., & Duran, R. L. (1982). Gender orientation as a correlate of communicative competence. *Southern Speech Communication Journal, 48,* 51-64.

White, R. H. (1959). Motivation reconsidered: The concept of competence. *Psychological Review, 66,* 297-333.

White, R. H. (1968). Sense of interpersonal competence: Two case studies and some reflections on origins. In W. G. Bennis, E. H. Schein, F. I. Steele, & D. E. Berlew (Eds.), *Interpersonal dynamics: Essays and readings on human interaction* (pp. 674-680);. Homewood, IL: Irwin.

White, R. H. (1974). Strategies of adaptation: An attempt at systematic description. In G. V. Coelho, D. A. Hamburg, & J. E. Adams (Eds.), *Coping and adaptation* (pp. 47-68). New York: Basic Books.

White, R. H. (1976). Strategies of adaptation: An attempt at systematic description. In R. H. Moos (Ed.), *Human adaptation: Coping with life crises* (pp. 17-32). Lexington, MA: D. C. Heath.

Wiemann, J. M. (1977). Explication and test of a model of communicative competence. *Human Communication Research, 3,* 195-213.

Wiemann, J. M. (1978). Needed research and training in speaking and listening literacy. *Communication Education, 27,* 310-315.

Wiemann, J. M., & Backlund, P. (1980). Current theory and research in communicative competence. *Review of Educational Research, 50,* 185-199.

Wiemann, J. M., & Kelly, C. W. (1981). Pragmatics of interpersonal competence. In C. Wilder-Mott & J. H. Weakland (Eds.), *Rigor and imagination: Essays from the legacy of Gregory Bateson* (pp. 283-297). New York: Praeger.

Wiemann, J. M., & Knapp, M. L. (1975). Turn-taking in conversations. *Journal of Communication, 25,* 75-92.

Wiener, M., Shilkret, R., & Devoe, S. (1980). "Acquisition" of communication competence: Is language enough? In M. R. Key (Ed.), *The relationship of verbal and nonverbal communication* (pp. 275-294). The Hague: Mouton.

Williams, C. L., & Ciminero, A. R. (1978). Development and validation of a heterosocial skill inventory: The survey of heterosexual interactions for females. *Journal of Consulting and Clinical Psychology, 46,* 1547-1548.

Williams, R. D. (1979). Criteria for competence. *Psychological Reports, 44,* 167-Wills, T. A., Weiss, R. L., & Patterson, G. R. (1974). A behavioral analysis of the determinants of marital satisfaction. *Journal of Consulting and Clinical Psychology, 42,* 802-811.

Wilmot, W. W. (1971). A test of the construct and predictive validity of three measures of ego involvement. *Speech Monographs, 38,* 217-227.

Wilmot, W. W. (1979). *Dyadic communication* (2nd ed.). Reading, MA: Addison-Wesley.

Wilson, T. D., & Capitman, J. A. (1982). Effects of script availability on social behavior. *Personality and Social Psychology Bulletin, 8,* 11-19.

Wine, J. D. (1981). From defect to competence models. In J. D. Wine & M. D. Smye (Eds.), *Social competence* (pp. 3-35). New York: Guilford Press.

Wish, M. (1979). Dimensions of dyadic communication. In S. Weitz (Ed.), *Nonverbal communication: Readings with commentary* (2nd ed., pp. 371-378). Oxford: Oxford University Press.

Wish, M., D'Andrade, R. G., & Goodnow, J.E., II. (1980). Dimensions of interpersonal communication: Correspondences between structures for speech acts and bipolar scales. *Journal of Personality and Social Psychology, 39,* 848-860.

Wish, M., & Kaplan, S. J. (1977). Toward an implicit theory of interpersonal communication. *Sociometry, 40,* 234-246.

Wolf, T. M., & Wenzl, P. A. (1982). Assessment of relationship among measures of social competence and cognition in educable mentally retarded-emotionally disturbed students. *Psychological Reports, 50,* 695-700.

Wolpe, J., & Lazarus, A. A. (1967). *Behavior therapy techniques: A guide to the treatment of neuroses.* Elmsford, NY: Pergamon.

Wolpert, E. A. (1955). A new view of rigidity. *Journal of Abnormal and Social Psychology, 51,* 589-594.

Wood, B. S. (1973). Competence and performance in language development. *Today's Speech, 21*(1), 23-30.

Wood, B. S. (1976). *Children and communication.* Englewood Cliffs, NJ: Prentice-Hall.

Woolfolk, R. L., & Denver, S. (1979). Perceptions of assertion: An empirical analysis. *Behavior Therapy, 10,* 404-411.

Wright, J. (1977). The development of instruments to assess behavior therapy training. *Journal of Behavior Therapy and Experimental Psychiatry, 8,* 281-286.

Wright, L., Bond, D., & Denison, J. W. (1968). An expanded sociometric device for measuring personal effectiveness. *Psychological Reports, 23,* 263-269.

Wright, L., & Dunn, T. (1970). Factor structure of the expanded sociometric device: A measure of personal effectiveness. *Educational and Psychological Measurement, 30,* 319-326.

Wright, M. J. (1980). Measuring the social competence of preschool children. *Canadian Journal of Behavioural Science, 12,* 17-32.

Wright, W., Morris, K. T., & Fettig, B. (1974). Comparative effects of social skill development. *Small Group Behavior, 5,* 211-221.

Wrubel, J., Benner, P., & Lazarus, R. S. (1981). Social competence from the perspective of stress and coping. In J. D. Wine & M. D. Smye (Eds.), *Social competence* (pp. 61-99). New York: Guilford Press.

Yardley, K. M. (1979). Social skills training—a critique. *British Journal of Medical Psychology, 52,* 55-62.

Zajonc, R. B. (1980). Feeling and thinking: Preferences need no inferences. *American Psychologist, 35,* 151-175.

Zakahi, W. R., & Duran, R. L. (1982). All the lonely people: The relationship among loneliness, communicative competence, and communication anxiety. *Communication Quarterly, 30*(3), 203-209.

Zanna, M. P., Olson, I. M., & Fazio, R. H. (1980). Attitude-behavior consistency: An individual difference perspective. *Journal of Personality and Social Psychology, 38,* 432-440.

Zeiss, A. M., Lewinsohn, P. M., & Muñoz, R. F. (1979). Nonspecific improvement effects in depression using interpersonal skills training, pleasant activity schedules, or cognitive training. *Journal of Consulting and Clinical Psychology, 47,* 427-439.

Zelen, S. L., & Levitt, E. E. (1954). Note on the Wesley rigidity scale: The development of a short form. *Journal of Abnormal and Social Psychology, 49,* 472-473.

Zigler, E., & Levine, J. (1981). Premorbid competence in schizophrenia: What is being measured? *Journal of Consulting and Clinical Psychology, 49,* 96-105.

Zigler, E., & Phillips, L. (1960). Social effectiveness and symptomatic behaviors. *Journal of Abnormal and Social Psychology, 61,* 231-238.

Zigler, E., & Phillips, L. (1961). Social competence and outcome in psychiatric disorder. *Journal of Abnormal and Social Psychology, 63,* 264-271.

Zigler, E., & Phillips, L. (1962). Social competence and the process-reactive distinction in psychopathology. *Journal of Abnormal and Social Psychology, 65,* 215-222.

Zigler, E., & Trickett, P. L. (1978). IQ, social competence, and evaluation of early childhood intervention programs. *American Psychologist, 33,* 789-798.

Zimmerman, A. R. (1980). *A competency model for curriculum design and development of basic speech courses.* Paper presented at the meeting of the Speech Communication Association, New York.

Zuroff, D. C., & Schwarz, J. C. (1978). An instrument for measuring the behavioral dimension of social anxiety. *Psychological Reports, 42,* 371-379.

NAME INDEX

Names appearing in this index represent only the first name listed for each citation, and do not include names listed in tables.

SUBJECT INDEX

Accommodation theory, 162-163

Adaptability and adaptation (see also behavioral flexibility), 25, 31, 35-37, 40-41, 44-45, 51, 63, 68-69, 71, 78, 87, 90, 107-108, 124, 130, 154

Adjustment, 25-26, 33-35, 46, 67, 149-150, 185

Altercentrism (see also other-orientation), 119-120, 131, 142

Anxiety, 22, 35, 42, 43, 53, 77, 119-120, 129,130, 147, 155, 178, 182
communication apprehension, 81
social anxiety, 41, 43, 81, 87, 131, 149

Appropriateness, 29, 35, 37, 64-69, 71, 78, 87, 92-94, 100-110, 114, 116, 124, 127, 128, 131, 140-142, 146, 147, 150, 157, 158, 160, 162, 179

Assertiveness, 41, 43, 47, 48, 53, 76, 129-131, 154, 175, 183

Attentiveness, 43, 155, 182

Attribution theory, 29, 158-159, 161

Behavioral flexibility, 20, 36, 81, 88, 90, 92, 94, 155

Cognitive complexity, 43, 44, 92, 108, 127-128, 155

Communication apprehension (see Anxiety)

Communicative competence, 32-35, 58, 60-67, 71, 75, 76, 79, 80, 175

Competence (see communicative competence, competence-performance distinction, competency levels, fundamental competence,

interpersonal competence, linguistic competence, relational competence, social competence, social skills, strategic competence)

Competence-performance distinction, 58-60, 63, 64

Competency levels, 12

Confirmation, 87, 140, 141

Consciousness, 20, 36, 75-84, 97
self-consciousness

Context (situation), 15, 18, 31, 35, 37, 53, 63-66, 68, 71, 77, 80, 84-93, 97, 106-110, 117, 120, 121, 128, 131, 140, 142-151, 154, 156, 158, 166, 174-176, 180, 183, 189

Control, 54, 55, 70, 166

Education, 12, 14, 82, 180-185

Effectance motivation, 11, 37-39

Effectiveness, 15, 18, 26, 29, 31, 36, 37, 39, 40, 44, 52, 54-57, 67, 68, 70, 71, 74, 79, 84, 89, 93, 94, 100-106, 109-110, 113, 115, 116, 126, 127, 141, 142, 153, 160-162, 183

Empathy, 43, 45, 46, 48-49, 52, 54, 68, 69, 75, 81, 86-88, 107, 127-128, 154, 155, 166

Expressiveness, 42, 87, 124, 131, 126

Functions (functional communication), 19, 67, 102, 112-113, 137-142, 174, 178-179, 181-183

Fundamental competence, 34-40, 54, 57, 67, 70

Generative grammar, 58-61

Goals, 19, 35, 54-57, 67, 68, 71, 76,

ABOUT THE AUTHORS

BRIAN H. SPITZBERG is currently Assistant Professor at North Texas State University, Denton, Texas. He received his Ph.D. in communication arts and sciences from the University of Southern California in 1981. His research interests include competence, impression management, loneliness, conflict, and the psychology of communication. His works include numerous scholarly papers presented at professional conventions and several articles published in books and journals.

WILLIAM R. CUPACH is Assistant Professor in the Department of Communication at Illinois State University. He received his Ph.D. from the University of Southern California in 1981. His research interests include communication competence, interpersonal relationship development dissolution processes, and conflict management. Cupach has authored or coauthored numerous papers presented at professional conferences, and has published in the *Western Journal of Speech Communication.*